Memories of the Russian Court

MEMORIES OF
THE RUSSIAN COURT

THE MACMILLAN COMPANY
NEW YORK · BOSTON · CHICAGO · DALLAS
ATLANTA · SAN FRANCISCO

MACMILLAN & CO., LIMITED
LONDON · BOMBAY · CALCUTTA
MELBOURNE

THE MACMILLAN CO. OF CANADA, LTD.
TORONTO

THE EMPRESS OF RUSSIA IN HER HAPPY YEARS.

MEMORIES OF
THE RUSSIAN COURT

BY
ANNA VIROUBOVA

MACMILLAN AND CO., LIMITED
ST. MARTIN'S STREET, LONDON
1923

PRINTED IN THE UNITED STATES OF AMERICA

TO MY EMPRESS,
WITH LOVE AND FIDELITY ETERNAL

"When you are reproached—bless; when per-secuted—be patient; when calumniated—com-fort yourself; when slandered—rejoice; this is your road and mine" Words of St. Seraphine.

ALEXANDRA FEODOROVNA, from *Tobolsk,*

March 20, 1918

Yea, though I walk through the valley of the shadow of death I shall not fear. Thy rod and Thy staff shall comfort me.

ILLUSTRATIONS

Note· With very few exceptions all these photographs were taken by members of the Imperial Family and by Mme. Viroubova, all of whom were experts with the camera.

MEMORIES OF
THE RUSSIAN COURT

MEMORIES OF THE RUSSIAN COURT

CHAPTER I

IT is with a prayerful heart and memories deep and reverent that I begin to write the story of my long and intimate friendship with Alexandra Feodorovna, wife of Nicholas II, Empress of Russia, and of the tragedy of the Revolution, which brought on her and hers such undeserved misery, and on our unhappy country such a black night of oblivion.

But first I feel that I should explain briefly who I am, for though my name has appeared rather prominently in most of the published accounts of the Revolution, few of the writers have taken the trouble to sift facts from fiction even in the comparatively unimportant matter of my genealogy. I have seen it stated that I was born in Germany, and that my marriage to a Russian officer was arranged to conceal my nationality. I have also read that I was a peasant woman brought from my native Siberia to further the ambitions of Rasputine. The truth is that I am unable to produce an ancestor who was not born Russian. My father, Alexander Sergievitch Tanieff, during most of his life, was a functionary of the Russian Court, Secretary of State, and Director of the Private *Chancellerie* of the Emperor, an office held before him by his father and his grandfather. My mother was a daughter of General Tolstoy, aide-de-camp of Alexander II. One of my immediate ancestors was Field Marshal Koutousoff, famous in the Napoleonic Wars. Another, on my mother's side, was Count Kontaisoff, an intimate friend of the eccentric Tsar Paul, son of the great Catherine.

Notwithstanding my family's hereditary connection with the Court our own family life was simple and quiet. My father, aside from his official duties, had no interests apart from his home and his music, for he was a composer and a pianist of more than national fame. My earliest memories are of home evenings, my brother Serge and my sister Alya (Alexandra) studying their lessons under the shaded lamp, my dear mother sitting near with her needlework, and my father at the piano working out one of his compositions, striking the keys softly and noting down his harmonies. I thank God for that happy childhood which gave me strength of soul to bear the sorrows and sufferings of after years.

Six months in every year we spent in the country near Moscow on an estate which had been in the family for nearly two hundred years. For neighbors we had the Princes Galatzine and the Grand Duke and Grand Duchess Serge, the last named being the older sister of the Empress. I hardly remember when I did not know and love the Grand Duchess Elizabeth, as she was familiarly called. As small children she petted and spoiled us all, often inviting us to tea, the feast ending in a grand frolic in which we were allowed to search the rooms for toys which she had

ingeniously hidden. It was at one of these children's
teas that I first saw the Empress Alexandra. Quite
unexpectedly the Tsarina was announced and the
beautiful Grand Duchess Elizabeth, leaving her small
guests, ran eagerly to greet her. The time was near
the beginning of the reign of Nicholas II and Alexandra Feodorovna, and the Tsarina was at the very
height of her youthful beauty. My childish impression of her was of a tall, slender, graceful woman,
lovely beyond description, with a wealth of golden
hair and eyes like stars, the very picture of what an
Empress should be.

For my father the young Empress soon conceived a
warm liking and confidence and she named him as
vice president of the committee of *Assistance par le
Travail*. During this time we lived in winter in the
Michailovsky Palace in Petrograd, and in summer in
a small villa in Peterhof on the Baltic Sea. From conversations between my mother and father I learned a
great deal of the life of the Imperial Family. The
Empress impressed my father both by her excessive
shyness and by her unusual intelligence. She was
above all a motherly woman and often combined
baby-tending with serious business affairs. With the
little Grand Duchess Olga in her arms she discussed
all kinds of business with my father, and while with
one hand rocking the cradle where lay the baby Tatiana she signed letters and papers of consequence.
Sometimes while thus engaged there would come a
clear, musical whistle, like a bird call. It was the
Emperor's special summons to his wife, and at the
first sound her cheek would turn to rose, and, regard-

less of everything, she would fly to answer it. That birdlike whistle of the Emperor I became very familiar with in later years, calling the children, signaling to me. It had a curious, appealing, resistless quality, peculiar to himself.

Perhaps it was a common love of music which first drew the Empress and our family into a bond of friendship. All of us children received a thorough musical education. From childhood we were taken regularly to concerts and the opera, and our home, especially on Wednesday evenings, was a rendezvous for all the musicians and composers of the capital. The great Tschaikovsky was a friend of my father, and I remember many others of note who were frequent guests at tea or dinner.

Apart from music we received an education rather more practical than was the average at that time. In the Russia of my childhood a girl of good family was supposed to acquire a few pretty accomplishments and nothing much besides. Accomplishments I and my sister were given, but besides music and painting, for which my sister had considerable talent, we were well grounded in academic studies, and we finished by taking examinations leading to teachers' diplomas. I may say also that even in our drawing-room accomplishments we were obliged to be thorough, and when my father ventured to show some of our work to the Empress she expressed warm approval. "Most Russian girls," she said, "seem to have nothing in their heads but officers."

The Empress, coming from a small German Court where everyone at least tried to occupy themselves usefully, found the idle and listless atmosphere of Russia little to her taste. In her first enthusiasm of power she thought to change things a little for the better. One of her early projects was a society of handwork composed of ladies of the Court and society circles, each one of whom should make with her own hands three garments a year to be given to the poor. The society, I am sorry to say, did not long flourish. The idea was too foreign to the soil. Nevertheless the Empress persisted in creating throughout Russia industrial centers, *maisons de travail,* where the unemployed, both men and women, and especially unfortunate women who, through errors of conduct, lost their positions, could find work.

Life at Court was by no means serious. In fact it was at that time very gay. At seventeen I was presented, first to the Empress Dowager who lived in a palace in Peterhof known as the Cottage. Extremely shy at first, I soon accustomed myself to the many brilliant Court functions to which my mother chaperoned my sister and myself. We danced that first winter, I remember, at no less than twenty-two balls besides attending many receptions, teas, and dinners. Perhaps it was partly the fatigue of all this social dissipation which made so serious the illness with which in the ensuing summer I was stricken. Typhus, that scourge of Russia, struck down at the same time my brother Serge and myself. My brother's illness ran a normal course and he made a rapid recovery, but for three months I lay at death's door. After the fever succeeded many complications, inflammation of the lungs and kidneys, and an affection of the brain whereby I lost both speech and hearing. In the midst of my suffering I had a vivid dream in which the saintly Father John of Kronstadt appeared to me and told me to have courage and that all would finally be well.

This Father John of Kronstadt, whom all true Russians reverence as a saint, I remembered as having thrice been at our house in my early childhood. The gentle majesty of his presence, the beauty of his benign countenance had so deeply impressed me that now, in my desperate illness, it seemed to me that he, more than the skilled physicians and the devoted sisters who attended me, had power of help and healing. In some way I managed to convey to my parents that I wanted Father John, and they immediately telegraphed begging him to come. It was some days before the message reached him, as he was away from home on a mission, but as soon as he received word of our need he hastened to Peterhof. As in a vision I sensed his coming long before he reached the house, and when he came I greeted him without astonishment with a feeble movement of my hand. Father John knelt down beside my bed, praying quietly, a corner of his long stole laid over my burning head. At length he rose, took a glass of holy water, and to the consternation of the nurses sprinkled it freely over me and bade me sleep. Almost instantly I fell into a deep sleep, and when I awoke next day I was so much better that all could see that I was on the road to recovery.

In September of that year I went with my mother first to Baden and afterwards to Naples. We lived in the same hotel with the Grand Duke and Grand Duchess Serge who were very much amused to see me in a wig, my long illness having rendered me temporarily almost bald. After a quiet but happy season in southern Italy I returned to Russia quite restored to health. The winter of 1903 I remember as a round of gaieties and dissipations. In January of that year I received from the Empress the diamond-studded *chiffre* of maid of honor, which meant that, following my marriage, I would have permanent entry to all Court functions. Not immediately but very soon afterwards I was called to duty to the person of the Empress, and there began then that close and intimate friendship which I know lasted with her always and which will remain with me as long as God permits me to live.

I would that I could paint a picture of the Empress Alexandra Feodorovna as I knew her before the first shadow of doom and disaster fell upon unhappy Russia. No photograph ever did her justice because it could reproduce neither her lovely color nor her graceful movements. Tall she was, and delicately, beautifully shaped, with exquisitely white neck and shoulders. Her abundant hair, red gold, was so long that she could easily sit upon it when it was unbound. Her complexion was clear and as rosy as a little child's. The Empress had large eyes, deep gray and very lustrous. It was only in later life that sorrow and anxiety gave her eyes the melancholy with which they are usually associated. In youth they wore an expression of constant merriment which explained her family nickname of "Sunny," a name by the way nearly always used by the Emperor. I began almost from the first day of our association to love and admire her, as I have loved her ever since and always shall.

The winter of 1903 was very brilliant, the season culminating in a famous ball in costumes of Tsar Alexis Michailovitch, who reigned in the seventeenth century. The ball was given first in the Hermitage, the great art gallery adjoining the Winter Palace, but so immense was its success that it had to be twice repeated, once in the *Salle de Concert* of the palace and again in the large ballroom of the Schermetieff Palace. My sister and I were two of twenty young girls selected to dance with twenty youthful cavaliers in an ancient Russian dance which required almost as much rehearsal as a ballet. The rehearsals were quite important society events, all the mothers attending, and the Empress often looking on as interested as any of us.

That summer I again fell ill in our villa in Peterhof, and I remember particularly that this was the first time the Empress ever visited our house. She drove in a low pony chaise, coming up to my sickroom all in white with a big white hat and in the best of spirits. Needless to say, her unexpected visit did me a world of good, as did her second visit at our home in the country when she left me a gift of holy water from Saroff, a place greatly venerated by Russians. That winter with its artless pleasures, and the pleasant summer which followed, marked the end of an era in Russia. Immediately afterwards came the catastrophe of the Japanese War, so needlessly entered into. This war was the beginning of a long line of disasters which ended in the supreme disaster of 1917. I must confess that at the time the Japanese War made no

THE EMPRESS DRIVING IN HER PONY CHAISE.
PETERHOF, 1909.

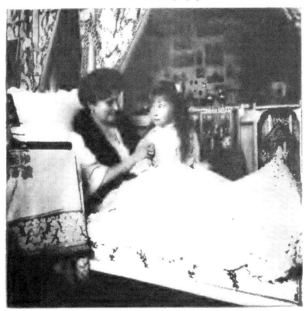

THE EMPRESS WITH GRAND DUCHESS TATIANA IN
HER BEDROOM, TSARSKOE SELO. FAVORITE IKONS
IN BACKGROUND.

ALEXANDER SERGIEVITCH TANIEFF,
Director of the Tsar's Private Chancellerie, Father of Anna Viroubova.

very deep impression on young girls who, like myself, faced life lightly like happy children. We resigned ourselves to an almost complete cessation of balls and parties, and we put aside our pretty gowns for the sober dress of working sisters. The great salons of the Winter Palace were turned into workrooms and there every day society flocked to sew and knit for our soldiers and sailors fighting such incredible distances away, as well as for the wounded in hospitals at home and abroad. My mother, who was one of the heads of committees giving out work to be done at home, was constantly busy, and we obediently followed her example.

Every day the Empress came to inspect the work, often sitting down at a table and sewing diligently with the others. This was shortly before the birth of the Tsarevitch and I have a clear picture in my mind of the Empress looking more than ever fine and delicate, her tall figure clad in a loose robe of dark velvet trimmed in fur. Behind her chair, bringing into splendid relief her bright gold hair, stood a huge negro servant, gorgeous in scarlet trousers, gold-embroidered jacket, and white turban. This negro, Jim, was one of four Abyssinians who stood guard before the doors of the private apartments. They were not soldiers and they had no functions except to open and close the doors, and to signify by a sudden, noiseless entrance into a state apartment that one of their Majesties was about to appear. The Abyssinians were in fact simply one of the left-overs from the days of Catherine the Great, in whose times dwarfs and negroes and other exotics figured as a part of Court ceremonials. They remained not because Nicholas II or the Empress wanted them, but because, as I shall later explain, it was practically impossible to change any detail of Russian Court life.

The following summer the heir was born amid the wildest rejoicings all over the Empire. I remember the Empress telling me with what extraordinary ease the child was brought into the world. Scarcely half an hour after the Empress had left her boudoir for her bedroom the baby was born and it was known that, after many prayers, there was an heir to the throne of the Romanoffs. The Emperor, in spite of the desperate sorrow brought upon him by a disastrous war, was quite mad with joy. His happiness and the mother's, however, was of short duration, for almost at once they learned that the poor child was afflicted with a dread disease, rather rare except in royal families where it is only too common. The victims of this malady are known in medicine as hæmophiliacs, or bleeders. Frequently they die soon after birth, and those who survive are subject to frightful suffering, if not to sudden death, from slight injuries to blood vessels, internal as well as external. The whole short life of the Tsarevitch, the loveliest and most amiable child imaginable, was a succession of agonizing illnesses due to this congenital affliction. The sufferings of the child were more than equaled by those of his parents, especially of his mother, who hardly knew a day of real happiness after she realized her boy's fate. Her health and spirits began to decline, and she developed a chronic heart trouble. Although the boy's affliction was in no conceivable way her fault, she dwelt morbidly on the fact that the disease is transmitted through the mother and that it was common in her family. One of her younger brothers suffered from it, also her uncle Leopold, Queen Victoria's youngest son, while all three sons of her sister, Princess Henry of Prussia, were similarly afflicted. One of these boys died young and the other two were lifelong invalids.

Everything possible, everything known to medical science, was done for the child Alexei. The Empress nursed him herself, as indeed, with the assistance of professional women, she had nursed all her children. Three trained Russian nurses were in attendance, with the Empress always superintending. She bathed the babe herself, and was with him so much that the Court, ever censorious of her, complained that she was more of a nurse than an Empress. The Court, of course, did not immediately understand the serious condition of the infant heir. No parents, be their estate high or low, are ready all at once to reveal a misfortune such as that one. It is always human to hope that things are not as desperate as they seem, and that in time some remedy for the illness will be found. The Emperor and Empress guarded their secret from all except relatives and most intimate friends, closing their eyes and their ears to the growing unpopularity of the Empress. She was ill and she was suffering, but to the Court she appeared merely cold, haughty, and indifferent. From this false impression she never fully recovered even after the explanation of her suddenly acquired silence and melancholy became generally known.

CHAPTER II

IN one of the earliest days of 1905 my mother received a telegram from Princess Galatzine, first lady in waiting, saying that my immediate presence at Court was required. The Princess Orbeliani, also a lady in waiting, was seriously ill, and some one was needed to replace her in attendance on Her Majesty. I left at once for Tsarskoe Selo, then, as always, the favorite home of the Imperial Family, and on my arrival was conducted to the apartments in the palace known as the Lyceum. The rooms were small and dark with windows looking out on a little church. It was the first time I had ever been away from home, and in any surroundings I should have been homesick and forlorn, but in these unfriendly surroundings my spirits were with some excuse depressed.

The time of my coming to Court was unpropitious, the Imperial Family and all connections being in deep mourning for the Grand Duke Serge who, on the morning of February 4, had been barbarously assassinated. The Grand Duke Serge, uncle of Nicholas II, had been Governor of Moscow. He was undoubtedly a reactionary, and his rule was said to have been harsh. Certain it is that his administrative methods earned him the intense enmity of the Social Revolutionaries and he had long lived in danger of assassination. His wife, the Grand Duchess Elizabeth, was devoted to him in spite of his somewhat difficult temperament, and she never willingly allowed him to leave the palace of the Kremlin unaccompanied. Usually she went with him herself, but on this fatal February morning he, being in a dark mood, left the palace without her knowledge. Suddenly a great explosion shook all the windows, and the poor Grand Duchess, springing from her chair, cried out in an agonized voice: "It is Serge!"

Rushing out into the court she saw a horrible sight, the body of her husband scattered in a hundred bleeding fragments over the snow. The bomb had literally torn the unfortunate man to pieces, so that in the dismembered mass of flesh and blood there was nothing recognizable of what had been, only a few minutes before, a strong and dominating man.

The terrorist who threw the bomb was promptly arrested, tried, and sentenced to death. It was entirely characteristic of the Grand Duchess Elizabeth that in the midst of her grief and horror she still found room in her heart to pity the misguided wretch sitting in his cell waiting his miserable end. The Grand Duchess insisted on visiting the man in prison, assuring him of her forgiveness, and praying for him on the stone floor of his cell. Whether or not he joined in her prayers I do not know. The Social Revolutionaries prided themselves on being irreligious and very many of them were Jews.

The Court weighed down by this terrible tragedy was a sad enough place for a homesick girl like myself. Like all the other ladies in waiting I wore a black dress with a long veil, and when at length I was received by the Empress I found her, too, dressed in deep mourning. After this first formal reception I saw very little of the Empress, all her time being devoted to her sister, the Grand Duchess Elizabeth, and to Princess Henry of Prussia, who was visiting her. The Empress Dowager also came, so that the suite was thrown together in what for me was not altogether a pleasant association. My special duty, as I discovered, was attendance on the old Princess Orbeliani, whose illness, I am bound to admit, did not sweeten her disposition. But as she was dying of that terribly trying malady, creeping paralysis, I am ashamed, even now, to criticize her. For the other *dames d'honneur*, however, I have no hesitation to say that they were not on their best behavior. Being entirely a stranger at Court and unacquainted with insincerities which afterwards I came to know only too well, I suffered keenly from the cutting remarks of my colleagues. My French, which I own I spoke rather badly, came in for a great deal of ridicule. On the whole it was rather an unhappy period in my young life.

The one bright spot that I remember was a drive with the Empress to which I was summoned by telephone. It was a warm day in early spring and the snow around the tree roots along the road was thawing in the pale sunlight. We drove in an open carriage, a big Cossack, picturesquely uniformed, riding behind. It was my first public appearance with Royalty and I was a little confused as to how to behave in the presence of the low-bowing crowds that lined the way. The Empress, however, soon put me at my ease, chatting of simple things, talking of her children, especially of the infant heir, at that time about eight months old. Our drive was not very long because the Empress had to hurry back to superintend a dancing lesson of the young Grand Duchesses. I remember when I returned to the apartment of the invalid Princess Orbeliani, she commented rather maliciously on the fact that I was not invited to attend the dancing lesson. But by that time, alas! I knew that had I been invited her comment might have been more malicious still. Still I must not speak badly of the poor Princess, for in spite of her illness and approaching death she was very brave and kinder than most people in her circumstances would have been.

Lent came on and in the palace church there were held every Wednesday and Friday special services for the Imperial Family. I asked and was given permission to assist in these services and I found great solace in them. At that time also I became warmly attached to a maid of honor of the Grand Duchess Serge, Princess Scnkovsky, a woman of rare character. She had recently lost her mother and was in a sad mood. Almost everyone, in fact, was sad at this time. The Grand Duchess Serge, although she bore her tragedy with dignity and courage, went about with a white face and eyes in which horror still lingered. On religious holidays she laid aside her black robes and appeared all in white like a madonna.

The Princess Irene of Prussia (Princess Henry) was still in mourning for her little son who had died of the same incurable disease which afflicted the Tsarevitch. She spoke to me with emotion of the child, to whom she had been deeply attached.

My duty came to an end in Holy Week, and I went to the private apartments to make my farewell of the Empress. She received me in the nursery, the baby Tsarevitch in her arms, and I cannot forget how beautiful the child appeared or how healthy and normal. He had a wealth of golden hair, large blue eyes, and an expression of intelligence rare in so young a child. The Empress was kindness itself. At parting she kissed me, and gave me as a souvenir of my first service a locket set in diamonds. Yet for all her gracious kindness how gladly I left that night for my beloved home.

The following summer, which as usual we spent at Peterhof, I saw much more of the Empress than in my month of attendance on her. With my mother and sister I again worked daily in the workrooms established for the wounded in the Japanese War, and there almost daily the Empress came to sew with the other women. Once every week she visited the hospitals at Tsarskoe Selo, and twice that summer, at her request, I accompanied her to her foundation hospital for training nurses. The Empress in the military hospitals was at her very best. Passing from bedside to bedside, speaking as tenderly as a mother to the sick and suffering men, sitting down to a game of checkers with convalescent officers, it was difficult to imagine how anyone could ever call her cold or shy. She was altogether charming and as she passed all eyes followed her with love and gratitude. To me she was everything that was good and kind, and into my heart there was born a great emotion of love and loyalty that made me determine that I would devote my whole life to the service of my Sovereigns. Soon after I was to know that they, too, desired that I should be intimately associated with their household. The first intimation came in the form of an invitation to spend two weeks on the Royal yacht which was about to leave for a cruise in Finnish waters. We left on the small yacht *Alexandria,* and at Kronstadt transferred to the larger yacht *Polar Star.* We were a fairly large company on board, among others Prince Obolensky, Naval Minister, Admiral Birileff, Count Tolstoy, Admiral Chagin of the Emperor's staff, and Mademoiselle Schneider and myself in attendance on Her Majesty. A little to my embarrassment I was placed at table next the Emperor with whom I was not at all acquainted. It is true that I had often seen him at Tsarskoe and at Peterhof riding, or walking with his kennel of English collies, eleven magnificent animals in which he took great pride. But this time, on the *Polar Star,* was the first time I had been brought into personal contact with him. With the Empress I felt more at home, and this he knew, for he began almost at once to speak to me of her and of her great help to him in the pain and anxiety of the Japanese War. "Without her," he said with feeling, "I could never have endured the strain."

The war was again recalled by a visit on board the yacht from Count Witte, fresh from the Portsmouth Conference. As a reward for his work done there he received for the first time his title by which the world now knows him. During dinner he related with great gusto all his experiences in the United States, his triumph over the Japanese delegates, his popularity with the Americans, appearing very happy and satisfied with himself. The Emperor complimented him warmly, but Count Witte for all his talents was never a favorite with the Sovereigns.

Life on board the *Polar Star* was very informal, very lazy and agreeable. We sailed through the quiet waters of the Baltic, every day going ashore for walks, the Emperor and his staff sometimes shooting a little, but more often spending the time climbing rocks, hunting mushrooms and berries in the woods and meadows, and playing with the children to whom this country holiday was heavenly pleasure. Living long hours in the open air and indulging in so much vigorous exercise made me desperately sleepy so that I found myself drowsy at dinner and almost dead for sleep by the time the eleven o'clock tea hour came round. Everyone found my drowsiness a source of never-ending amusement, and once, after I had actually fallen asleep at tea and had nearly pitched out of my chair, the Emperor presented me with a silver matchbox with which he said I might prop my eyes open.until bedtime.

There was, of course, a piano in the salon of the yacht, and the Empress and I found a new bond in our common love of music. We spent hours playing four-hand pieces, all our dearly loved classics, Bach, Beethoven, Tschaikovsky, and others. In our quiet hours with our music, and especially before going to bed, the Empress and I had many intimate conversations. As if to relieve a heart too much constrained to silence and solitude the Empress confided in me freely the difficulties of her life. From the first day of her coming to the Russian Court she felt herself disliked, and this was all the more a grief and mortification to her because her marriage with the Emperor was a true love match, and she ardently desired that their union should increase in the Russian people the loyalty and devotion they undoubtedly felt in those days for the House of Romanoff.

All the stories of the reluctance of Alexandra Feodorovna to marry Nicholas II are absurdly untrue. As a small child she had been taken to Petrograd to the marriage of her older sister Elizabeth and the Grand Duke Serge. With the Grand Duchess Xenia, sister of Nicholas, she formed a warm friendship, and with the young heir himself she was on the best of terms. One day he presented her with a pretty little brooch which from very shyness she accepted but afterwards repenting, she returned, squeezing the gift into his hand in the course of a children's party. The young Tsarevitch, much offended, or rather much hurt, passed the brooch on to his sister Xenia who, not knowing its history, cheerfully accepted it.

The attraction so early established increased with years and ripened into romantic love, yet Alexandra Feodorovna hesitated to accept Nicholas as her betrothed because of the change of religion which was necessary. Her home life at this time was not particularly happy. Her mother, Princess Alice of England, had died in her childhood, and now her father, the reigning Grand Duke of Hesse, died suddenly of a stroke of paralysis. Her brother Ernest, who inherited the title and who was of course her guardian, had made an unhappy marriage with Princess Victoria of Coburg, and the home life of the family was not particularly pleasant. Later this marriage was dissolved, and in 1908 Grand Duke Ernest was happily united to Princess Eleanor of Sohmslich. It was at his first marriage that Alexandra Feodorovna again met the Tsarevitch, and from this time on he became a suitor. After their formal betrothal the young pair spent some happy weeks with Queen Victoria in England, where the match met with the approval of all the English relatives.

Emperor Alexander III was at this time lying mortally ill in the Summer Palace Livadia, in the Crimea, and when his condition became hopeless Alexandra Feodorovna, as the future Tsarina, was summoned to join the Imperial Family at his bedside. The dying Tsar rose from his sickbed and, dressed in full uniform, gave her the greeting due her dignity as a royal bride. From the rest of the family, unfortunately, she had a less cordial reception. The Empress and her ladies in waiting, Princess Oblensky and Countess Voronzoff, were distant and formal, and the rest of the Court, as might be expected, followed their example. The whole atmosphere of the palace seemed to the young girl unwholesome and unsympathetic. Upstairs lay the dying Emperor, while below the suite lunched and dined and followed ordinary pursuits very much as though nothing untoward was happening. To Alexandra Feodorovna, accustomed to the intimacy of a small and much less formal Court, this behavior seemed unfeeling and unkind.

The end came suddenly one day when the Emperor, at the moment almost free from pain or weakness, was sitting in his armchair. The Empress Marie, quite overcome, fainted in the arms of Alexandra, who in that hour of extreme sorrow, prayed sincerely that she and her future mother-in-law might be drawn together in bonds of affection. But this, alas! was never to be.

The days that followed were gray and desolate for the young bride. The funeral procession of Alexander III wound slowly and solemnly from the Crimea to Petrograd, a journey of many days. The young Emperor, absorbed in his new duties, had little time to devote to the lonely, homesick girl, and indeed they hardly met before the morning of their marriage, a few days after the state funeral of the dead Emperor. The marriage took place in the church of the Winter Palace, and those who witnessed it have said that the bride, in her rich satin robes, looked very pale and unhappy. As she herself told me, the wedding seemed only a continuation of the long funeral ceremonies she had so lately attended.

Thus came Alexandra Feodorovna to Russia, nor did the weeks that followed her arrival bring her any happiness. To her friend Countess Rantsau, lady in waiting to Princess Henry of Prussia, she wrote:

I feel myself completely alone, and I am in despair that those who surround my husband are apparently false and insincere. Here nobody seems to do his duty for duty's sake, or for Russia, but only for his own selfish interests and for his own advancement. I weep and I worry all day long because I feel that my husband is so young and so inexperienced. He does not at all realize how they are all profiting at the expense of the State. What will come of it in the end? I

am alone most of the time.   My husband is all day occupied
and he spends his evenings with his mother.

This was true, as Nicholas was very inexperienced
and his mother's influence and, it must be said, her
knowledge of affairs were very potent.   All during the
first year the Emperor and the two Empresses lived
together in the Annitchkoff Palace on the Nevski
Prospekt.   Alexandra Feodorovna comforted herself
with the thought that summer would bring her a real
honeymoon in the Crimea.   Meanwhile she and her
young husband went for an occasional sledge ride together, about the only time granted them for confidences.   Fortunately the first baby came soon and
the second was soon expected.   That autumn in
the Crimea the Emperor was stricken with typhus and
his wife insisted upon nursing him herself, hardly
permitting his personal servant to assist her.   Christmas was celebrated in his sickroom, his recovery having set in some weeks before.   During these days of
convalescence they went on solitary walks together, and
the Emperor began to read with his wife, to confide in
her with affection.   When they went back to Petrograd it was with every cloud dispelled, and the Empress a radiantly happy wife.   However, the somewhat
cold and distant manner acquired in the first unhappy
months of her stay in Russia remained with her.   Russia seemed to her an unfriendly land, and she was
never able to present to it her really sunny and amiable
disposition.

Not all of these confidences did the Empress im-
part to me on that first cruise I was privileged to

share with her on the *Polar Star*. Little by little, then
and later, I learned the story of her unhappy youth.
But what she told me that summer seemed to relieve
her mind, and she was more cheerful at the ending of
the cruise than at the beginning. The commander
of the yacht was good enough to tell me that I had
broken down the wall of ice that seemed to surround
Her Majesty, and that now she could be more easily
approached. At the close of the voyage the Emperor
said: "You are to go with us every year after this."

But dearest of all in my memory were the words
of the Empress at parting: "Dear Annia, God has
sent me a friend in you." And so I remained ever
afterwards, not a courtier, not long a lady in waiting,
or even a maid of honor, or in any capacity an official
member of the Court, but merely a devoted and an
intimate friend of Alexandra Feodorovna, Empress
of Russia.

CHAPTER III

SHORTLY after our return to Peterhof I went abroad with my family, stopping first at Karlsruhe, Baden, to visit my grandmother, and afterwards going on to Paris. The Empress had given me letters to her brother, the Grand Duke of Hesse, and to her eldest sister, Princess Victoria of Battenberg, both of whom I saw before leaving Germany. The seat of the Grand Duke of Hesse was Wolfsgarten near Darmstadt, a beautiful place surrounded by extensive gardens laid out according to the Grand Duke's own plans. After my first luncheon at the palace, during which the Grand Duke asked me many questions about the Empress and her life at the Court of Russia, I walked in the gardens with Mme. Grancy, hofmistress of the Court of Hesse, a gracious and charming woman. She showed me the toys and other pathetic relics of the little Princess Elizabeth, only child of the Grand Duke's first marriage, who had died in Russia after an acute illness of a few hours. I also saw the white marble monument which the people of Hesse had raised to the memory of the child.

To the second luncheon I attended at the old Schloss came the Princess Victoria of Battenberg with her lovely daughter Louise. Etiquette at Hesse was of the severest order and I observed with some astonishment that the Princess Victoria curtsied deeply to her sister-in-law, Princess Eleanor, who though much younger than herself, was the wife of the reigning Grand Duke. The old Princess was a very clever woman and a brilliant conversationalist, although, to tell the truth, as she spoke very rapidly I lost a great deal of what she said. I remember her questioning me rather closely about the political situation in Russia, and although I was not very enlightening on the subject she was good enough to invite me and my sister to lunch with her at Jugenheim in the neighborhood of Darmstadt. Both the brother and the sister of the Empress entrusted me with letters to her, and I took them with me to Paris, not knowing that it would be a long time before I should be able to deliver them.

For in the midst of these pleasant days, all unknown to me, the tide of trouble and unrest was rising high in Russia. Beginning with a railroad strike in Finland, a succession of labor troubles and revolutionary demonstrations extending over a large territory brought about a serious crisis which for a time tied up most of the railroads and prevented our return to Russia. Of the cause of the trouble, and above all, of its ultimate consequences, I must say that I remained in complete ignorance. That the situation was grave of course I realized, and my heart went out to the Emperor on whom the responsibility of restoring order largely rested. But that this railroad strike, for that is all it seemed to amount to, was the beginning of a revolution never crossed my mind. I longed to get back to the Empress who I knew would be sharing the anxiety of the Emperor, but as a matter of fact I did not get back until after the manifesto of

October, 1905, had been signed and delivered to a startled world.

This October manifesto, relinquishing the principle of autocracy, creating for the first time a Duma of the Empire, was the result of many councils, some of them dramatic, not to say violent. Count Witte and Grand Duke Nicholas were determined that the Emperor should sign the manifesto, a thing which he was reluctant to do, not because he clung to his privileges as autocrat of all the Russias, though I know that this is the motive still attributed to him by almost all the world. The Tsar hesitated to create a house of popular representation because he knew how ill prepared the Russian people were for self-government. He knew the dense ignorance of the masses, the fanatical and ill-grounded socialism of the intelligentsia, the doctrinaire theories of the Constitutional Democrats. I can say with positive knowledge that Nicholas II fervently desired the progress of his country towards a high civilization, but in 1905 he felt very serious doubts of the wisdom of radical changes in the Russian system of government. At last, however, overborne by his ministers, he signed the manifesto. It is said that the Grand Duke Nicholas, in one of the last councils, lost all control of himself and drawing a revolver threatened to shoot himself on the spot unless the manifesto was signed. Whether this actually occurred or not I do not know, but from what was told me later by the Empress the scenes with the Grand Dukes and the ministers were painful in the extreme. When in one of the final councils the actual form of the national assembly was decided upon the Emperor, with a hand trembling with emotion, signed his name to the fateful document, all in the room rose and bowed to him in token of their continued fidelity.

The Empress told me that while these trying scenes were in progress she sat in her boudoir alone save for her near relative the Grand Duchess Anastasie, both of whom felt that in the stormy council chamber a child was being dangerously brought into the world. Yet all the prayers of the Empress, as well as those of the Emperor, were that the new policy of popular representation would bring peace to troubled Russia.

The Duma was elected, the Socialists alone of political parties repudiating it as too "bourgeois." I was present with all the Empress's household, in the Throne Room of the Winter Palace on the opening day of the Duma when the Tsar welcomed the deputies, and I remember with what a strong, steady voice, and with what clear enunciation, the opening speech was read. Of the proceedings of the first Duma I have no very definite recollections, because they were marked with endless and very wordy discussions rather than with any attempt at constructive action. Everyone knows that the Duma was dissolved by Imperial order after a short life of two months.

Of these momentous political events which rocked Russia and were featured prominently in every newspaper in the world only faint echoes reached the inner circle of the Russian Court. This may sound incredible to readers in republican countries where the press is entirely uncensored and where public opinion in educated in politics. In the Russia of 1906 the reading public was a comparatively small one and the press was poorly representative of the really intelligent people of the Empire. Few men and fewer women of my class attached any particular interest to the Duma, the best we hoped for it being that in time it would become an efficient working agency, like the parliaments of western European countries, adapted, of course, to Russian needs. The first Duma we thought of only as a rather foolish debating society.

The Empress and I were engaged, at that time, with singing lessons, our teacher being Mme. Tretskaia of the Conservatoire. The Empress was gifted with a lovely contralto voice, which, had she been born in other circumstances, might easily have given her a professional standing. My voice being a high soprano we sang many duets. Sometimes my sister joined us and as she also sang well we formed a trio singing many of the lovely arrangements for three voices by Schumann and others. Occasionally came also an English friend of the Empress, a talented violinist, and among us we arranged concerts which gave us the greatest pleasure, although we always had to hold them in another building of the palace called the Farm in order not to disturb the Emperor, who, for some strange reason, did not like to hear his wife sing.

When summer came and while the Duma was talking out its brief existence we again took up our sea life, this time on board the large royal yacht the *Standert*. We cruised for two months, the Emperor frequently going ashore for tennis and other amusements, but occupied two days of each week with papers and state documents brought to him by messenger from Petrograd. The Empress and I were almost constantly together walking on shore, or sitting on deck reading, or watching the joyful play of the children, each of whom had a sailor attendant to keep them from falling overboard or otherwise suffering mishap. The special attendant of the little Alexei was a big, good-natured sailor named Derevanko, a man seemingly devoted to the child. It was in fact Derevanko who taught Alexei to walk, and who during periods of great weakness following severe attacks of his malady carried the boy most tenderly in his arms. All of these sailors at the end of a cruise received watches and other valuable presents from the Emperor, yet most of them, even Derevanko, when the revolution came, turned on their Sovereigns with meanest treachery.

On my days of regular service, Wednesdays and Fridays, for I was then a regularly appointed lady in waiting, I dined with the Imperial Family, and at that time I formed a close friendship with General Alexander Orloff, an old companion in the Royal Hussars with the Emperor. After dinner the Emperor and General Orloff usually played billiards, while the Empress and I read or sewed under the warm lamplight. Those were happy evenings, full of bright talk and laughter, and I came to regard General Orloff as one of my best friends. Already the hateful hand of jealousy and gossip had been directed against me by people who could not understand, or who, from motives of palace politics, deliberately misunderstood the Empress's preference for my society. Practically every monarch has some close personal friend, absolutely disassociated with politics and social intrigue, but I have noticed that these friendships are always misunderstood and frequently bitterly resented. I used to take my small troubles to General Orloff, at least they seem small now after years of real trouble and affliction. But even after these bitter years of sorrow and affliction the kindly counsels of the good old general often come back to me, as they did then, like a friendly hand laid on my hot and resentful heart.

I was then, in 1906, a fully grown and mature young woman and, as I could not help knowing, I was the subject of many conversations in the family circle because of my indifference to marriage. I had, I suppose, the normal amount of attention from men, and the usual number of suitors, but none of the young officers and courtiers with whom I danced and chatted made any special appeal to my imagination. There was one young naval officer, Alexander Virouboff, who after December, 1906, came to our house almost every day, paying me the most marked attentions. One day at luncheon he spoke with pride of the very good service to which he had just been appointed, and very soon afterwards I found myself greeted on all sides as his affianced. In February there was a ball in which I was formally presented as a bride, and in the after whirl of dinners, presents, new gowns and jewels, I began to share the excitement, if not the happiness, of those around me. The Empress approved the match, my parents approved, and no one except my old friend General Orloff expressed even a faint doubt of the wisdom of the marriage. But on the day when he spoke to me frankly, advising me to think seriously before taking such a serious step, the Empress entered the room and said in a decided voice that I had given my word and that therefore I should not be given any discouragement.

I was married on the 30th of April, 1907, in the palace church at Tsarskoe Selo. The night before I slept ill and in the early morning I awoke in a mood of sadness and depression. The events of the day passed more like a dream than a reality. As in a dream I allowed myself to be dressed in my white satin wedding gown and floating veil, and still in a dream I knelt before their Majesties who blessed me, holding over my head a small ikon. Then began the marriage procession through the long corridors to the church. First walked Count Fredericks, master of ceremonies of the Court. Then came their Majesties, arm in arm, with my little boy cousin, Count Karloff, carrying a holy image. Then I, walking with my father. I must have shown by my excessive pallor the anxiety I felt, for on the stairs the Empress looked at me with concern and having caught my eye smiled brightly and glanced upward reassuringly at the bright sky.

During the ceremony I stood quite still like a manikin, gazing at my bridegroom as at some stranger. I had one moment of faint amusement when the officiating priest, who was very near-sighted, mistook the best man for the bridegroom addressing us affectionately as "my dear children." The Empress, as my matron of honor, stood at my left hand with the four young Grand Duchesses, and two others, the children of Grand Duke Paul. One of these was the Grand Duke Dmitri, who was destined to grow up to take part in the assassination of Rasputine. On the day of my marriage he was just a dear little boy, wide-eyed with the excitement of being one of a wedding party. After the ceremony there was tea with the Emperor and the Empress, and as usual when she and I parted there was an affectionate little note pressed into my hand How like an angel she looked to me that day, and how hard it was for me to turn away from her and to go away with my husband. There was a family dinner that night in our home in Petrograd, and afterwards we went away for a month into the country.

It is a hard thing for a woman to tell of a marriage which from the first proved to be a complete mistake, and I shall say only of my husband that he was the victim of family abnormalities which in more than one instance manifested themselves in madness. My husband's nervous system had suffered severely in the rigors of the Japanese War, and there were many occasions when he was not at all responsible for what he did. Often for days together he kept his bed refusing to speak to anyone. One night things became so threatening that I could not forbear telephoning my fears to the Empress, and she, to my joy, responded by driving instantly to the house in her evening gown and jewels. For an hour she stayed with me comforting me with promises that the situation should, in one way or another, be relieved.

In August the Emperor and Empress invited us both to go for a cruise on the *Standert,* and sailing

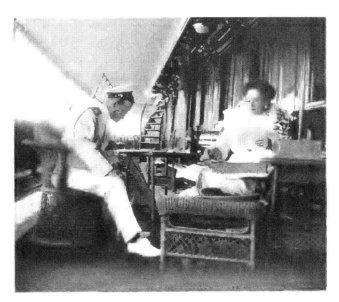

THE EMPEROR AND EMPRESS IN A QUIET HOUR ON BOARD
THE *STANDERT*. Photograph by Mme. Viroubova.

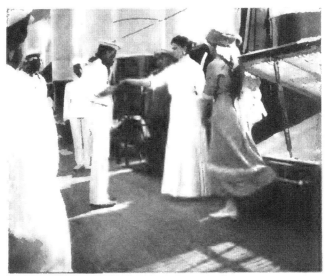

THE EMPRESS DISTRIBUTING PRESENTS AT THE END OF
A CRUISE ON THE IMPERIAL YACHT *STANDERT*.

through the blue Finnish fjords it did seem for a time that I should find peace.   But one day a terrible thing happened, possibly an accident, but if so a very strange one, as we had on board an uncommonly able Finnish pilot.   We were seated on deck at tea, the band playing, a perfectly calm sea running, when we felt a terrific shock which shook the yacht from stem to stern and sent the tea service crashing to the deck.   In great alarm we sprang to our feet only to feel the yacht listing sharply to larboard.   In an instant the decks were alive with sailors obeying the harsh commands of the captain, and helping the suite to look to the safety of the women and childen.   The fleet of torpedo boats which always surrounded the yacht made speed to the rescue and within a few minutes the children and their nurses and attendants were taken off.   Not knowing the exact degree of the disaster, the Empress and I hastened to the cabins where we hurriedly tied up in sheets all the valuables we could collect.   We were the last to leave the poor *Standert,* which by that time was stationary on the rocks.

We spent the night on a small vessel, the *Asia,* the Empress taking Alexei with her in one cabin and the Emperor occupying a small cabin on deck.   The little Grand Duchesses were crowded in a cabin by themselves, their nurses and attendants finding beds where they could.   The ship was far from clean and I remember the Emperor, rather disheveled himself, bringing basins of water to the Empress and me in which to wash our faces and hands.   We had some kind of a dinner about midnight and none of us passed an especially restful night.   The next day came the yacht

Alexandria on which we spent the next two weeks. A fortnight was required to get the ill-fated *Standert* off the rocks on which she had so mysteriously been driven. From the *Alexandria* and later to the *Polar Star,* to which we had been transferred, we watched the unhappy yacht being carefully removed from her captivity. We had not been very comfortable on the *Alexandria* because there was not nearly enough cabin room for our rather numerous company. The Empress occupied a cabin, the Tsarevitch and his sailor another one adjoining. The four little Grand Duchesses did as well as they could in one small cabin, while the Emperor slept on a couch in the main salon. As for me, I slept in a bathroom. Most of the suite found quarters on a Finnish ship which stood by.

After our return to Peterhof my husband became worse rather than better and his physician advised him to spend some time in a sanatorium for nervous patients in Switzerland. He left, but on coming back to Russia was noticeably in worse condition than before. In the hope that active service would be of benefit to his shattered nerves and disordered brain he was ordered to sea, but even this expedient proved of little benefit. After a year of intense suffering and humiliation my unhappy marriage, with the full approval of their Majesties and of my parents, was dissolved.

I kept my little house in Tsarskoe Selo, its modest furnishings beautified by many gifts from the Empress. Among these gifts were some charming pictures and six exquisitely embroidered antique chairs. A silver-laden tea table helped to make the salon cozy, and I have many happy memories of intimate teas to which the Empress sent fruit and the Emperor the cherry brandy which he especially affected.

The little house, however, was far from being the luxurious palace in which I have often been pictured as living. As a matter of fact, it was frightfully cold in winter because the house had no stone foundation but rested on the frozen earth. Sometimes when the Emperor and Empress came to tea we sat with our feet on the sofa to keep warm. Once the Emperor jokingly told me that after a visit to my house he kept himself from freezing only by going directly to a hot bath.

The summer of 1908 the Emperor and Empress paid an official visit to England, but on their return they sent for me and again I spent a happy holiday on the yacht. Not altogether happy, however, for towards the end of the cruise my poor friend General Orloff, then near his death from tuberculosis, came to say good-bye to his Sovereigns. Correct in his uniform and all his orders the fine old soldier bade us all a brave farewell before leaving for Egypt, where he well knew that his end awaited him. Peace to his honored ashes. He lies buried at Tsarskoe Selo, where the Emperor and Empress often visited his grave. Poor Orloff, he too suffered from the malicious gossip of the Court where his honest admiration of the Empress was deliberately misinterpreted and as-soiled. I can bear witness, and I do, that his greatest devotion was to the Emperor, his old comrade in arms, the friend of his youthful days.

CHAPTER IV

IN the autumn of 1909 I went for the first time to
Livadia, the country estate of the Imperial Family
in the Crimea. This part of Russia, dearer to all of the
Tsars than any other, is a small peninsula, almost an
island, surrounded on the west and south by the Black
Sea and on the east by the Sea of Asov. A range of
high hills protects it from the cold winds of the north
and gives it a climate so mild and bland as to be almost
sub-tropical. The Imperial estate, which occupies
nearly half the peninsula, has always been left as far
as possible in its natural condition of unbroken forests,
wild mountains, and valleys. There was at the time of
which I write but one short railroad in the whole of the
Crimea, a short line running from Sevastopol, the principal port of the Black Sea, northward to Moscow.
All other journeys had to be taken by carriage, motor
cars, or on horseback.

The natural beauties of the Crimea would be difficult to exaggerate. The mountains, dark with pines,
snow-covered during most of the year, make an imposing background for the profusion of flowering
trees, shrubs and vines, making the valleys and plains
one continuous garden. The vineyards of the Crimea
are, or were previous to the Revolution, equal to any
in Italy or southern France. What they became afterwards God knows. But certainly up to the summer of

1914, when I saw them last, the vine-clad hills and valleys of the Crimea were an earthly Paradise, as lovely and as peaceful as the mind can picture. From the grapes of the Crimea were distilled the best wines in Russia, among others an excellent champagne and a delicious sweet wine of the muscat variety.

Almost every kind of fruit flourished in the valleys, and in spring the wealth of blossoms, pink and white, of apples, cherries, peaches, almonds, made the whole countryside a perfumed garden, while in autumn the masses of golden fruit were a wonder to behold. Flowers bloomed as though they were the very soul of the fair earth. Never have I seen such roses. They spread over every building in great vines as strong as ivy, and they scattered their rich petals over lawns and pathways in fragrance at times almost overpowering. There was another flower, the glycinia, which grew on trailing vines in grapelike clusters, deep mauve in hue, the favorite color of the Empress. This flower, too, was intensely fragrant, as were the violets which in spring literally carpeted the plains. Imagine these valleys and plains, with their vineyards and orchards, their tall cypress trees and trailing roses, sloping down to a sea as blue as the sky and as gentle as a summer day, and you have a picture, imperfectly as I have painted it, of the country retreat of the Romanoffs. Here of all places in Russia they were loved and revered. The natives of the peninsula were Tartars, the men very tall and strong and the women almost invariably handsome. They were Mohammedans, and it was only within late years that the women had discarded their veils. Both men and women wore very picturesque dress, the men wearing round black fur caps and short embroidered coats over tight white trousers. It was the fashion for the women to dye their hair a bright red, over which they wore small caps and floating veils and adorning themselves with a wealth of silver bangles. These Tartars were an honest folk, absolutely loyal to the Tsar. They were wonderful horsemen, comparing favorably with the best of the Cossacks, and their horses, through long breeding and training, were natural pacers. To see a cavalcade of Tartars sweep by was to imagine a race of Centaurs come back to earth, so absolutely one was every horse and man.

The palace, as I saw it in 1909, was a large, old wooden structure surrounded by balconies, the rooms dark, damp, and unattractive. The only really sunny and cheerful room in the whole house was the dining room, where twice a day the suite met for luncheon and dinner. The Emperor usually presided at these meals, but the Empress being in bad health lunched privately with the Tsarevitch. The Empress had been for some time a victim of the most alarming heart attacks which she bravely concealed, not wishing the public to know her condition. Oftentimes when I remarked the blue whiteness of her hands, her quick, gasping breaths, she silenced me with a peremptory "Don't say anything. People need not know." However, I was intensely relieved when at last she consented to have the daily attention of a special physician, this being the devoted Dr. Botkine, who accompanied the family in their Siberian exile, and shared their fate, whatever that fate may have been. Dr. Botkine, although a very able physician, was not a man of great social prominence, and when, at the Empress's request, I went to apprise him of his appointment as special medical adviser to their Majesties, he received the news with astonishment almost amounting to dismay. He began his administration by greatly curtailing the activities of the Empress, keeping her quietly in bed for long periods, and insisting on the use of a rolling chair in the gardens, and a pony chaise for longer jaunts abroad.

Life at Livadia in 1909 and in after years was simple and informal. We walked, rode, bathed in the sea, and generally led a healthful country life, such as the Tsar, eminently an outdoor man and a lover of nature, enjoyed to the utmost. We roamed the woods gathering wild berries and mushrooms which we ate at our al fresco teas, cooking the mushrooms over little campfires of twigs and dried leaves. The Emperor and his suite hunted a little, rode much, and played very good tennis. In this latter sport I was often the Emperor's partner and a very serious affair I had to make of each game. No conversation was allowed, and we played with all the gravity and intensity of professionals.

We had each year many visitors. In 1909 came sometimes to lunch the Emir of Bokhara, a big, handsome Oriental in a long black coat and a white turban glittering with diamonds and rubies. He seemed intensely interested in the comparative simplicity of Russian royal customs, and when he departed for his own land he distributed presents in true Arabian Nights' profusion, costly diamonds and rubies to their

Majesties, and to the suite orders and decorations set with jewels. Nevertheless the souvenir of the Emir's visit to Livadia which I most prized was a photograph of himself for which he obligingly posed in the gardens. This photograph and hundreds of others which I took during the twelve years I spent with the Imperial Family I was obliged to leave behind me when I fled, a hunted refugee, across the Russian frontier. I have no hope of ever seeing any of them again.[1]

The 20th of October, the anniversary of the death of Alexander III, was always remembered by a solemn religious service held in the room where he died, the armchair in which he breathed his last being draped in heavy black. This death chamber was not in the main palace but in a smaller house adjoining, one which in 1909 was used as a lodging for the suite. The last part of our stay in the Crimea that year was not very gay. The Emperor left us for an official visit to the King of Italy, and on the day of his departure the Empress, greatly depressed, shut herself up in her own room refusing to see anyone, even the children. It was always to her an intolerable burden that she and the Emperor were obliged by etiquette to part from each other in public and to meet again after each absence in full view of the suite and often of the staring multitude.

This autumn was made sad also by one of the all too frequent illnesses of the unfortunate little Tsarevitch. The sufferings of the child on these occasions were so acute that everyone in the palace was

[1] Happily many of these photographs were later recovered and appear among illustrations of this volume.

rendered perfectly miserable. Nothing much could be done to assuage the poor boy's agony, and nothing except the constant love and devotion of the Empress gave him the slightest relief. We who could do nothing else for him took refuge in prayer and supplication in the little church near the palace. Mlle. Tutcheva, maid of honor to the young Grand Duchesses, read the psalms, while the Empress, the older girls, Olga and Tatiana, two of the Tsar's aides, and myself assisted in the singing. In the midst of our anxiety and distress during this illness of Alexei my father paid us a brief visit, bringing important reports to the Emperor, and this was at least a momentary bright hour in the sorrow of my existence. At Christmas time the Court returned to Tsarskoe Selo, both the Empress and the Tsarevitch by this time much improved in health.

The next time I went with their Majesties to the Crimea we found the estate transformed and greatly beautified by the substitution of a palace of white marble for the ancient and gloomy wooden buildings. The new palace was the work of the eminent architect, Krasnoff, who had also designed the palaces of the Grand Dukes Nicholas and George. In the two years Krasnoff had indeed worked marvels, not only in the palace, which was a gem of Italian Renaissance architecture, but in many smaller buildings, the whole constituting a town in itself, harmonious in material and design.

I shall never forget the day we landed in Yalta, and the glorious drive through the bright spring sunshine to the palace. Before the carriage rode an old Tartar of the Crimea, one of the tribe I described earlier in this chapter. To ride before the Tsar's carriage was an ancient prerogative of these honest and loyal people, a prerogative which had to be resigned when carriages gave way to motor cars No Tartar horse could have kept pace with, much less have preceded, a motor car of Nicholas II, for he always insisted on driving at a terrifying speed. But as late as 1911 he kept up the old custom of driving from Yalta to Livadia.

We drove, as I say, through the dazzling sunshine and under the fresh green trees of springtime until the white palace, set in gardens of blooming flowers and vines, burst on our delighted eyes. Russian fashion we proceeded first to the church, from whence in procession we followed the priests to the anointing and blessing of the new dwelling. The first day I spent with the Empress superintending the hanging of pictures and ikons, placing familiar and homely objects, photographs and souvenirs, so necessary to make a dwelling place out of an empty house, even though it be a royal palace. On the second floor were the private apartments of the family, including a small salon. The apartments of the Empress were furnished in light wood and pink chintzes and many vases and jars always kept full of the pink and mauve flowers she loved. From the windows of her boudoir one looked out on the wooded hills, and from the bedroom there was an enchanting view of the sparkling sea. To the right of the Empress's boudoir was the Emperor's study, furnished in green leather with a large writing table in the center of the room. On this floor also was the family dining room, the bedrooms of the Tsarevitch and of the Grand Duchesses and their attendants, a large day room for the use of the children, and a big white hall or ballroom, seldom used.

Below were the rooms of state, drawing rooms and dining rooms, all in white, the doors and windows opening on a marble courtyard draped with roses and vines which almost covered an antique Italian well in the center of the court. Here the Emperor loved to walk and smoke after luncheon, chatting with his guests or with members of the household. The whole palace, including the rooms of state, were lightly, beautifully furnished in white wood and flowered chintzes, giving the effect of a hospitable summer home rather than a palace.

That autumn was marked by a season of unusual gaiety in honor of the coming of age, at sixteen, of the Grand Duchess Olga, who received for the occasion a beautiful diamond ring and a necklace of diamonds and pearls. This gift of a necklace to the daughter of a Tsar when she became of age was traditional, but the expense of it to Alexandra Feodorovna, the mother of four daughters, was a matter of apprehension. Powerless to change the custom, even had she wished to do so, she tried to ease the burden on the treasury by a gradual accumulation of the jewels. By her request the necklaces, instead of being purchased outright when the young Grand Duchesses reached the age of sixteen, were collected stone by stone on their birthdays and name days. Thus at the coming-out ball of the Grand Duchess Olga she wore a necklace of thirty-two superb jewels which had been accumulating for her from her babyhood.

It was a very charming ball that marked the introduction to society of the oldest daughter of the Tsar. Flushed and fair in her first long gown, something pink and filmy and of course very smart, Olga was as excited over her début as any other young girl. Her hair, blonde and abundant, was worn for the first time coiled up young-lady fashion, and she bore herself as the central figure of the festivities with a modesty and a dignity which greatly pleased her parents. We danced in the great state dining room on the first floor, the glass doors to the courtyard thrown open, the music of the unseen orchestra floating in from the rose garden like a breath of its own wondrous fragrance. It was a perfect night, clear and warm, and the gowns and jewels of the women and the brilliant uniforms of the men made a striking spectacle under the blaze of the electric lights. The ball ended in a cotillion and a sumptuous supper served on small tables in the ballroom.

This was a beginning of a series of festivities which the Grand Duchess Olga and a little later on her sister Tatiana enjoyed to their utmost, for they were not in the least like the conventional idea of princesses, but simple, happy, normal young girls, loving dancing and parties and all the frivolities which make youth bright and memorable. Besides the dances given at Livadia that year, large functions attended by practically everyone in the neighborhood who had Court entrée, there were a number of very brilliant balls given in honor of Olga and Tatiana after the family returned to Tsarskoe Selo. Two of these were given by the Grand Dukes Peter and George and the girls enjoyed them so much that they begged for another before Christmas. This time it was Grand Duke Nicholas who provided a most regal entertainment, preceded by a dinner for the suite, to which I was invited. I went because the Empress wished it, but I went rather unwillingly knowing that the atmosphere was not a friendly one. Their Majesties were at that time particularly friendly with Grand Duke George and his wife who was Princess Marie of Greece, as formerly they had been with Grand Dukes Peter and Nicholas and their wives, the Montenegran princesses, Melitza and Stana, of whom more must be written later on.

In relating the events of the coming of age of Olga and Tatiana I must not forget to mention affairs of almost equal consequence which occurred in the Crimea in that season of 1911. The climate of the Crimea was ideal for tuberculosis patients, and from her earliest married life the Empress had taken the deepest interest in the many hospitals and sanatoria which nestled among the hills, some of them almost within the confines of the Imperial estate. Before the beginning of the reign of Nicholas II and Alexandra Feodorovna these hospitals existed in numbers but they were not of the best modern type. Not satisfied with these institutions the Empress out of her own private fortune built and equipped new and improved hospitals, and one of the first duties laid on me when I first visited the Crimea was to spend hours at a time visiting, inspecting and reporting on the condition of buildings, nursing and care of patients. I was particularly charged with discovering patients who were too poor to pay for the best food and nursing, and one of each summer's activities when the family visited the Crimea was a bazaar or other entertainment for the benefit of these needy ones. Four great bazaars organized and largely managed by the Empress I particularly remember. The first of these was held in 1911 and the others in 1912, 1913, and 1914. For all of these bazaars the Empress and her ladies worked very hard and from the opening day the Empress, however precarious the condition of her health, always presided at her own table, disposing of fine needlework, embroidery, and art objects with energy and enthusiasm. The crowds around her booth were enormous, the people pressing forward almost frenziedly to touch her hand, her sleeve, her dress, enchanted to receive their purchases from the hand of the Empress they adored, for she was adored by the real Russian people, whatever the intriguing Court and the jealous political rivals of her husband thought of her. Often the crowd at these bazaars would beg for a sight of Alexei, and smiling with pleasure the Empress would lift him to the table where the child would bow shyly but sweetly, stretching out his hands in friendly greeting to the worshipping crowds. Indeed the people loved all the Imperial Family then, whatever changes were made in the minds of the many by the horrible sufferings of the War, by propaganda, and by the mania of the Revolution. The great mass of the Russian people loved and were loyal to their Sovereigns. No one who knew them at all can ever forget that.

Perhaps they were more universally loved in the Crimea than elsewhere because of the simplicity of their lives and the close touch they were able to keep with the people of the country. We went to Livadia again in 1912, in 1913, and last of all in the spring and summer of 1914. We arrived in 1912 in the last week of Lent, I think the Saturday before Palm Sunday. Already the fruit trees were in full bloom and the air was warm with spring. Twice a day we attended service in the church, and on Thursday of Holy Week, a very solemn day in the orthodox Russian calendar, their Majesties took communion, previously turning from the altar to the congregation and bowing on all sides. After this they approached the holy images and kissed them. The Empress in her white gown and cap looked beautiful if somewhat thin and frail, and it was very sweet to see the little Alexei helping his mother from her knees after each deep reverence. On Easter eve there was a procession with candles all through the courts of the palace and on Easter Sunday for two hours the soldiers, according to old custom, gathered to exchange Easter kisses with the Emperor and to receive each an Easter egg. Children from the schools came to salute in like manner the Empress. For their Majesties it was a long and fatiguing ceremony, but they carried it through with all graciousness, while the Imperial household looked on.

Such was the intimate, the patriarchal relation between the Tsar and his people, and such was the real soul of Russia before the Revolution. I have often read, in books written by Western authors, that the Tsar and all the Imperial Family lived in hourly terror of assassination, that they knew themselves hated by their people and were righteously afraid of them. Nothing could possibly be farther from the truth.

Certainly neither Nicholas II nor Alexandra Feodorovna feared their people.   The constant police
supervision under which they lived annoyed them un-
speakably, and never were they happier than when
practically unattended they moved freely among the
Russian people they loved.   In connection with the
Empress's care for the tuberculosis patients in the
Crimea there was one day every summer known as
White Flower Day, and on that day every member of
society, unless she had a very good excuse, went out
into the towns and sold white flowers for the benefit
of the hospitals.   It was a day especially delightful to
the Empress and, as they grew old enough to partici-
pate in such duties, to all the young Grand Duchesses.
The Empress and her daughters worked very hard on
White Flower Day, spending practically the whole
day driving and walking, mingling with the crowd and
vending their flowers as enthusiastically as though
their fortunes depended on selling them all.   Of course
they always did sell them all.   The crowds surged
around them eager and proud to buy a flower from
their full baskets.   But the buyers were no whit happier
than the sellers, that I can say with assurance.

Of course life in the Crimea was not all simplicity
and informality.   There were a great many visitors,
most of them of rank too exalted to be treated with
informality.   I remember in particular visits of Grand
Duke Ernest of Hesse, brother of the Empress, and
his wife, Princess Eleanor.   I remember also visits
of the widowed Grand Duchess Serge, who had become
a nun and was now abbess of a wonderful convent in
Moscow, the House of Mary and Martha.   When she

visited Livadia masses were said daily in the palace church. I ought not, while speaking of visitors, to omit mention of the old Prince Galitzin, a very odd person, but strongly attached to the Tsar, to whom he presented a part of his own estate, some distance to Livadia, and to which we made a special excursion on the royal yacht. Another memorable excursion was to the estates of Prince Oldenbourg on the coast of Caucasia. The sea that day was very rough and by the time we reached our destination the Empress was so prostrated that she could not go ashore. It was a pity because she missed what to all the others was a remarkable spectacle, a grand holiday of the Caucasians who, in their picturesque costumes, crowded down to the shore to greet their Sovereigns. The whole countryside was in festival, great bonfires burning in all the hills and on all the meadows wild music and the most fascinating of native dances.

Such was life in the Crimea in the old, vanished days. Simple, happy, kind, and loyal, all that was best in Russia.

CHAPTER V

THESE yearly visits to the Crimea were diversified with holiday voyages on the *Standert,* and visits to relatives and close friends in various countries. In 1910 their Majesties visited Riga and other Baltic ports where they were royally welcomed, afterwards voyaging to Finnish waters where they received as guests the King and Queen of Sweden. This was an official visit, hence attended with considerable ceremony, exchange visits of the Sovereigns from yacht to warship, state dinners and receptions. At one of these dinners I sat next the admiral of the Swedish fleet, who was much depressed because during the royal salute to the Emperor one of his sailors had accidentally been killed.

In the autumn of 1910 the Emperor and Empress went to Nauheim, hoping that the waters would have a beneficial effect on her failing health. They left on a cold and rainy day and both were in a melancholy state, partly because of separation from the beloved home, and partly because of the quite apparent weakness of the Empress. On her account the Emperor showed himself deeply disturbed. "I would do anything," he said to me, "even to going to prison, if she could only be well again." This anxiety was shared by the whole household, even by the servants who stood in line on the staircase saying their farewells,

COALING IN AT YALTA, THE CRIMEA, 1911. THE EMPEROR, GRAND DUCHESSES OLGA AND ANASTASIE, MME VIROUBOVA AND OFFICERS OF THE YACHT *STANDART*. Photograph by the Empress.

THE EMPEROR, GRAND DUCHESSES OLGA AND MARIE STROLLING THROUGH HOM-
BURG IN 1910. THE EMPEROR OUT OF UNIFORM WAS ALMOST SAFE FROM
RECOGNITION.

kissing the shoulder of the Emperor and the gloved hand of the Empress.

I heard almost daily from Frieberg, where the family were stopping, letters from the Emperor, the Empress, and the children, telling me of their daily life. At length came a letter from the Empress suggesting that I join my father at Hombourg, not far distant, that we might have opportunity for occasional meetings. As soon as I arrived I telephoned the château at Frieberg, and the next day a motor car was sent to fetch me. I found the Empress improved in health but looking thin and tired from the rather rigorous cure. The Emperor, in his civilian clothes, looked unfamiliar and strange, but he wore the conventional citizen's garb because he as well as the Empress wished to remain as far as possible private persons. When the health of the Empress permitted she, with Olga and Tatiana, enjoyed going unattended to Nauheim, walking unnoticed through the streets, and gazing admiringly into shop windows like ordinary tourists. Once the Emperor and the young Grand Duchesses motored over to Hombourg and for a short hour walked about quite happily unobserved. Only too soon, however, the Emperor was recognized and our whole small party, was obliged to flee precipitously before the gathering crowds and the ever enterprising news photographers. On some of our outings the Emperor was more fortunate. Once when we were wandering along a country road on the outskirts of Hombourg a wagon passing us dropped suddenly into the road a heavy box. The carrier, try as he would, could not succeed in lifting the box back to its place until the Emperor went forward and, exerting all his strength, helped the man out of his difficulty. The carrier thanked his Majesty with every expression of respect and gratitude, recognizing him as a gentleman but never dreaming, of course, of his exalted station. To my expressions of amused enjoyment of the situation the Emperor said to me gravely: "I have come to believe that the higher a man's station in life the less it becomes him to assume any airs of superiority. I want my children to be brought up in this same belief."

Soon after this I returned to Russia to visit my sister, who had just borne her first baby, a little girl named for the Grand Duchess Tatiana, who acted as godmother for the child. My stay was not long, as letters from the Empress called me to Frankfort in order to be near her. On my arrival at Frankfort a surprise awaited me in the form of an invitation from the Grand Duke Ernest of Hesse to stay with his Imperial guests at his castle. At the castle gates I was welcomed by Mme. Grancy, the charming hofmistress of the Hessian Court, and by Miss Kerr, a bright and clever English girl, maid of honor to Princess Victoria. Miss Kerr took me at once to my apartments, near her own, and I quickly made myself at home. That night at dinner I sat between the Emperor and our host, the Grand Duke of Hesse. The company, which was most distinguished, included Prince Henry of Prussia, who that evening happened to be in rather a disagreeable mood, Princess Irene, Princess Victoria of Battenberg, and her beautiful daughter Princess Louise, Prince George of Greece,

and the two semi-invalid sons of Prince and Princess
Henry. The Empress was not present, being excused
on account of her cure. Besides, it was understood
that the Empress almost never appeared at state
dinners.

The Grand Duke of Hesse I have always liked extremely both for his amiable disposition and for his
many accomplishments. He was, and is still, an unusually gifted musician, a painter, and an artist crafts-
man seriously interested in the great pottery in Darmstadt, where his own designs are used. He has always
been a man of liberal social ideals and his popularity
among the people of Hesse not even the German Revolution has been powerful enough to overthrow. His
wife, Princess Eleanor, when I knew her, was dignified
and gracious and gifted with a genuine talent for dress.
Prince Henry of Prussia, brother of the Kaiser and
brother-in-law of the Empress, was a tall and handsome man, but inclined to be—let us say—tempera-
mental. At times he was overbearing and very satiri-
cal, and at others friendly and charming. His wife
was a small woman, simple in manner and of a kindly,
unselfish nature. Princess Alice, daughter of Princess
Victoria of Battenberg and wife of Prince Andrew of
Greece, was a beautiful woman but unhappily quite
deaf.

The Castle of Frieberg, which stands on a high hill
overlooking a low valley and the little red-roofed
town of Nauheim, is an ancient structure not particularly attractive either inside or out. There was nothing much for Grand Duke Ernest's guests to do in the
way of amusement except to walk and drive. Of the

Empress I saw rather less than we had planned, but sometimes late in the evenings the Emperor, the Empress, and myself met for Russian tea and for familiar talks before bedtime.

In October or November their Majesties returned to Tsarskoe Selo, the Empress greatly benefited by her cure. How happy we were to be once more at home, the Empress in her charming boudoir hung with mauve silk and fragrant with fresh roses and lilacs, I in my own little house which I dearly loved even though the floors were so cold. The opal-hued boudoir of the Empress, where we spent a great deal of our time, was a lovely, quiet place, so quiet that the footsteps of the children and the sound of their pianos in the rooms above were often quite audible. The Empress usually lay on a low couch over which' hung her favorite picture, a large painting of the Holy Virgin asleep and surrounded by angels. Beside her couch stood a table, books on the lower shelf, and on the upper a confusion of family photographs, letters, telegrams, and papers. It was undeniably a weakness of the Empress that she was not in the least systematic about her correspondence. Intimate letters, it is true, she answered promptly, but others she often left for weeks untouched. About once a month Madeleine, the principal maid of the Empress, would invade the boudoir and implore her mistress to clear up this heap of neglected correspondence. The Empress usually began by begging to be left alone, but in the end she always gave in to the importunities of the invaluable Madeleine. The Empress of course had a private secretary, Count Rostovseff, but it was one of her peculiarities that she preferred to handle her letters and telegrams before her secretary, and he seemed to accustom himself with ease to her dilatory ways.

It would be difficult to imagine two people more widely different on points of this kind than Nicholas II and Alexandra Feodorovna. Their private apartments were very close together, the Emperor's study, billiard and sitting room and his dressing room with a fine swimming bath, almost adjoining the apartments of the Empress. The big antechamber to the study, well furnished with chairs and tables and many books and magazines, looked out on a court, and here people who had business with the Emperor waited until they were summoned to his private room. The study was a perfect model of orderliness, the big writing table having every pen and pencil exactly in its place. The large calendar also with appointments written carefully in the Emperor's own hand was always precisely in its proper place. The Emperor often said that he wanted to be able to go into his study in the dark and put his hand at once on any object he knew to be there. The Emperor was equally particular about the appointments of his other rooms. The dressing table in the white-tiled bathroom, separated from the sitting room by a corridor and a small staircase, was as much a model of neatness as the study table, nor could the Emperor have tolerated valets who would not have kept his rooms in a condition of perpetual good order. Of course the ample *garderobes,* where the gowns, wraps, hats, and jewels of the Empress and the innumerable uniforms of the Emperor were kept, were always in order because they were in the care of experienced servants and were rarely if ever visited by others than their responsible guardians.

The Emperor's combined billiard and sitting room was not very much used because the Emperor spent most of his leisure hours in his wife's boudoir. But it was in the billiard room that the Emperor kept his many albums of photographs, records of his reign. These albums bound in green with the Imperial monogram, contained photographs taken over a period of twenty years. The Empress had her own albums full of equally priceless records, priceless from the historian's standpoint at any rate, and each of the children had their own. There was an expert photographer attached to the household whose only duty was to develop and print these photographs, which were, in almost every case, mounted by the royal photographer's own hand. This work used to be done, as a rule, on rainy days, either in the palace or on board the *Standert*. The Emperor, as usual, was neater about this work of pasting photographic prints than any other member of the household. He could not endure the sight of the least drop of glue on a table. As might be expected of so orderly a person the Emperor was slow about almost everything he did. When the Empress wrote a letter she did it very quickly, holding her portfolio on her knees on her *chaise longue*. When the Emperor wrote a letter it was a matter of hours before it was completed. I remember once at Livadia the Emperor retiring to his study at two o'clock to write an important letter to his mother. At five, the Empress afterwards told me, the letter remained unfinished.

The private life of the Imperial Family in these years before the War was quiet and uneventful. The Empress never left her room before noon, it being her custom, since her illness, to read and write propped up on pillows on her bed. Luncheon was at one o'clock, the Emperor, his aide-de-camp for the day, the children, and an occasional guest attending. After luncheon the Emperor went at once to his study to work or to receive visitors. Before tea time he usually went for a brisk walk in the open.

At half past two I came to the Empress, and if the weather was fine and she well enough, we went for a drive or a walk. Otherwise we read or worked until five, when the family tea was served. Tea was a meal in which there was never the slightest variation. Always appeared the same little white-draped table with its silver service, the glasses in their silver standards, and for the rest simply plates of hot bread and butter and a few English biscuits. Never anything new, never any surprises in the way of cakes or sweetmeats. The only difference in the Imperial tea table came in Lent, when butter and even bread made with butter disappeared, and a small dish or two of nuts was substituted. The Empress often used gently to complain, saying that other people had much more interesting teas, but she who was supposed to have almost unlimited power, was in reality quite unable to change a single deadly detail of the routine of the Russian Court, where things had been going on almost exactly the same for generations. The same arrangement of furniture in the state rooms, the same braziers of incense carried by footmen in the long corridors, the same house messengers in archaic costumes of red and gold with ostrich-feathered caps, and for all I know the same plates for hot bread and butter on the same tea table, were traditions going back to Catherine the Great, or Peter, or farther still perhaps.

Every day at the same moment the door opened and the Emperor came in, sat down at the tea table, buttered a piece of bread, and began to sip his tea. He drank every day two glasses, never more, never less, and as he drank he glanced over his telegrams and newspapers. The children were the only ones who found tea time at all exciting. They were dressed for it in fresh white frocks and colored sashes, and spent most of the hour playing on the floor with toys kept especially for them in a corner of the boudoir. As they grew older needlework and embroidery were substituted for the toys, the Empress disliking to see her daughters sitting with idle hands.

From six to eight the Emperor was busy with his ministers, and he usually came directly from his study to the eight o'clock family dinner. This was never a ceremonial meal, the guests, if any, being relatives or intimate friends. At nine the Empress, in the rich dinner gown and jewels she always wore, even on the most informal evenings, went to the bedroom of the Tsarevitch to hear him say his prayers and to tuck him into bed for the night. The Emperor worked until eleven, and until that hour the Empress, the two older Grand Duchesses, and I read, had a little music, or otherwise passed the time. Perhaps it is worth recording that bridge, or in fact any other card games, we never played. Nobody in the family cared at all for cards, and only a little, once in a while, for dominoes. At eleven the evening tea was served, and after that we separated, the Emperor to write his diary for the day, the Empress and the children to bed and I for home. All his life the Emperor kept a daily record of events, but like all the private papers of the Imperial Family, the diaries were seized by the Revolutionary leaders and probably (although I still hope to the contrary) destroyed. The diaries of Nicholas II, apart from any possible sentimental associations, should be possessed of great historical value.

Monotonous though it may have been, the private life of the Emperor and his family was one of cloudless happiness. Never, in all the twelve years of my association with them, did I hear an impatient word or surprise an angry look between the Emperor and the Empress. To him she was always "Sunny" or "Sweetheart," and he came into her quiet room, with its mauve hangings and its fragrant flowers, as into a haven of rest and peace. Politics and cares of state were left outside. Never were we allowed to speak of them. The Empress, on her part, kept her own troubles to herself. Never did she yield to the temptation to confide in him her perplexities, the foolish and spiteful intrigues of her ladies in waiting, nor even lesser troubles concerning the education and upbringing of the children. "He has the whole nation to think about," she often said to me. The only care she brought to the Emperor was the ever precarious health of Alexei, but this the whole family constantly felt, and it had to be spoken of very often. The Imperial

Family was absolutely united in love and sympathy.   I
like to remember of the children, who adored their
parents, that they never felt the slightest resentment
of their mother's attachment for me.   Sometimes I
think the little Grand Duchess Marie, who especially
worshipped her father, felt a little jealous when he
invited me, as he often did, to accompany him on walks
in the palace gardens.   This may be imagination, and
at all events the child's slight jealousy never interfered with our friendship.

I think the Emperor liked to walk with me because
he had need to talk to someone he trusted of purely
personal cares which troubled his mind and which
he could share with few.   Some of these cares were of
old origin, but had never been forgotten.   I remember
once he began to tell me, almost without any preface,
of the dreadful disaster which attended his coronation,
a panic, induced by bad management of the police, in
the course of which scores of people were crushed to
death.   At the very hour of this fatal accident the
coronation banquet took place, and the Emperor and
Empress, despite their grief and horror, were obliged
to take part in it exactly as though nothing had happened.   The Emperor told me with what difficulty
they had concealed their emotions, often having to
hold their serviettes to their faces to hide their streaming tears.

One of the happiest memories of my life at Tsarskoe Selo were the evenings when the Emperor, all
cares past and present forgot, sat with us in the Empress's boudoir reading aloud from the work of Tolstoy, Tourgenieff, or his favorite Gogol.   The Emperor

read extremely well, with a pleasant voice and a re-
markably clear enunciation. In the years of the Great
War, so full of anguish and apprehension, the Emperor found relief in reading aloud amusing stories
of Averchenko and Teffy, Russian humorists who perhaps have not yet been translated into foreign tongues.

Before the War the Emperor was pictured far and
wide as a cruel tyrant deliberately opposed to the interests of his people, while the Empress appeared as a
cold, proud woman, a *malade imaginaire*, wholly indifferent to the public good. Both of these pictures
are cruelly misrepresentative. Nicholas II and his
wife were human beings, with human faults and failings like the rest of us. Both had quick tempers, not
invariably under perfect control. With the Empress
temper was a matter of rapid explosion and equally
sudden recovery. She was often for the moment
furiously angry with her maids whom too often she discovered in insincerities and deceit. The Emperor's
anger was slower to arouse and much slower to pass.
Ordinarily he was the kindest and simplest of men,
not in the least proud or over-conscious of his exalted
position. His self-control was so great that to those
who knew him little he often appeared absent-minded
and indifferent. The fact is he was so reserved that
he seemed to fear any kind of self-revealment. His
mind was singularly acute, and he should have used it
more accurately to gauge the characters of persons
surrounding him. It was entirely within his mental
powers to sense the atmosphere of gossip and calumny
that surrounded the Court during the last years, and
certainly it was within his power to put a stop to idle

and malicious talk.   But it was rarely possible to arouse him to its importance.   "What high-minded person would believe such nonsense?" was his usual comment.   Alas! he little realized how few were the really high-minded people who, in the last years of the Empire, surrounded his person or that of the Empress.

Sometimes the Emperor found himself obliged to take cognizance of the malicious gossip which made the Empress desperately unhappy and in the end poisoned the minds of thousands of really well-meaning and loyal Russians.   Beginning as far back as 1909 the tide of treachery had begun to rise, and one of the earliest of those responsible for the final disaster, I regret to say, was a woman of the highest aristocracy, one long trusted and affectionately regarded by the Imperial Family.   Mlle. Sophie Tutcheff, a protégée of the Grand Duchess Serge, and a lady who was a general over-governess to the children, was perhaps the first of all the intriguing courtiers of whom I have positive knowledge.   Mlle. Tutcheff belonged to one of the oldest and most powerful families in Moscow, and she was strongly under the influence of certain bigoted priests, especially that of her cousin, Bishop Vladimir Putiata, who for ten years had lived in Rome as official representative of the Russian Church.   It was he, I firmly believe, who inspired in Mlle. Tutcheff her antipathy to the Empress and her evil reports concerning the life of the Imperial Family.   Mlle. Tutcheff, either of her own accord or encouraged by her relative, was continually opposed to what she called the English upbringing of the Imperial children.   She wished to change the whole system, make it entirely Slav and free from any imported ideas.

Mlle. Tutcheff was, I believe, the first person to create what afterwards became the international Rasputine scandal. At the time of her residence in the palace at Tsarskoe Selo Rasputine's influence had scarcely been felt at all by the Emperor or Empress, although he was an intimate friend of other members of the Romanoff family. But Mlle. Tutcheff spread abroad a series of the most amazing falsehoods in which Rasputine figured as a constant visitor and virtually the spiritual guardian of the Imperial Family. I do not wish to repeat these stories, but merely to give an idea of their preposterous nature I will say that she represented Rasputine as having the freedom of the nurseries and even the bedchambers of the young Grand Duchesses. According to tales purported to have their origin with her, Rasputine was in the habit of bathing the children and afterward talking with them, sitting on their beds.

I do not think the Emperor believed all these rumors, but he did believe that Mlle. Tutcheff was guilty of malicious gossip of his family, and he therefore summoned her to his study and rebuked her severely, asking her how she dared to spread idle and untrue stories about his children. Of course she denied having done anything of the sort, but she admitted that she had spoken ill of Rasputine. "But you do not know the man," protested the Emperor, "and in any case, if you had criticisms to make of anyone known to this household you should have made them to us and not to the public." Mlle. Tutcheff admitted that she did not know Rasputine, and when the Emperor suggested that before she spoke evil of him it might be well for her to meet him she haughtily replied: "Never will I meet him."

For a short time after this Mlle. Tutcheff remained at Court, but being a rather stupid and very obstinate woman, she continued her campaign of intrigue. She managed to influence Princess Oblensky, long a favorite lady in waiting, until she entirely estranged her from the Empress. She even began to speak to the children against their own mother, until the Empress, who felt herself powerless against the woman, actually refused to visit the nurseries, and when she wanted her children near her sent for them to come to her private apartments. Too well she knew the Emperor's extreme reluctance to dismiss any person connected with the Court, and she waited in silent pain until the scandal grew to such proportions that the Emperor could no longer ignore it. Then Mlle. Tutcheff was summarily dismissed and sent back to her home in Moscow.

So powerful was the influence of the Tutcheff family that this incident was magnified beyond all proper proportions, and the former over-governess of the Imperial children was represented as a poor victim of Rasputine, a man whom she had never seen and who probably never knew of her existence. The last I ever heard of Mlle. Tutcheff, who, by the way, was a niece of the esteemed poet Tutcheff, she was living in Moscow, under the special protection of the Bolshevik Government. Her cousin, the former Bishop Vladimir Putiata, I understand has for several years been

a great favorite of those Communists who have prose-
cuted such brave and fearless opponents of church
despoilment as the unhappy Patriarch Tikhon and
others.

Of the Emperor I think it ought to be said that his
education, under his governor, General Bogdanovitch,
was calculated to weaken the will of any boy and to
encourage in Nicholas II his natural reserve and what
might be called indolence of mind. But this I know
of him that after his marriage he became much more
resolute of temper and much more gentle of manner
than other members of his family. It is certain that
he loved Russia and the Russian people with his whole
soul, and yet, under the political system for centuries
in force, he had often to leave to people whom he
knew only superficially many important details of government. Unquestionably it was a fault of the Emperor that he was over-confident, and only too ready
to believe what was told him by people whom he personally liked. He was impulsive in most of his acts
and sometimes made important nominations on the impression of a moment. It goes without saying that
many of his officials took advantage of this over-
confidence and sometimes acted in his name without
his knowledge or authority.

Only too well for her own happiness and peace of
mind did the Empress Alexandra Feodorovna understand her husband. She knew his kind heart, his love
for his country and his people, but she knew also how
easily influenced he could be by men in whom he reposed confidence. She knew that too often his acts
were governed by the last person he happened to con-

sult. But for all this I wish to say that the Emperor never appeared to his friends as a weak man. He had qualities of leadership with very limited opportunities to exercise those qualities. In his own domain he was "every inch an Emperor." The whole Court, from the Grand Dukes down to the last petty official and intriguing maid of honor, recognized this and stood in real awe of their Sovereign. I have a keen recollection of an episode at dinner in which a certain young Grand Duke ventured to utter an ill-founded grievance against a distinguished general who had dared to rebuke his Highness in public. The Emperor instantly recognized this as a mere display of temper and egoism, and his contempt and indignation knew no bounds. He literally turned white with anger, and the unfortunate young Grand Duke trembled before him like an offending servant. Afterwards the still indignant Emperor said to me: "He may thank God that the Empress and you were present. Otherwise I could not have held myself in hand." Towards the end of the Russian tragedy in 1917 the Emperor had learned to hold himself almost too well in hand, to subdue and to conceal the commanding personality of which he was naturally possessed. It would have been far better if he had used his personality and his great charm of manner to offset the tide of intrigue and revolution which in the midst of a world war overcame the Empire.

As long as I knew him, whether in the privacy of the palace at Tsarskoe Selo, in the informal life of the Crimea, on the Imperial yacht, in public or in private, I was always conscious of the strong personality of the Emperor. Everybody felt it. I can instance one occasion at a great reception of the Tauride Zemstvo when two men present were deliberately resolved to behave in a disrespectful manner to the Emperor. But the moment he entered the room these men found themselves completely overpowered. Their manner changed and they showed in every subsequent word and action their shame and regret. At one time a group of Social Revolutionaries were able to put on a cruiser which the Emperor was to visit a sailor charged with his Sovereign's assassination. But when the opportunity came the man literally could not do the deed. For his "weakness" this poor wretch was afterwards murdered by members of his party.

The character of the Empress was quite different from that of her husband. She was less lovable to the many, and yet of a stronger fiber. Where he was impulsive she was usually cautious and thoughtful. Where he was over-optimistic she was inclined to be a bit suspicious, especially of the weak and self-indulgent aristocracy. It was generally believed that the Empress was difficult to approach, but this was never true of sincere and disinterested souls. Suffering always made a strong appeal to the Empress, and whenever she knew of anyone sad or in trouble her heart was instantly touched. Few people, even in Russia, ever knew how much the Empress did for the poor, the sick, and the helpless. She was a born nurse, and from her earliest accession took an interest in hospitals and in nursing quite foreign to native Russian ideas. She not only visited the sick herself, in hospitals, in homes, but she enormously increased the efficiency of the hospital system in Russia. Out of her own private funds the Empress founded and supported two excellent schools for training nurses, especially in the care of children. These schools were founded on the best English models, and were under the general supervision of the famous Dr. Rauchfuss and of head nurse Miss Puchkine, a near relative of the great poet Puchkine. I could enlarge at length on the many constructive philanthropies of the Empress, paid for by herself, hospitals, homes, and orphanages, planned in almost every detail by herself, and constantly visited and inspected. After the Japanese War she built a *Hôtel des Invalides,* in which hundreds of disabled men were taught trades. She also built a number of cottages with gardens for wounded soldiers and their families, most of these war philanthropies being under the supervision of a trusted friend, Colonel the Count Shoulenbourg of the Empress's favorite Lancers.

The Empress possessed a heart and a mind utterly incapable of dishonesty or deceit, consequently she could never tolerate either in other people. This naturally got her heartily disliked by people of society to whom deceit was a matter of long practice. Another quality condemned in the Empress because entirely misunderstood, was her care as to expenses. Brought up in the comparative poverty of a small German Court, the Empress never lost the habit of a cautious use of money. Quite as in private families, where economy is an absolute necessity, the clothing of the young Grand Duchesses when outgrown by the elders were handed down to the younger girls. In the matter of selecting gifts for guests, for relatives, or at holidays for the suite, the Emperor simply selected from the rich assortment sent to the palace objects which best pleased him. The Empress, on the other hand, always examined the price cards and considered before choosing whether the jewel or the fur or the bijou, whatever it was, was worth what was asked for it. The difference between the Emperor and the Empress in regard to money was a difference in experience. The Emperor, all his life, had had everything he wanted without ever paying a single ruble for anything. He never had any money, never needed any money. I can recall but one solitary instance in which the Tsar of all the Russias ever even felt the need of touching a kopeck of his illimitable riches. It was in 1911 when their Majesties began to attend services at the Feodorovsky Cathedral at Tsarskoe Selo. In this church it was the custom to pass through the congregations alms basins into which everyone, of course, dropped a contribution, large or small. The Emperor alone was entirely penniless, and embarrassed by his unique situation he made a representation to the proper authorities, after which at exact monthly intervals he was furnished with four gold pieces for the alms basin of the Feodorovsky Cathedral. If he happened to attend an extra service he had to borrow his contribution from the Empress.

But if the Emperor carried no money in his pockets it was well enough known that he commanded vast sums, and it was characteristic of the sycophants who surrounded him that he was constantly importuned for "loans," for money to help out gambling or otherwise impecunious officers who, aware of the Emperor's great love for the army, played on it to their advantage. One day when the Emperor was taking his usual brisk walk through the grounds before tea a young officer who had managed to conceal himself in the shrubbery sprang out, threw himself on his knees, and threatened to kill himself on the spot unless the Emperor granted him a sum of money to clear the desperate wretch of some reckless deed. The Emperor was frightfully enraged—but he sent the man the money demanded.

The Empress had always handled money and knew quite well how to spend it wisely. From the depths of her honest soul she despised the use of money to buy loyalty and devotion For a long time after my first formal service as maid of honor, with the usual salary, I received from her Majesty literally nothing at all. From my parents I had the income from my dowry, four hundred rubles a month, a sum entirely inadequate to pay the running expenses of my small establishment with its three absolutely indispensable servants, and at the same time to dress myself properly as a member of the Court circle. The Empress's brother, Grand Duke Ernest of Hesse, was one of the first of her intimates to point out to her the difficulties of my position, and to suggest to her that I be given a position at Court. The suggestion was not welcomed by Alexandra Feodorovna. "Is it not possible for the Empress of Russia to have one friend?" she cried bitterly, and she reminded her brother that her relation and mine were not without precedent in Russia. The Empress Dowager had a friend, Princess Oblensky; also the Empress Marie Alexandrovna, wife of Alexander III, had in Mme. Malzoff an intimate associate, and neither of these women had had any Court functions. Why should she not cherish a friendship free from all material considerations? However, after her brother and also Count Fredericks, Minister of the Court, had pointed out to her that it was scarcely proper that the Empress's best friend and confidante should wear made-over gowns and go home from the palace on foot at midnight because she had no money for cabs, the Empress began to relent a little. At first her change of attitude took the form of useful gifts bestowed at Christmas and Easter, dress patterns, furs, gloves, and the like. Finally one day she asked me to discuss with her the whole subject of my expenses. Making me sit down with pencil and paper, she commanded me to set forth a complete budget of my monthly expenditures, exactly what I paid for food, service, light, fire, and clothing. The domestic budget, apart from my small income, came to two hundred and seventy rubles a month, and at the orders of the Empress I was thereafter furnished monthly with the exact sum of two hundred and seventy rubles. It never occurred to her to name the amount in round numbers of three hundred rubles. Nor did it occur to me except as a matter of faint amusement. Of course I was often embarrassed for money even after I became possessed of this regular income, and even later when it was augmented by two thousand rubles a year for rent, and it often wrung my heart to have to say no to appeals for money. I knew that I appeared selfish and hard-hearted. The truth was that I was simply impecunious.

CHAPTER VI

THE year 1912, although destined to end in the
almost fatal illness of the Tsarevitch, began happily for the Imperial Family. Peaceful and busy were
the winter and spring, the Emperor engaged as usual
with the affairs of the Empire, the Empress, as far as
her health permitted, superintending the education of
her children, and all of them busy with their books and
their various tutors. Of the education and upbringing
of the children of Nicholas II and the Empress Alexandra Feodorovna it should be said that while nothing
was omitted to make them most loyal Russians, the
educational methods employed were cosmopolitan.
They had French, Swiss, and English tutors, but all
their studies were under the superintendence of a Russian, the highly cultured M. Petroff, while for certain
branches such as physics and natural science they were
privately instructed in the gymnasium of Tsarskoe Selo.
The first teacher of the Imperial children, she from
whom they received their elementary education, was
Miss Schneider, familiarly called "Trina," a native of
one of the Baltic states of the Empire. Miss
Schneider first came into service, years before the marriage of the Emperor and Empress, as instructor in
the Russian language to Elizabeth, Grand Duchess
Serge. Afterwards she taught Russian to the young
Empress, and was retained at Court as reader to her

Majesty. "Trina" was rather a difficult person in some ways, taking every advantage of her privileged position, but she was undeniably valuable and was heart and soul in her devotion to the family. She accompanied them to Siberia and there disappeared with them.

Perhaps the most valued of the instructors was M. Pierre Gilliard, whose book "Thirteen Years at the Russian Court" has been published in several languages and has been very well received M. Gilliard, a Swiss gentlemen of many accomplishments, came first to Tsarskoe Selo as teacher of French to the young Grand Duchesses. Afterwards he became tutor to the Tsarevitch. M. Gilliard lived in the palace, and enjoyed to the fullest extent the confidence and affection of their Majesties. Mr. Gibbs, the English tutor, was also a great favorite. Both of these men followed the family into exile and remained faithful and devoted friends until forcibly expelled by the Bolsheviki.

In his book M. Gilliard has recorded that he was never able to teach the Grand Duchesses to speak a fluent French. This is true because the languages used in the family were English and Russian, and the children never became interested in any other languages. "Trina" was supposed to teach them German but she had less success with that language than M. Gilliard with French. The Emperor and Empress spoke English almost exclusively, and so did the Empress's brother, the Grand Duke of Hesse and his family. Among themselves the children usually spoke Russian. The Tsarevitch alone, thanks to his constant association with M. Gilliard, mastered the French language.

Every detail of the education of her children was supervised by the Empress, who often sat with them for hours together in the schoolroom. She herself taught them sewing and needlework, her best pupil being Tatiana, who had an extraordinary talent for all kinds of handwork. She not only made beautiful blouses and other garments, embroideries and crochets, but she was able on occasions to arrange her mother's long hair, and to dress her as well as a professional maid. Not that the Empress required as much dressing as the ordinary woman of rank and wealth. She had that kind of Victorian modesty that forbade any intrusion on the privacy of her dressing room. All that her maids were allowed to do was to dress her hair, fasten her boots, and put on her gown and jewels. The Empress had great taste in dress and always chose her jewels to finish rather than to ornament her costumes. "Only rubies to-day," she would command, or "pearls and sapphires with this gown."

The Empress and the children have been represented as surrounded by German servants, but this accusation is absolutely false. The chief woman of the household was Mme. Geringer, a Russian lady who came daily to the palace, ordered gowns, did all necessary shopping, paid bills, and attended to any business required by the Empress. The chief maid of the Empress was Madeleine Zanotti, of English and Italian parentage, whose home before she came to Tsarskoe Selo was in England. Madeleine was a woman of middle age, very clever, and as usual with one in her position, inclined to be tyrannical. Madeleine had charge of all the gowns and jewels of the Empress, and as I think I have related, she was often critical of her mistress's indolent habits in regard to correspondence, etc. A second maid was Tutelberg, "Toodles," a rather slow and quiet girl from the Baltic. She and Madeleine were mortal enemies, but they agreed on one thing at least, and that was that they would not wear caps and aprons. The Empress good-naturedly acquiesced and permitted simple black gowns and ribbon bows in the hair for her chief maids. There were three under maids, all Russians, and all perfectly devoted to the Imperial Family. These girls, who wore the regulation caps and white aprons, cared for the rooms of the Empress and the children. All the maids, when the Revolution came, remained faithful to the family, and one of them, as I shall tell later, performed the dangerous service of smuggling letters in and out of Siberia. One girl, Anna Demidoff, shared the fate of the family in 1918.

The Emperor had three valets, one of whom, Shalferoff, who had served Alexander III, turned spy during the Revolution. Another, old Raziesh, also a former servant of Alexander III, died in the service of Nicholas II, and was replaced by Chemoduroff, a fine and very loyal man. The third valet's name was Katoff. All three, as their names testify, were Russians, as were also the three men in the service of the Empress, Leo and Kondratief, both of whom died during the early days of the Revolution, and Volkoff, who followed the Royal exiles as far into

Siberia as he was permitted by the Provisional Government.

The children's nurses were Russians, the head nurse being Marie Vechniakoff. Others I remember well were Alexandra, nicknamed "Shoura," a great favorite with the girls, Anna and Lisa, kind, faithful girls who spoke no word of any language except Russian. There were, of course, hundreds of house servants, and to my knowledge most, if not all of them, were Russians. The chef was a Frenchman, Cubat, a very great man in his profession. Sometimes, when an especially splendid dish had been prepared, Cubat was wont to introduce it, as it were, by standing magnificently in the doorway, clad in immaculate white linen, until the dish was served. Cubat became very wealthy in the Tsar's service, and now lives happily and luxuriously in his native France. He was, I believe, truly loyal to the Imperial Family, which is more than can be said for most of the servants. Their children were educated at the expense of the Emperor, and the majority, instead of choosing useful trades, elected to go to the universities, where they nearly all became Revolutionists. In my father's opinion this was due to the fact that the Russian universities and higher schools offered little if any technical training. Recognizing this, the Empress created in Petrograd a technical school for boys and girls of the whole Empire. In this school the students were trained to become teachers in many useful handicrafts, and in addition to this normal academy the Empress established in many governments schools where boys and girls were perfected in the beautiful peasant arts of embroidery, dyeing, carving, and painting. I give these details because I think it only just to offset with facts the lying slanders of sensational writers who could not possibly have known anything of the intimate life of the Imperial Family of Russia but who have substituted propaganda for truth.

None of these sensational writers knew or tried to know how simple, not to say rigorous, was the régime followed by the Imperial children. All of them, even the delicate little Tsarevitch, slept in large, well-aired nurseries, on hard camp beds without pillows and with the least possible allowance of bedclothing. They had cold baths every morning and warm ones only at night. As a consequence of this simple life their manners were unassuming and natural without a single trace of *hauteur*. Although in 1912 the four girls were rapidly approaching womanhood—Olga was in her eighteenth year and Tatiana was nearly sixteen— their parents continued to regard them as children. The two older girls were spoken of as "the big ones," and were given many grown-up privileges, as for example, concerts and the theater to which the Emperor himself escorted them. The two younger Grand Duchesses and the Tsarevitch, "the little ones," were still in the nursery.

In the darkness of the mystery which surrounds the fate of these innocent children it is with poignant emotion that I recall them as they appeared, so full of life and joy, in those distant, yet incredibly near, days before the World War and the downfall of Imperial Russia. Of the four girls, Olga and Marie were essentially Russian, altogether Romanoff in their inheritance. Olga was perhaps the cleverest of them all, her mind being so quick to grasp ideas, so absorbent of knowledge that she learned almost without application or close study. Her chief characteristics, I should say, were a strong will and a singularly straightforward habit of thought and action. Admirable qualities in a woman, these same characteristics are often trying in childhood, and Olga as a little girl sometimes showed herself wilful and even disobedient. She had a hot temper which, however, she early learned to keep under control, and had she been allowed to live her natural life she would, I believe, have become a woman of influence and distinction. Extremely pretty, with brilliant blue eyes and a lovely complexion, Olga resembled her father in the fineness of her features, especially in her delicate, slightly tipped nose.

Marie and Anastasie were also blonde types and very attractive girls. Marie had splendid eyes and rose-red cheeks. She was inclined to be stout and she had rather thick lips which detracted a little from her beauty. Marie had a naturally sweet disposition and a very good mind. All three of these girls were more or less of the tomboy type. They had something of the innate brusqueness of their Romanoff ancestors, which displayed itself in a tendency to mischief. Anastasie, a sharp and clever child, was a very monkey for jokes, some of them at times almost too practical for the enjoyment of others. I remember once when the family was in their Polish estate in winter the children were amusing themselves at snowballing. The imp which sometimes seemed to possess Anastasie led her to throw a stone rolled in a snowball straight

THE EMPEROR AND TSAREVITCH WALKING ON BOARD
THE *STANDERT*. Photograph by the Empress.

THE TSAR, TSARINA, AND ALEXEI IN THE GARDENS
OF TSARSKOE SELO, 1913.

THE TSAREVITCH IN COSSACK UNIFORM WITH
HIS SAILOR, DEREVANKO.

at her dearly loved sister Tatiana. The missile struck
the poor girl fairly in the face with such force that she
fell senseless to the ground. The grief and horror of
Anastasie lasted for many days and permanently cured
her of her worst propensities to practical jokes.

Tatiana was almost a perfect reincarnation of her
mother. Taller and slenderer than her sisters, she
had the soft, refined features and the gentle, reserved
manners of her English ancestry. Kindly and sympathetic of disposition, she displayed towards her
younger sisters and her brother such a protecting
spirit that they, in fun, nicknamed her "the governess."
Of all the Grand Duchesses Tatiana was with the
people the most popular, and I suspect in their hearts
she was the most dearly loved of her parents. Certainly she was a different type from the others even in
appearance, her hair being a rich brown and her eyes
so darkly gray that in the evening they seemed quite
black. Of all the girls Tatiana was most social in her
tastes. She liked society and she longed pathetically
for friends. But friends for these high born but unfortunate girls were very difficult to find. The Empress
dreaded for her daughters the companionship of over-
sophisticated young women of the aristocracy, whose
minds, even in the schoolroom, were fed with the
foolish and often vicious gossip of a decadent society.
The Empress even discouraged association with
cousins and near relatives, many of whom were un-
wholesomely precocious in their outlook on life.

I would not give the impression that these young
daughters of the Emperor and Empress were forced
to lead dull and uneventful lives. They were allowed

to have their little preferences for this or that handsome young officer with whom they danced, played
tennis, walked, or rode.   These innocent young ro-
mances were in fact a source of amusement to their
Majesties, who enjoyed teasing the girls about any
dashing officer who seemed to attract them.   The
Grand Duchess Olga, sister of the Emperor, sympathized with her nieces' love of pleasure and often arranged tea parties and tennis matches for them, the
guests, of course, being of their own choice.   We had
some quite jolly tea parties in my little house also.
In the matter of dress, so important to young and
pretty girls, the Grand Duchesses were allowed to indulge their own tastes.   Mme. Brisac, an accomplished
French dressmaker, made gowns for the Imperial
Family, and through her the latest Paris models
reached the palace.   The girls, however, inclined towards simple English fashions, especially for outdoor wear.   In summer they dressed almost entirely in
white.   Jewels they were too young to wear except on
very great occasions.   Each girl received on her
twelfth birthday a slender gold bracelet which was
afterwards always worn, day and night, "for good
luck."   I have described in a previous chapter the
Russian custom of presenting each Grand Duchess, on
her coming of age, with a pearl and diamond necklace, but this was worn only at state functions or very
formal balls.

Alexei, the only son of the Emperor and Empress,
a more tragic child than the last Dauphin of France,
indeed one of the most tragic figures in history, was,
apart from his terrible affliction, the loveliest and most

attractive of the whole family. Because of his delicate health Alexei began life as a rather spoiled child. His chief nurse, Marie Vechniakoff, a somewhat over-emotional woman, made the mistake of indulging the child in every whim. It is easy to understand why she did so, because nothing more heart-rending could be imagined than the little boy's moans and cries during his frequent illnesses. If he bumped his head or struck a hand or foot against a chair or table the usual result was a hideous blue swelling indicating a subcutaneous hemorrhage frightfully painful and often enduring for days or even weeks.

At five Alexei was placed in charge of the sailor Derevanko, who for a long term of years remained his constant body servant and companion. Derevanko, while devoted to the boy, did not spoil him as his women nurses had done, and the man was so patient and resourceful that he often did wonders in alleviating the child's pain. I can still in memory hear the plaintive, suffering voice of Alexei begging the big sailor to "lift my arm," "put my leg up," "warm my hands," and I can see the patient, calm-eyed man working for hours on end to give the maximum of comfort to the little pain-racked limbs.

As Alexei grew older his parents carefully explained to him the nature of his illness and impressed on him the necessity of avoiding falls and blows. But Alexei was a child of active mind, loving sports and outdoor play, and it was almost impossible for him to avoid the very things that brought him suffering. "Can't I have a bicycle?" he would beg his mother. "Alexei, you know you can't." "Mayn't I play ten-

nis?" "Dear, you know you mustn't." Often these
hard denials of the natural play impulse were followed
by a gush of tears as the child cried out: "Why can
other boys have everything and I nothing?"

Suffering and self-denial had their effect on the character of Alexei. Knowing what pain and sacrifice
meant, he was extraordinarily sympathetic towards
other sick people. His thoughtfulness of others was
shown in his beautiful courtesy to women and girls and
to his elders, and in his interest in the troubles of
servants and dependents. It was a failing of the Emperor that even when he sympathized with the troubles
of others he was rather slow to take action, unless
indeed the matter was really serious. Alexei, on the
contrary, was always for immediate action. I remember an instance when a boy in service at the palace
was discharged for some reason which I have quite
forgotten. The story somehow reached the ears of
Alexei, who immediately took sides with the boy and
gave his father no rest until the whole case was reviewed and the culprit was forgiven and restored to
duty. Alexei usually defended all offenders, yet when
the day came when his parents, in deep distress, told
him that Father Gregory, that is, Rasputine, had been
killed by members of his own family the boy's grief
was swallowed up in rage and indignation. "Papa,"
he exclaimed, "is it possible that you will not punish
them? The assassins of Stolypine were hanged."

I ask the reader to remember that the Imperial
Family firmly believed that they owed much of
Alexei's improving health to the prayers of Rasputine.
Alexei himself believed it. Several years before Ras-

putine had assured the Empress that when the boy was twelve years old he would begin to improve and that by the time he was a man he would be entirely well. The undeniable fact is that after the age of twelve Alexei did begin very materially to improve. His illnesses became farther and farther apart and before 1917 his appearance had changed marvelously for the better. He resembled in no way the invalid sons of his mother's sister, Princess Henry of Prussia, who suffered from his own terrible malady. What the best physicians of Europe had been unable to do in their case some mysterious force had done in the case of the Tsarevitch. His parents to whom the young boy was as their very heart's blood believed that the healing hand of God had wrought the cure, and that it was in answer to the supplication of one whose spirit was able to rise in higher flight than theirs or any other's. They knew of course that the boy was not yet entirely well, but they believed that he was getting well. Alexei believed this also and it is certain that he looked forward to a healthy, normal manhood.

Alexei, like his father, dearly loved the army and all the pageants of military display. He had every kind of toy soldier, toy guns and fortresses, and with these he played for hours, with his sailor companion Derevanko, or "Dina" as the boy called him, and with the few boy companions he was allowed. Two of these boys were sons of "Dina," and a third was the son of one of the family physicians, by coincidence also named Derevanko. In the last years before the Revolution a few carefully selected boys, cadets from the

Military School, were called to the palace to play with Alexei. These boys were warned of the danger of any rough play, and all were .extremely mindful of their responsibility. It was because no other type of boy could be trusted to play with Alexei that the Empress did not often invite to the palace the children of the Grand Dukes. They were Romanoffs, brusque and rude in their manners, thoughtless of the feelings of others, and the Empress literally did not dare to leave them alone with her son. But because of her caution she was bitterly assailed by her enemies who spoke sneeringly of her preference for "low born" children over the aristocratic children of the family.

The Emperor and Empress and all the children were passionately fond of pets, especially dogs. The Emperor's inseparable companion for many years was a splendid English collie named Iman, and when in the natural course of time this dog died the Emperor was inconsolable. After that he had a fine kennel of collies but he never made a special pet of any dog. The favorite dog of the Empress was a small, shaggy terrier from Scotland. This dog's name was Eira, and, to tell the truth, I did not like the little animal at all. His disagreeable habit of darting from under chairs and snapping at people's heels was a trial to my nerves   Nevertheless the Empress doted on him, carried him under her arm even to the dinner table, and amused herself greatly talking to and playing with the dour little creature. When he fell ill and had to be mercifully killed she wept in real grief and pity. Alexei's pets were two, a silky little spaniel named Joy and a beautiful big gray cat, the gift of

General Voyeikoff. It was the only cat in the household and it was a privileged animal, even being allowed to sleep on Alexei's bed. There were two other dogs, Tatiana's French bull and a little King Charlie which I contributed to the menagerie. Both of these dogs went with the family to Siberia, and Jimmie, the King Charles spaniel, was found shot to death in that dreadful deserted house in Ekaterinaburg.

How far, how unbelievably far away now seem those peaceful days of 1912, when we were watching the Tsar's daughters growing towards womanhood, and even in our minds speculating on possible marriages for them. Their prospects as far as marriage was concerned, I must say, were rather vague. Foreign matches, because of religion and even more because of the girls' devotion to home and country, were almost out of the question, and suitable husbands in Russia seemed to be entirely lacking. There was a time in his boyhood when Dmitri, son of the Tsar's uncle, Grand Duke Paul, was a great favorite with the Imperial Family. But Dmitri as he grew older became so dissipated that he quite cut himself off from the prospect of an alliance with any of the Grand Duchesses. There had once been a faint possibility of an engagement between Olga and Crown Prince Carol of Rumania. As early as 1910 the beautiful Queen Marie and her son visited Russia for the purpose of introducing the young people, but nothing came of the visit. In 1914 the family made a return visit to Rumania on the *Standert*, the Rumanian Royal family, including the old Queen, "Carmen Sylva," meeting the yacht at Constanza, on the Black Sea, and making a

splendid fête which lasted for three days   This time
the matter was seriously broached to Olga who, in her
usual quick, straightforward manner, declined the
match.   In 1916 Prince Carol again visited the Russian Court, and now his young man's fancy rested on
Marie.   He made a formal proposal for her hand,
but the Emperor, declaring that Marie was nothing
more than a schoolgirl, good-naturedly laughed the
Prince's proposal aside.

Not all these proposals ended so merrily.   One day
coming as usual to Peterhof, I found the Empress in
tears.   A formal proposal had just been received from
the old Grand Duchess, Marie Pavlovna, aunt of the
Emperor, for a marriage between her son Boris Vladimirovitch and Grand Duchess Olga.   This young
man, Prince Boris, was much better known in question-
able circles in Paris than in the Court of Russia and the
mere suggestion of a marriage with one of her daughters was enough to reduce the Empress to mortified
tears.   Of course the proposal was rejected, greatly
to the wrath of Grand Duchess Marie Pavlovna, a
Russian *grande dame* of the old school in which the
debauchery of young men was regarded as a perfectly
natural phenomenon.   She never forgave the slight,
as she chose to consider it, and later became one of
the most active of the circle of intriguers which, from
the safety of a foreign embassy in Petrograd, plotted
the ruin of the Imperial Family and of their country.

In the summer of 1912 the family and their immediate household, including myself, went on another
long cruise in Finnish waters.   During the cruise the
yacht was visited by the Empress Dowager of whom

previously I had seen but little. I write with some hesitation about the Empress Dowager, who is still living, and for whom I entertain all due respect. She was, as I remember her then, a small, slender woman, not beautiful certainly, not as attractive as her sister, Queen Alexandra of England, but with a great deal of presence and, when she chose to exert it, considerable personal charm. The Emperor she apparently loved less than her other children, especially her son, Grand Duke Michail, and the Empress I fear she loved not at all. To the children she was affectionate but a trifle distant. I am sure that she resented the fact that the first four children were girls, and there is little doubt that she felt bitterly the affliction of the heir. Possibly she felt in her secret heart that it should have been her own strong son Michail who was the acknowledged successor of Nicholas II. I say this from my own conjecture and observations and not from positive knowledge. Yet after events, I think, confirmed my opinion.

The Dowager Empress after the death of Alexander III relinquished with rather bad grace her position of reigning Empress. In fact she never did relinquish it altogether, always taking precedence on public occasions of Alexandra Feodorovna. Just why the Tsar consented to this I never knew, but certain it is that always, when the Imperial Family made a state entrance the Tsar appeared first with his mother on his arm, the Empress following on the arm of one of the Grand Dukes. Society generally approved this procedure, the Empress Mother enjoying all the popularity which the Empress lacked There were actually in Russia two Courts, a large one represented by society and the Grand Dukes, and a small one represented by the intimate circle of the Emperor and Empress. In the one everything done by the Empress Mother was right and by the shy and retiring Empress wrong. In the small Court it was exactly the other way around, except that even in the palace a certain amount of petty intrigue always existed.

The visit to Finnish waters by the Empress Mother in 1912 was marred by no coldness or disharmony. When we went ashore for tennis the Emperor admonished us all to play as well as we could, "because Mama is coming." We lunched aboard her yacht and she dined with us on the *Standert.* On the 22d of July, which was her name day, as well as that of the little Grand Duchess Marie, she spent most of the day on the Emperor's yacht, and after luncheon I took a photograph of her sitting with her arm around the Emperor's shoulders, her two little Japanese spaniels at their feet. She made us dance for her on deck, photographing us as we danced. After tea the children performed for her a little French playlet which seemed to delight her. Yet that evening at dinner I could not help noticing how her fine eyes, so kind and smiling towards most of the company, clouded slightly whenever they were turned to the Emperor or the Empress. Still I must record that later, passing the open door of Alexei's cabin, I saw the Empress Mother sitting on the edge of the child's bed talking gaily and peeling an apple quite like any loving grandmother.

I do not pretend to understand the Empress

Dowager or her motives, but, as far as I can judge, her chief weakness was love of power. She carried her insistence on precedence so far that the *chiffres* of the maids of honor of both Empresses bore the initials M. A. instead of A M., which was the proper order. She wanted to be first in everything and could not bear to abdicate either power or influence. She never, I believe, understood her son's preference for a quiet, family life, or the changed and softened manners he acquired under the influence of his wife.

CHAPTER VII

IN the autumn of 1912 the family went to Skerne-vizi, their Polish estate, in order to indulge the Emperor's love for big-game hunting. In the vast forests surrounding the estate all kinds of game were preserved and the sport of hunting there was said to be very exciting. During the war these woods and all the game were destroyed by the Germans, but until after 1914 Skernevizi was a favorite retreat of the Emperor. I had returned to my house in Tsarskoe Selo but I was not allowed long to remain there. A telegram from the Empress conveyed the disquieting news that Alexei, in jumping into a boat, had injured himself and was now in a serious condition. The child had been removed from Skernevizi to Spala, a smaller Polish estate near Warsaw, and to Warsaw I accordingly traveled. Here I was met by one of the Imperial carriages and was driven to Spala. Driving for nearly an hour through deep woods and over a heavy, sandy road I reached my destination, a small wooden house, something like a country inn, in which the suite was lodged. Two rooms had been set apart for me and my maid, and here I found Olga and Tatiana waiting to help me get settled. Their mother, they said, was expecting me, and without any loss of time I went with them to the palace.

I found the Empress greatly agitated. The boy

was temporarily improved but was still too delicate to be taken back to Tsarskoe Selo. Meanwhile the family lived in one of the dampest, gloomiest palaces I have ever seen. It was really a large wooden villa, very badly planned as far as light and sunshine were concerned. The large dining room on the ground floor was so dark that the electric lights had to be kept on all day. Upstairs to the right of a long corridor were the rooms of the Emperor and Empress, her sitting room in bright English chintzes being one of the few cheerful spots in the house. Here we usually spent our evenings. The bedrooms and dressing rooms were too dark for comfort, but the Emperor's study, also on the right of the corridor, was fairly bright.

As long as the health of little Alexei continued fairly satisfactory the Emperor and his suite went stag hunting daily in the forests of the estate. Every evening after dinner the slain stags were brought to the front of the palace and laid out for inspection on the grass. The huntsmen with their flaring torches and winding horns standing over the day's bag made, I was told, a very picturesque spectacle. The Emperor and his suite and most of the household used to enjoy going out after dinner to enjoy this fine sight. I never went myself, having a foolish love of animals which prevents enjoyment of the royal sport of hunting. I even failed to appreciate, as the head of the estate, kind Count Velepolsky, thought I should, the many trophies of the chase with which the corridors and apartments of the palace were adorned.

What I did enjoy was the beautiful park which surrounded the palace, and the rapid little river Pilitsa that flowed through it. There was one leafy path through which I often walked in the mornings with the Emperor. This was called the Road of Mushrooms because it ended in a wonderful mushroom bench. The whole place was so remote and peaceful that I deeply sympathized with their Majesties' irritation that even there they could never stir abroad without being haunted by the police guard.

Although Alexei's illness was believed to have taken a favorable turn and he was even beginning to walk a little about the house and gardens, I found him pale and decidedly out of condition. He occasionally complained of pain, but the doctors were unable to discover any actual injury One day the Empress took the child for a drive and before we had gone very far we saw that indeed he was very ill He cried out with pain in his back and stomach, and the Empress, terribly frightened, gave the order to return to the palace. That return drive stands out in my mind as an experience of horror. Every movement of the carriage, every rough place in the road, caused the child the most exquisite torture, and by the time we reached home he was almost unconscious with pain. The next weeks were endless torment to the boy and to all of us who had to listen to his constant cries of pain. For fully eleven days these dreadful sounds filled the corridors outside his room, and those of us who were obliged to approach had often to stop our ears with our hands in order to go about our duties. During the entire time the Empress never undressed, never went to bed, rarely even lay down for an hour's rest. Hour after hour she sat beside the bed where the half-conscious child lay huddled on one side, his left leg drawn up so sharply that for nearly a year afterwards he could not straighten it out. His face was absolutely bloodless, drawn and seamed with suffering, while his almost expressionless eyes rolled back in his head. Once when the Emperor came into the room, seeing his boy in this agony and hearing his faint screams of pain, the poor father's courage completely gave way and he rushed, weeping bitterly, to his study. Both parents believed the child dying, and Alexei himself, in one of his rare moments of consciousness, said to his mother: "When I am dead build me a little monument of stones in the wood."

The family's most trusted physicians, Dr. Rauchfuss and Professor Fedoroff and his assistant Dr. Derevanko, were in charge of the case and after the first consultations declared the Tsarevitch's condition hopeless. The hemorrhage of the stomach from which he was suffering seemed liable to turn into an abscess which could at any moment prove fatal. We had two terrible moments in which this complication threatened. One day at luncheon a note was brought from the Empress to the Emperor who, pale but collected, made a sign for the physicians to leave the table. Alexei, the Empress had written, was suffering so terribly that she feared the worst was about to happen. This crisis, however, was averted. On the second occasion, on an evening after dinner when we were sitting very quietly in the Empress's boudoir, Princess Henry of Prussia, who had come to be with her sister in her trouble, appeared in the doorway very white and agitated and begged the members of the suite to re-

tire as the child's condition was desperate. At eleven
o'clock the Emperor and Empress entered the room,
despair written on their faces. Still the Empress declared that she could not believe that God had abandoned them and she asked me to telegraph Rasputine for his prayers. His reply came quickly. "The
little one will not die," it said. "Do not allow the
doctors to bother him too much." As a matter of
fact the turning point came a few days later, the pain
subsided, and the boy lay wasted and utterly spent,
but alive.

Curiously enough there was no church on this Polish
estate, but during the illness of the Tsarevitch a chapel
was installed in a large green tent in the garden. A
new confessor, Father Alexander, celebrated mass and
after the first celebration he walked in solemn procession from the altar to the sickroom bearing with him
holy communion for the sick boy. The Emperor and
Empress were very much impressed with Father Alexander and from that time on they retained him in their
private chapel at Tsarskoe Selo. He was a good man
but not a brave one, for when the Revolution came,
and the Emperor and the Empress sent for him to
come to them, he confessed himself afraid to go.
Poor man! His caution, after all, did not save him.
He was shot by the Bolsheviki a year or two afterwards, on what pretext I do not know.

The convalescence of Alexei was slow and weari-
some. His nurse, Marie Vechniakoff, had grown so
hysterical with fatigue that she had to be relieved,
while the Empress was so exhausted that she could
hardly move from room to room. The young Grand

Duchesses were tireless in their devotion to the poor invalid, as was also M. Gilliard, who read to him and diverted him hours on end. Gradually the distracted household assumed a more normal aspect. The Emperor, in Cossack uniform, began once more to entertain the officers of his Varsovie Lancers, commanded by a splendid soldier, General Mannerheim, of whom the world has heard much. As Alexei's health continued to improve there was even a little shooting, and a great deal of tennis which the girls, after their long confinement to the house, greatly enjoyed. All of us began to be happy again, but one day the Emperor called me into his study and showed me a telegram from his brother, Grand Duke Michail, in which the latter announced his morganatic marriage to the Countess Brassoff, of whom the Emperor strongly disapproved. It was not the marriage itself that so strongly disturbed the Emperor, but that Michail had solemnly given his word of honor that it would never take place. "He broke his word—his word of honor," the Emperor repeated again and again.

Another blow which the Emperor received at this time was the suicide of Admiral Chagin, commandant of the *Standert* and one of the closest friends of the family. The Admiral shot himself on account of an unhappy love affair, and deeply as the Emperor mourned his death he was even more indignant at the manner of it Russians, I know, are inclined to morbidity, and suicide with them is not an uncommon thing. But Nicholas II always regarded it as an act of dishonor. "Running away from the field of battle," was his characterization of such an act, and when he heard of Chagin's suicide he gave way to a terrible mood of anger and grief. Speaking of both Michail and Chagin he said bitterly: "How, in the midst of the boy's illness and all our trouble, how could they have done such things?" The poor Emperor, to whom every failure of those he loved and trusted came as an utterly unexpected blow, how near was his hour of complete and final disillusionment of nearly all earthly loyalties.

We had a few weeks of peaceful enjoyment before leaving Spala that autumn The girls, bright and happy once more, rode every morning, the crisp air and the exercise coloring their cheeks and raising their spirits high. The Emperor tramped the woods, sometimes with me as his companion, and on one of these outings we both had a narrow escape from drowning. The Emperor took me for a row on the river which, as I have said, had a very rapid currrent. Intent on keeping the boat well into the current, the Emperor ran us into a small island, and for a few seconds escape from an ignominious upset seemed impossible. I was th ʾroughly frightened, the Emperor not a little em-

ᵈ, and ardor for water sports was, for a time,

r   ·ened in both of us.

ober 21 (Russian Calendar) we celebrated the accession to the throne with high mass and holy communion, and a few days later the doctors decided that Alexei was well enough to be moved to Tsarskoe Selo. The Imperial train was made ready and their Majesties decided that I was to travel on it with the rest of the suite. This was, as a matter of fact, contrary to strict etiquette, and the announcement created among the ladies in waiting much consternation, not to say rancor. There is no question that being a regularly appointed lady in waiting to royalty and having nothing to do when a mere friend of the exalted one happens to be at hand is a bit irritating, so I cannot really blame the Empress's ladies for objecting to me as a traveling companion. The Imperial train, now used, one hears, by the inner circle of the Communists, was composed of a number of luxurious carriages, more like a home than a railway train. In the carriage of the Emperor and Empress the easy chairs and sofas were upholstered in bright chintz and there were books, family photographs, and all sort of familiar trinkets. The emperor's study was in his favorite green leather, and adjoining their dressing rooms was a large and perfectly equipped bathroom. In this carriage also were rooms for the personal attendants of their Majesties. The Grand Duchesses and their maids had a similar carriage, and Alexei's carriage, which had compartments for the maids of honor and myself, was furnished with every imaginable comfort. The last carriage was the dining wagon with a small anteroom where the inevitable zakouski, the Russian table of *hors d'œuvres,* was served At the long dining table the Emperor sat with his daughters on either hand, while facing him were Count Fredericks and the ladies in waiting. Throughout the journey of nearly two days the Empress was served in her own room or beside the bed where Alexei lay, very weak, but bright and cheerful once more.

This chapter may well close with one of the open-

ing events of 1913, the Jubilee of the Romanoffs, cele-
brating the three hundredth anniversary of their
reign.   In February the Court moved from Tsarskoe
Selo to the Winter Palace in Petrograd, a place they
disliked because of the vast gloominess of the building and the fact that the only garden was a tiny space
hardly large enough for the children to play or to
exercise in.   On reaching Petrograd the family drove
directly across the Neva to Christ's Chapel, the little
church of Peter the Great, where is, or was, preserved
a miraculous picture of the Christ, very old and highly
revered.   The public had not been notified that the
Imperial Family would first visit this chapel, but their
presence quickly became known and they drove back
to the Winter Palace through excited, but on the
whole undemonstrative, masses of people, a typical
Petrograd crowd.

The actual celebration of the Jubilee began with a
solemn service in the Cathedral of Our Lady of Kazan,
which everyone familiar with Petrograd remembers
as one of the most beautiful of Russian churches.   The
vast building was packed to its utmost capacity, and
that means a much larger crowd than in ordinary
churches, since in Russia the congregation stands or
kneels through the entire service.   From my position
I had a very good view of both the Emperor and the
Tsarevitch, and I was puzzled to see them raise their
heads and gaze long at the ceiling, but afterwards they
told me that two doves had appeared and had floated
for several minutes over their heads.   In the religious
exaltation of the hour this appeared to the Emperor
a symbol that the blessing of God, after three cen-

THE EMPEROR AND EMPRESS IN OLD SLAVONIC DRESS.
1913 JUBILEE.

THE INVALID EMPRESS ON HER BALCONY AT PETERHOF.

turies, continued to rest on the House of Romanoff. There followed a long series of functions at the palace, with deputations coming from all over the Empire, the women appearing at receptions and dinners in the beautiful national dress, which were also worn by the Empress and her daughters. The Empress, for all her weariness, was regal in her richly flowing robes and long-veiled, high *kokoshnik,* the Russian national headdress, set with magnificent jewels. She also wore the wide-ribboned order of St. Andrew, which was her sole privilege to wear, and at the most formal of the state dinners she wore the most splendid of all the crown jewels. The young Grand Duchesses were simply but beautifully gowned on all occasions, and they wore the order of Catherine the Great, red ribbons with blazing diamond stars. The crowds were enormous in all the great state rooms, the Imperial Family standing for hours while the multitudes filed past with sweeping curtsies and low bows. So long and fatiguing were these ceremonies that at the end the Empress was literally too fatigued to force a smile. Poor little Alexei also, after being carried through the rooms and obliged to acknowledge a thousand greetings, was taken back to his room in a condition of utter exhaustion.

There were state performances at the theater and the opera, Glinka's "Life for the Tsar" being sung to the usual tumult of applause and adulation, but for all that I felt that there was in the brilliant audience little real enthusiasm, little real loyalty. I saw a cloud over the whole celebration in Petrograd, and this impression, I am almost sure, was shared by the

Empress. She told me that she could never feel happy in Petrograd. Everything in the Winter Palace reminded her of earlier years when she and her husband used to go happily to the theater together and returning would have supper in their dressing gowns before the fire talking over the events of the day and evening. "I was so happy then," she said plaintively, "so well and strong. Now I am a wreck."

Much as both she and the Emperor desired to shorten their stay in Petrograd, they were obliged to remain several weeks after the close of the official celebration because Tatiana, who unwisely had drunk the infected water of the capital, fell ill of typhoid and could not for some time be moved. With her lovely brown hair cut short, we finally went back to Tsarskoe Selo, where she made good progress back to health.

In the spring began the celebration of the Jubilee throughout the Empire. The visit to the Volga, especially to Kostrama, the home of the first Romanoff monarch, Michail Feodorovnitch, was a magnificent success, the people actually wading waist deep in the river in order to get nearer the Imperial boat. It was the same through all the surrounding governments, crowds, cheers, acclamations, prayers, and great choruses singing the national hymn, ~very evidence of love and loyalty. I particularly remember when the cortège reached the town of Pereyaslovl, in the Vladimir Government, because it was from there that my father's family originated, and some of his relatives took part in the day's celebration. The Empress, to my regret, was not present, being confined to her bed on the Imperial train, ill and fatigued, yet under obligation to be ready for special ceremonies in Moscow. It would need a more eloquent pen than mine adequately to describe those days in Moscow, the Holy City of Russia. The weather was perfect, and under the clear sunshine the floating flags and banners, the flower-trimmed buildings, and the numberless decorations made up a spectacle of unforgettable beauty. Leaving his car at some distance from the Kremlin, the Emperor entered the great gate on foot, preceded by chanting priests with waving censers and holy images. Behind the Emperor and his suite came the Empress and Alexei in an open car through crowds that pressed hard against the police lines, while overhead all the bells of Moscow pealed welcome to the Sovereigns. Every day it was the same, demonstrations of love and fealty it seemed that no time or circumstance could ever alter.

CHAPTER VIII

NINETEEN-FOURTEEN, that year of fate for all the world, but more than all for my poor country, began its course in Russia, as elsewhere, in apparent peace and tranquillity. With us, as with other civilized people, the tragedy of Sarajevo came as a thrill of horror and surmise. I do not know exactly what we expected to follow that desperate act committed in a distant province of Austria, but certainly not the cataclysm of a World War and the ruin of three of the proudest empires of earth. Very shortly after the assassination of the Austrian heir and his wife the Emperor had gone to Kronstadt, headquarters of the Baltic fleet, to meet French and British squadrons then on cruise in Russian waters.[1] From Kronstadt he proceeded to Krasnoe, near Petrograd, the great summer central review center of the old Russian Army where the usual military maneuvers were in progress. Returning to Peterhof, the Emperor ordered a hasty departure to Finland because, he said, the political horizon was darkening and he

[1] So little did any of the Allied rulers and statesmen anticipate the World War that in July, 1914, President Poincaré accompanied the French fleet on its cruise to the Baltic. Many festivities were arranged for him, and he was regally entertained by the Emperor. When receiving the ambassadors President Poincaré spoke gravely of the troubled political situation, but he said nothing to indicate that he expected war.

needed a few days of rest and distraction. We sailed
on July 6 (Russian Calendar) and had a quiet cruise,
the last one we were ever destined to enjoy. Not that
we intended it to be our last, for returning to Peterhof, from whence the Emperor hurried again to the
reviews, we left nearly all our luggage on the yacht.
The Empress, however, in one of her fits of melancholy, told me that she felt that we would never again
be together on the *Standert*.

The political skies were indeed darkening. The
Serbian murders and the unaccountably arrogant attitude of Austria grew in importance every succeeding
day, and for many hours every day the Emperor was
closeted in his study with Grand Duke Nicholas, Foreign Minister Sazonoff and other Ministers, all of
whom urged on the Emperor the imperative duty of
standing by Serbia. During the short intervals of the
day when we saw the Emperor he seemed half dazed
by the momentous decision he was called upon to make.
A few days before mobilization I went to lunch at
Krasnoe with a friend whose husband was on the Russian General Staff. In the middle of luncheon this
officer, Count Nosstiz, burst into the room exclaiming:
"Do you know what the Emperor has done? Can you
guess what they have made him do? He has promoted
the young men of the Military Academy to be officers,
and he has sent the regiments back to their casernes
to await orders All the military attachés are tele-
graphing their Governments to ask what it means.
What can it mean except war?"

From my friend's house I went almost at once back
to Peterhof and informed the Empress what I had

heard. Her amazement was unbounded, and over and over she repeated that she did not understand, that she could not imagine under what influence the Emperor had acted. He was still at the maneuvers, and although I remained late with the Empress I did not see him that night. The days that followed were full of suspense and anxiety. I spent most of my time playing tennis—very badly—with the girls, but from my occasional contacts with the Empress I knew that she was arguing and pleading against the war which apparently the Emperor felt to be inevitable. In one short talk I had with him on the subject he seemed to find a certain comfort in the thought that war always strengthened national feeling, and in his belief Russia would emerge from a truly righteous war stronger and better than ever. At this time a telegram arrived from Rasputine in Siberia, which plainly irritated the Emperor. Rasputine strongly opposed the war, and predicted that it would result in the destruction of the Empire. But the Emperor refused to believe it and resented what was really an almost unprecedented interference in affairs of state on the part of Rasputine.

I think I have spoken of the Emperor's aversion to the telephone. Up to this time none of his studies were ever fitted with telephones, but now he had wires and instruments installed and spent a great deal of time in conversations with Ministers and members of the military staff. Then came the day of mobilization, the same kind of a day of wild excitement, waving street crowds, weeping women and children, heartrending scenes of parting, that all the warring countries saw and ever will remember. After watching

hours of these dreadful scenes in the streets of Peterhof I went to my evening duties with the Empress only
to find that she had remained in absolute ignorance
of what had been taking place. Mobilization! It was
not true, she exclaimed. Certainly armies were moving, but only on the Austrian frontiers. She hurried
from the room and I heard her enter the Emperor's
study. For half an hour the sound of their excited
voices reached my ears. Returning, the Empress
dropped on her couch as one overcome by desperate
tidings. "War!" She murmured breathlessly. "And
I knew nothing of it. This is the end of everything."
I could say nothing. I understood as little as she the
incomprehensible silence of the Emperor at such an
hour, and as always, whatever hurt her hurt me. We
sat in silence until eleven when, as usual, the Emperor
came in to tea, but he was distraught and gloomy and
the tea hour also passed in almost complete silence.

The whole world has read the telegrams sent to
Nicholas II by ex-Emperor William in those beginning
days of the war. Their purport seemed to be sincere
and intimate, begging his old friend and relative to
stop mobilization, offering to meet the Emperor for
a conference which yet might keep the peace. Historians of the future will have to decide whether those
tenders were made in good faith or whether they were
part of the sinister diplomacy of that wicked war.
Nicholas II did not believe in their good faith, for he
replied that he had no right to stop mobilization in
Russia when German mobilization was already a matter of fact and that at any hour his frontiers might
be crossed by German troops. After this interval

the Emperor seemed to be in better spirits. War
had come indeed, but even war was better than the
threat and the uncertainty of the preceding weeks.
The extreme depression of the Empress, however, continued unrelieved. Up to the last moment she hoped
against hope, and when the German formal declaration
of war was announced she gave way to a perfect
passion of weeping, repeating to me through her tears:
"This is the end of everything." The state visit of
their Majesties to Petrograd soon after the declaration really seemed to justify the Emperor's belief that
the war would arouse the national spirit, so long latent,
in the Russian people. Never again do I expect to
behold such a sight as the streets of Petrograd presented on that day. To say that the streets were
crowded, thronged, massed, does not half express it.
I do not believe that one single able-bodied person in
the whole city remained at home during the hours spent
in the capital by the Sovereigns. The streets were almost literally impassable, and the Imperial motor
cars, moving at snail's pace from quay to palace
through that frenzied sea of people, cheering, singing the national hymn, calling down blessings on the
Emperor, was something that will live forever in the
memories of all who witnessed it. The Imperial
cortège was able, thanks to the police, to reach the
Winter Palace at last, but many of the suite were
halted by the crowds at the entrance to the great square
in front of the palace and had to enter at a side door
opening from the small garden to the west.

Inside the palace the crowd was relatively as great
as that on the outside. Apparently every man and

woman who had the right to appear at Court were massed in the corridors, the staircases, and the state apartments. Slowly their Majesties made their way to the great *Salle de Nicholas,* the largest hall in the palace, and there for several hours they stood receiving the most extraordinary tokens of homage from thousands of officials, ministers, and members of the *noblesse,* both men and women. Te Deums were sung, cheers and acclamations arose, and as the Emperor and Empress moved slowly through the crowds men and women threw themselves on their knees, kissing the hands of their Sovereigns with tears and fervent expressions of loyalty. Standing with others of the suite in the *Halle de Concert,* I watched this remarkable scene, and I listened to the historic speech of the Emperor which ended with the assurance that never would there be an end to Russian military effort until the last German was expelled from the beloved soil. From the *Salle de Nicholas* the Sovereigns passed to a balcony overlooking the great square. There with the Tsarevitch at their side they faced the wildly exulting people who with one accord dropped to their knees with mute gestures of love and obedience. Then as countless flags waved and dipped there arose from the lips and hearts of that vast assembly the moving strains of our great hymn: "God Save the Tsar."

Thus in a passion of renewed love and patriotism began in Russia the war of 1914. That same day the family returned to Peterhof, the Emperor almost immediately leaving for the casernes to bid farewell to regiments leaving for the front. As for the Empress, she became overnight a changed being. Every bodily

ill and weakness forgotten, she began at once an extensive plan for a system of hospitals and sanitary
trains for the dreadful roll of wounded which she knew
must begin with the first battle. Her projected chain
of hospitals and sanitary centers reached from Petrograd and Moscow to Charkoff and Odessa in the extreme south of Russia. The center of her personal
activity was fixed in a large group of evacuation hospitals in and around Tsarskoe Selo, and there, after
bidding farewell to my only brother, who immediately
left for the southern front, I joined the Empress.
Already her plans were so far matured that ten sanitary trains, bearing her name and the children's, were
in active service, and something like eighty-five hospitals were open, or preparing to open, in Tsarskoe
Selo, Peterhof, Pavlovsk, Louga, Sablino, and neigh-
boring towns. The Empress, her two older daughters,
and myself immediately enrolled under a competent
woman surgeon, Dr. Gedroiz, as student nurses, spending two hours of every afternoon under theoretical instruction, and the entire hours of the morning in ward
work in the hospitals. For the benefit of those who
imagine that the work of a royal nurse is more or less
in the nature of play I will describe the average routine
of one of those mornings in which I was privileged
to assist the Empress Alexandra Feodorovna and the
Grand Duchesses Olga and Tatiana, the two last-
named girls of nineteen and seventeen. Please remember that we were then only nurses in training.
Arriving at the hospital shortly after nine in the morning we went directly to the receiving wards where the
men were brought in after having first-aid treatment in

the trenches and field hospitals. They had traveled far and were usually disgustingly dirty as well as blood-stained and suffering. Our hands scrubbed in antiseptic solutions we began the work of washing, cleaning, and bandaging maimed bodies, mangled faces, blinded eyes, all the indescribable mutilations of what is called civilized warfare. These we did under the orders and the direction of trained nurses who had the skill to do the things our lack of experience prevented us from doing. As we became accustomed to the work, and as both the Empress and Tatiana had extraordinary ability as nurses, we were given more important work. I speak of the Empress and Tatiana especially because Olga within two months was almost too exhausted and too unnerved to continue, and my abilities proved to be more in the executive and organizing than in the nursing end of hospital work. I have seen the Empress of Russia in the operating room of a hospital holding ether cones, handling sterilized instruments, assisting in the most difficult operations, taking from the hands of the busy surgeons amputated legs and arms, removing bloody and even vermin-infected dressings, enduring all the sights and smells and agonies of that most dreadful of all places, a military hospital in the midst of war. She did her work with the humility and the gentle tirelessness of one dedicated by God to a life of ministration. Tatiana was almost as skillful and quite as devoted as her mother, and complained only that on account of her youth she was spared some of the more trying cases. The Empress was spared nothing, nor did she wish to be. I think I never saw her happier than on the day, at the end of our two months' intensive training, she marched at the head of the procession of nurses to receive the red cross and the diploma of a certificated war nurse.

From that time on our days were literally devoted to toil. We rose at seven in the morning and very often it was an hour or two after midnight before we sought our beds. The Empress, after a morning in the operating room of one hospital, snatched a hasty luncheon and spent the rest of the day in a round of inspection of other hospitals. Every morning early I met her in the little Church of Our Lady of Znamenie, where we went for prayers, driving afterwards to the hospitals. On the days when the sanitary trains arrived with their ghastly loads of wounded we often worked from nine until three without stopping for food or rest. The Empress literally shirked nothing. Sometimes when an unfortunate soldier was told by the surgeons that he must suffer an amputation or undergo an operation which might be fatal, he turned in his bed calling out her name in anguished appeal. "Tsaritsa! Stand near me. Hold my hand that I may have courage." Were the man an officer or a simple peasant boy she always answered the appeal. With her arm under his head she would speak words of comfort and encouragement, praying with him while preparations for the operation were in progress, her own hands assisting in the merciful work of anesthesia. The men idolized her, watched for her coming, reached out bandaged hands to touch her as she passed, smiling happily as she bent over their pillows. Even the dying smiled as she knelt beside their beds murmuring last words of prayer and consolation.

In the last days of November, 1914, the Empress left Tsarskoe Selo for an informal inspection of hospitals within the radius of her especially chosen district. Dressed in the gray uniform of a nursing sister, accompanied by her older daughters, myself, and a small suite, she went to towns surrounding Tsarskoe Selo and southward as far as Pskoff, staff headquarters, where the younger Grand Duchess Marie Pavlovna was a hospital nurse. From there she proceeded to Vilna, Kovno, and Grodno, in which city she met the Emperor and with him went on to Dvinsk. The enthusiasm and affection with which the Empress was met in all these places and in stations along the route beggars description. A hundred incidents of the journey crowd my memory, each one worth the telling had I space to include them in this narrative. I remember, for example, the remarkable scene in the big fortress of Kovno, where acres of hospital beds were assembled and where the tall figure of the Empress, moving through those interminable aisles, was greeted like the visit of an angel. I never recall that journey without remembering the hospital at Grodno, where a gallant young officer lay dying of his wounds. Hearing that the Empress was on her way to the hospital, he rallied unexpectedly and declared to his nurses that he was determined to live until she came. Sheer will power kept life in the man's body until the Empress arrived, and when, at the door of the hospital, she was told of his dying wish to see her she hurried first to his bedside, kneeling beside it and receiving his last smile, his last gasping words of greeting and farewell.

After one very fatiguing day our train passed a sanitary train of the Union of Zemstvos moving south. The Empress, who should have been resting in bed at the time, ordered her train stopped that she might visit, to the surprise and delight of the doctors, this splendidly equipped rolling hospital. Another surprise visit was to the estate of Prince Tichkevitch, whose family supported on their own lands a very efficient hospital unit. It was impossible to avoid noticing how in the towns visited by the Empress, dressed as a simple sister of mercy, the love of the people was most manifest. In Grodno, Dvinsk, and other cities where she appeared with the Emperor there was plenty of enthusiasm, but on those occasions etiquette obliged her to lay aside her uniform and to dress as the wife of the Emperor. Much better the people loved her when she went among them in her nurse's dress, their devoted friend and sister. Etiquette forgotten, they crowded around her, talked to her freely, claimed her as their own.

Soon after returning from this visit of inspection the Empress accompanied by Grand Duchesses Olga and Tatiana, General Racine, Commander of the Palace Guards, a maid of honor and myself, set off on a journey to Moscow, where to my extreme sorrow and dismay I perceived for the first time unmistakable evidences of a spreading intrigue against the Imperial Family. At the station in Moscow the Empress was met by her sister, the Grand Duchess Serge and the latter's intimate friend and the executive of her convent, Mme. Gardieve. Welcome from the people there was none, as General Djounkovsky, Governor of

Moscow, had announced, without any authority whatsoever, that the Empress was in the city incognito
and did not wish to meet anyone. In consequence of
this order we drove to the Kremlin through almost
empty streets. Nevertheless the Empress began at
once the inspection of hospitals, accompanied by General Racine and her maid of honor, Baroness Bouk-
shoevden, daughter of the Russian Ambassador in
Denmark. During our stay in Moscow I was not as
constantly with the Empress as usual, our rooms in
the Kremlin being far apart. However, General
Odoevsky, the fine old Governor of the Kremlin, installed a telephone between our rooms, and on her free
evenings the Empress often summoned me to sit with
her in her dressing room, hung with light blue drap-
eries and looking out over the river and the ancient
roofs of Moscow. I lunched and dined with others
of the suite in an old part of the immense palace
known as the Granovita Palata, and here occurred
one night a disagreeable scene in which General Racine, in the presence of the whole company, administered a stinging rebuke to General Djounkovsky,
Governor of Moscow, for his responsibility for the
cold welcome accorded her Majesty. The Governor
turned very pale but made no answer to the accusation of General Racine. Already my mind was in a
tumult of trouble, more and more conscious of the
atmosphere of intrigue, plots, and conspiracies, the
end of which I could not see. In the coldness of
the Grand Duchess Serge, in my childhood such a
friend to me and to my family, her chilly refusal to
listen to her sister's denial of preposterous tales of

the political influence exerted by Rasputine, by the general animosity towards myself, I began dimly to realize that there was a plot to strike at her Majesty through Rasputine and myself. There was absolutely nothing I could do, and I had to watch with tearless grief the breach between the sisters grow wider and deeper until their association was robbed of most of its old intimacy. I knew well enough, or I was convinced that I knew, that the dismissed maid of honor, Mlle. Tutcheff, was at the bottom of the whole affair, her family being among the most prominent in Moscow. But I could say nothing, do nothing.

With great relief we saw our train leave Moscow for a round of visits in surrounding territory, and here again the enthusiasm with which the people welcomed the Empress was unbounded. In the town of Toula, for example, and a little farther on in Orel, the people were so tumultuous in their greeting, they crowded so closely around their adored Empress, that our party could scarcely make our way to church and hospital. Once, following the Empress out of a church, carrying in my hands an ikon which had been presented to her, I was fairly overthrown by the crowding multitude and fell halfway down the high flight of steps before friendly hands could get me to my feet. I did not mind this, being only too rejoiced at evidences of love and devotion which the simple people of Russia felt for their Empress. In one town where there were no modern carriages she was dragged along in an old coach of state such as a medieval bishop might have used, the coach being quite covered with flowers and branches. In the town of Charkoff hundreds of students met the train bearing aloft portraits of her Majesty. In the small town of Belgorod, where the Empress wished to stop in order to visit a very sacred monastery, I shall never forget the joy with which the sleepy ischvostiks hurried through the darkness of the night to drive us the three or four versts from the railway to the monastery. Nor can I forget the arrival at the monastery, the sudden flare of lights as the monks hastened out to meet and greet their Sovereign Empress. These were the people, the plain people of Russia, and the difference between them and the plotting officials we had left behind in Moscow was a sad and a terrible contrast.

On December 6 (Russian Calendar), the birthday of the Emperor, we met his train at Voronezh, where our parties joined in visits to Tambov, Riasan, and other towns where the people gave their Majesties wonderful greetings. In Tambov the Emperor and Empress visited and had tea with a charming woman of advanced age, Mme. Alexandra Narishkin, friend of Alexander III and of many distinguished men of her time. Mme. Narishkin, horrible to relate, was afterwards murdered by the Bolsheviki, neither her liberal mind nor her long services to her country, and especially to her humble friends in Tambov, sparing her from the blood lust of the destroyers of Russia.

The journey of their Majesties terminated at Moscow, where the younger children of the family awaited them. I can still see the slim, erect figure of Alexei standing at salute on the station platform, and the rosy, eager faces of Marie and Anastasie welcoming their parents after their long separation The united family drove to the Kremlin, this time not quite so inhospitably received. In the days following the Moscow hospitals and military organizations were visited in turn, and we included in these visits out of town activities of the Moscow Zemstvo (county council), canteens, etc. In one of these centers our host was Prince Lvoff, afterwards active in demanding the abdication of the Tsar, and I remember with what deference he received their Majesties, and the especial attention he paid to the Tsarevitch, whose autograph he begged for the visitors' book. Before we left Moscow the Empress paid two visits, one to the old Countess Apraxin, sister of the former first lady in waiting, Princess Galatzine and, with the Emperor, to the Metropolitan Makari, a good man, but mercilessly persecuted during the Revolution.

There was one small but significant incident which happened after our return to Tsarskoe Selo, near the end of the year 1914. It failed of its intended effect, but had it not failed it might have had a far-reaching influence on world events at that time. Looking back on it now, I sometimes wonder exactly what lay back of the plot, and who was responsible for its inception. One evening late in the year I received a visit from two war nurses lately released from a German prison where they had been taken with a portion of a captured Russian regiment. In much perturbation of spirit these nurses told me of a third nurse who had been captured and imprisoned with them. This woman they had come to distrust as she had been accorded many special favors by the Germans. She had been given good food and even champagne, and when the nurses were released she alone was conveyed to the frontier in a motor car, the others going on foot. While in prison this woman had boasted that she expected to be received by the Emperor, to whom she proposed to present the flag of the captured regiment. The other nurses declared that in their opinion his Majesty should be warned of the woman's dubious character.

Hardly knowing what to think of such an extraordinary story, I thought it my duty to lay the matter before General Voyeikoff, Chief Commander of the Palace Guards, and when I learned from him that the Emperor had consented to receive the nurse I begged that the woman be investigated before being allowed to enter the palace. The Emperor showed some vexation, but he consented. When General Voyeikoff examined the woman she made a display of great frankness, handing him a revolver which she said it had been necessary for her to carry at the front. General Voyeikoff, thinking it strange that the weapon had not been taken away from her by the Germans, immediately ordered a search of her effects. In the handbag which she would certainly have carried with her to the palace were found two more loaded revolvers. The woman was, of course, arrested, and although I cannot explain why, her arrest caused great indignation among certain members of the aristocracy who previously had received her at their homes. The whole onus of her arrest was placed on me, although the Emperor declared his belief that she was a German spy sent to assassinate him. That she was a spy I have never doubted, but in my own mind I have never even tried to guess from whence she came.

CHAPTER IX

A VERY few days after the events chronicled in the last chapter I became the victim of a railroad accident which brought me to the threshold of death and for many months made it impossible for me to follow the events of the war, or the growing conspiracy against the Sovereigns. At a little past five o'clock of the afternoon of January 2, 1915, I took the train at Tsarskoe for a short visit to my parents in Petrograd. With me in my carriage was Mme. Shiff, a sister of a distinguished officer of Cuirassiers. We sat talking the usual commonplaces of travel when suddenly, without a moment's notice, there came a tremendous shock and a deafening crash, and I felt myself thrown violently forward, my head towards the roof of the carriage, and both legs held as in a vise in the coils of the steam-heating apparatus. The overturned carriage lurched and broke in two like an eggshell and I felt the bones of my left leg snap sharply. So intense was the pain that I momentarily lost consciousness. Too soon my senses returned to me and I found myself firmly wedged in the wreckage of wood and iron, a great bar of steel crushing my face, and my mouth so choked with blood that I could not utter a sound. All I could do in my agony was silently to pray that God would give me the relief of a quick death, for I could not believe that any human being could endure such pain and live.

After what seemed to me an interminable length of time I felt the pressure on my face removed and a kind voice asked: "Who lies here?" As I managed to breathe my name the rescuers exclaimed in astonishment and alarm, and immediately began to endeavor to extricate me from my agonizing position. By means of ropes passed under my arms and using great care and gentleness they ultimately got me free and laid me on the grass. In a moment's flash I recognized one as a Cossack of the Emperor's special guard, an excellent man named Lichatchieff, and the other as a soldier of the railway battalion. Then I fainted. Ripping loose one of the doors of the railway carriage, the men placed me on it and carried me to a near-by hut already crowded with wounded and dying. Regaining consciousness for a moment, I begged in whispers that Lichatchieff would telephone my parents in Petrograd and their Majesties at the palace. This the good fellow did without delay, and he also brought to my corner one of the surgeons summoned to the wreck. The man gave me a rapid examination and said briefly: "Do not disturb her. She is dying." He left to attend to more hopeful cases, but the faithful soldiers still knelt beside me, straightening my crushed and broken legs and wiping the blood from my lips. In about two hours another doctor, this time the surgeon Gedroiz, under whom the Empress, her daughters, and myself had taken our nurses' training, approached the corner where I lay. I looked with a kind of terror into the face of this woman, for I knew

her to be no friend of mine. Simply giving my
wounded head a superficial examination she said carelessly that I was a hopeless case, and left me without
the slightest attempt to soothe my pain. Not until
ten o'clock that night, four hours after the collision
which had wrecked two trains, did any help reach me.
At that hour arrived General Racine from the palace
with orders from their Majesties to do everything possible in my behalf. At his imperative commands I
was again placed on a stretcher and carried to a relief
train made up of cattle cars. At the moment my poor
father and mother arrived from Petrograd and the
last things I remember were their sobs and a teaspoon-
ful of brandy mercifully poured down my throat.

At the end of the journey to Tsarskoe Selo I dimly
recognized the Empress and the four Grand Duchesses who had come to the station to meet the train.
Their faces were full of sympathy and grief, and as
they bent over me I found strength to whisper to them:
"I am dying" I believed it because the doctors had
said so, and because my pain was so great. Then came
the ordeal of being lifted into the ambulance and the
half-consciousness that the Empress was there too,
holding my head on her knees and begging me to have
courage. After that came an interval of darkness out
of which I awoke in bed and almost free from pain.
The Empress who, with my parents, remained near
me, asked me if I would like to see the Emperor. Of
course I replied that I would, and when he came I
pressed the hand he gave me. Dr. Gedroiz, who was
in charge of the ward, told everyone coldly to take
leave of me as I could not possibly live until morning.

"Is it so hopeless?" asked the Emperor. "She still has some strength in her hand."

Later on, I do not know exactly when, I opened my eyes quite clearly, and saw standing beside my bed the tall, gaunt form of Rasputine. He looked at me fixedly and said in a calm voice: "She will live, but will always be a cripple." A prediction which was literally fulfilled, for to this day I can walk only slowly and with the aid of a stout stick. I have been told that Rasputine recalled me from unconsciousness, but of his words I know only what I have recorded.

The next morning I was operated on and for the six weeks following I suppose I suffered as greatly as one can and live. My left leg which had sustained a double fracture, troubled me less than my back and my right leg which had been horribly wrenched and lacerated. My head wounds were also intensely painful and for a time I suffered from inflammation of the brain. My parents, the Empress, and the children came every day to see me, but despite their presence the neglect and unkindness of Dr. Gedroiz continued. The suggestion of the Empress that her trusted physician, Dr. Federoff, be brought into consultation was rudely repulsed by this woman, of whom I may finally say that she is now in high favor with the Bolsheviki whose ranks she joined in the autumn of 1917. Waited upon by none but the most inexperienced nurses, I do not know what might have become of me had not my mother brought to the hospital an old family nurse whom she absolutely insisted should take charge of me. Things went a little better after this, but happy was I when at the end of the sixth week, against the will of Dr. Gedroiz, I left that wretched hospital and was removed to my own home. There in the peace and security of my comfortable bed-room I enjoyed for the first time since my accident quiet and refreshing sleep.

It seems strange that the hostile and envious Court circle had deeply resented the daily visits of the Emperor and Empress to my bedside. To placate the gossipers the Emperor, before visiting me, used to make the rounds of all the wards. In spite of it all I had many visitors and many daily inquiries from the Empress Dowager and others. Very soon after my arrival home I was examined by skillful surgeons, among them Drs Federoff and Gagentorn, who pronounced my crushed right leg to be in a very bad condition and placed it in a plaster cast, where it remained for two months. The Empress visited me daily, but the Emperor I seldom saw because, as I learned indirectly, the War was going very badly on the Russian front, and the Emperor was almost constantly with the armies. In the last week before Lent he came to my bedside with the Empress, in accordance with an old Russian custom, before confession, to beg my forgiveness for possible wrongs done me during the year past. Their pious humility and also the white and careworn face of the Emperor filled me with emotion which later events served only to increase, for very momentous and trying hours were even then crowding the destiny of Nicholas II, Tsar of all the Russias.

A soldier of the sanitary corps, a man named Jouk, had been assigned to duty at my house, and as soon as I was able to leave my bed he took me daily in a wheeled chair to church, and to the palace. This was the summer of 1915, a time of great tribulation for the Russian Army, as every student of the World War is aware. Grand Duke Nicholai Nicholaievitch was pursuing a policy which rightly disturbed the Emperor, who constantly complained that the commander in chief of his armies sent the men forward without proper ammunition, without artillery support, and with no adequate preparations for safe retreat. Disaster after disaster confirmed the Emperor's fears. Fortress after fortress fell to the Germans. Kovno fell. Novogeorgiesk fell, and finally Warsaw itself fell. It was a terrible day when the Emperor, white and trembling, brought this news to the Empress as we sat at tea on her balcony in the warm autumn air. The Emperor was fairly overcome with grief and humiliation as he finished his tale. "It cannot go on any longer like this," he exclaimed bitterly, and then he went on to declare that in spite of ministerial opposition he was determined to take personal command of the army himself. Only that day Krivosheim, Minister of Agriculture, had addressed him on the impossible condition of Russian internal affairs. Nicholai Nicholaievitch, not content with military supremacy, had assumed almost complete authority over all the business of the Empire. There were in fact two governments in Russia, orders being constantly issued from military headquarters without the knowledge, much less the consent, of the Emperor.

Very soon after the fall of Warsaw it became clear to the Emperor that if he were to retain any dignity whatever he would have to depose Nicholai Nicholaievitch, and I wish here to state, without any reservation whatever, that this decision was reached by the Emperor without advice from Rasputine, myself, or any other person. Even the Empress, although she approved her husband's resolution, had no part in forming it. M. Gilliard has written that the Emperor was forced to his action by bad advisers, especially the Empress and Rasputine, but in this he is absolutely mistaken. M. Gilliard writes that the Emperor was told that Grand Duke Nicholai Nicholaievitch was plotting to confine his Sovereign in a monastery. I do not believe for a moment that Rasputine ever made such a statement, but he did, in my presence, warn the Emperor to watch Nicholai Nicholaievitch and his wife who, he alleged, were at their old practices of table-tipping and spiritism, which he thought to be a highly dangerous way to conduct a war against the Germans. As for me, I repeat that never once did I say or do anything to influence the Emperor in state affairs. I wish I could here reproduce a letter written to my father by the Emperor in which all the reasons for taking the step he did were explained. The letter, alas! was taken from me by the Bolsheviki after my father's death, and I suppose was destroyed.

On the evening when the Emperor met his ministers to announce his great decision I dined at the palace, and I was deeply impressed with the firmness of the Emperor's decision not to be overborne by arguments or vain fears on the part of timid statesmen As he arose to go to the council chamber the Emperor begged us to pray for him that his resolution should not falter. "You do not know how hard it has been for me to refrain from taking an active part in the command of my beloved army," he said at parting. Overcome and speechless, I pressed into his hand a tiny ikon which I had always worn around my neck, and during the long council which followed the Empress and I prayed fervently for the Emperor and for our distracted country.

As the time passed the Empress's anxiety grew so great that, throwing a cloak around her shoulders and beckoning me to follow, she went out on the balcony, one end of which gave on the council room. Through the lace of the window curtains we could see the Emperor sitting very upright, surrounded by his ministers, one of whom was on his feet speaking earnestly. Our eleven o'clock tea was served long before the Emperor, entirely exhausted, returned from the conference. Throwing himself in an armchair, he stretched himself out like a man spent after extreme exertion, and I could see that his brow and hands were wet with perspiration.

"They did not move me," he said in a low, tense voice. "I listened to all their long, dull speeches, and when all had finished I said: 'Gentlemen, in two days from now I leave for the Stavka.'" As he repeated the words his face lightened, his shoulders straightened, and he appeared like a man whose strength was suddenly renewed.

Yet one more struggle was before him. The Empress Dowager, whom the Emperor visited immediately after the ministerial conference, was by this time thoroughly imbued with the German-spy mania in which the Empress and Rasputine, not to mention myself, were involved. She believed the whole preposterous tissue of lies which had been built up and with all her might she struggled against the Emperor's decision to assume supreme command of the army. For over two hours a painful scene was enacted in the Empress Dowager's gardens, he trying to show her that utter disaster threatened the army and the Empire under existing conditions, and she repeating over and over again the wicked slanders of German plots which she insisted that he was furthering. In the end the Emperor left, terribly shaken, but with his resolution as strong as ever.

Before leaving for staff headquarters the Emperor and his family took communion together at the Feodorovsky Cathedral and at their last meal together he showed himself calm and collected as he had not been for some time; in fact, not since the beginning of the last disastrous campaign. From headquarters the Emperor wrote full accounts of the scenes which took place when he assumed personal command, and of the furious anger, not only of the deposed Nicholai Nicholaievitch but of all his staff, "Every one of whom," wrote the Emperor, "has the ambition himself to govern Russia."

I am not attempting to write a military history of those years, and I am quite aware of the fact that most published accounts of the Russian Army represent Nicholai Nicholaievitch as the devoted friend of the Allies and the Emperor as the pliant tool of German influences. It is undeniable, however, that almost as soon as Nicholai Nicholaievitch had been sent to the Caucasus and the Emperor took command of the Western Army a marked improvement in the general morale became apparent. Retreat at various points was stopped, the whole front strengthened, and a new spirit of loyalty to the Empire was manifest.

I wish to interpolate here, in connection with the Emperor's personal command of the army, a word on the immense service he rendered it at the beginning of the War in suppressing the manufacture and sale of vodka, the curse of the Russian peasantry. The Emperor did this entirely on his own initiative, without advice from his ministers or the Grand Dukes. The Emperor said at the time: "At least by this I will be remembered," and he was, because the condition of the peasants, the town workers, and of course the army became at once immeasurably better. In the midst of war-time privations the savings-banks accounts of the people increased enormously, and in the army there was none of the hideous debauchery which disgraced Russia in the Russo-Japanese War. As an eminent French correspondent long afterwards wrote: "It is to the dethroned Emperor Nicholas that we must accord the honor of having effected the greatest of all internal reforms in war-time Russia, the suppression of alcoholism."

In October the Emperor came to Tsarskoe Selo for a brief visit, and on his return he took with him to the Stavka the young Tsarevitch. This is the first time he had ever separated the boy from his mother, and the Empress was never happy except in the few minutes each day when she was reading the child's daily letter. At nine o'clock at night she went up to his bedroom exactly as though he were there and she was listening to his evening prayers. By day the Empress continued her tireless work in the hospitals from which, by reason of my accident, I had long been excluded. However, at this time, I received from the railroad as compensation for my injuries the considerable sum of eighty thousand rubles, and with the money I established a hospital for convalescent soldiers in which maimed and wounded men received training in various useful trades This, it is needless to say, became a great source of happiness to me, since I knew as well as the soldiers what it meant to be crippled and helpless. From the first my hospital training school was a most gratifying success, and my personal interest in it never ceased until the Revolution, after which all my efforts at usefulness and service ended in imprisonment and persecution.

Not this action of mine, patriotic though it must have appeared, no amount of devotion of the Empress to the wounded, sufficed to check the rapidly growing propaganda which sought to convict the Imperial Family and all its friends of being German spies. The fact that in England the Empress's brother-in-law, Prince Louis of Battenberg, German-born but a loyal Briton, was forced to resign his command in the British Navy was used with effect against the Empress Alexandra Feodorovna. She knew and resented keenly this insane delusion, and she did everything in her power to overcome it. I remember a day when the Empress received a letter from her brother Ernest, Grand Duke of Hesse, in which he implored her to do something to improve the barbarous conditions of German prisoners in Russia. With streaming tears the

Empress owned herself powerless to do anything at all in behalf of the unhappy captives She had organized a committee for the relief of Russian prisoners in Germany, but this had been fiercely attacked, especially in the columns of *Novy Vremya,* an influential organ of the Constitutional Democratic Party. In this newspaper and in general society the Empress's committee was accused of being a mere camouflage gotten up to shield her real purpose of helping the Germans. Against such attacks the Empress had no defense. Her secretary, Count Rostovseff, indeed tried to refute the story concerning the Empress's prison-camp committee, but the editors of *Novy Vremya* insolently refused to publish his letter of explanation.

The German-spy mania was extended from the palace to almost every Russian who had the misfortune to possess a name that sounded at all German. Count Fredericks and Minister Sturmer were among those who suffered calumny, although neither spoke a single German sentence. But the greatest sufferers were those barons of the Baltic Provinces whose ancestors had bequeathed them names of quite certain German origin. Many of these men were arrested and sent to die, or to suffer worse than death in exile. The sons and relatives of many of these very Baltic proprietors were at the time fighting loyally in the Russian Army. That there were German spies at work in Russia all during the War I have no reason to doubt, but they were the men who after 1917 invited in and exalted Lenine and Trotzky, and not the Empress and her friends, nor yet the persecuted estate owners of the Baltic Provinces. Did the Emperor's family call upon the Germans to rescue them from Siberia? Did any of the Baltic Provinces at Versailles ask to be united to Germany?

The army and navy still remained loyal to the Sovereigns. On one of his home visits to Tsarskoe Selo the Emperor brought with him as a proof of this the Cross of the Order of St. George, the highest of all Russian military decorations, which none could bestow except the Emperor, or the chief command of one of the armies in the field   In this case it was the gallant Southern Army which had voted to bestow it on the Emperor, and his pride and joy in it were humbly great.

CHAPTER X

TO one who has always held the honor and faith of the Russian people very dear, who has never doubted that after the last hideous phase of revolution and anarchism has passed, the Russian nation will emerge stronger and better than ever before, the writing of these next chapters is a duty inexpressibly painful. I must tell the truth, otherwise it would have been better for me never to have written at all. Yet to picture in anything like its true colors the decadence of Petrograd society from 1914 onward is a task from which any loyal Russian must shrink. Without a knowledge of these conditions, however, students of the Russian Revolution will never be able to understand why the fabric of government slipped so easily from the feeble hands of the Provisional Government to the ruthless and bloody grasp of the Bolshevists.

During the entire winter of 1915, when the War was being waged on all fronts with such disaster to the Allies, when millions of men, Russians, Frenchmen, Belgians, Englishmen, were giving up their lives in the cause of freedom, the aristocracy of the Russian capital was indulging in a reckless orgy of dancing, sports, dining, yes, and wining also in spite of the Emperor's edict against alcohol, spending enormous sums for gowns and jewels, and in every way ignoring the terrible fact that the world was on fire and that civilization was battling for its very life. In the palace the most frugal régime had been adopted. Meals were simple almost to parsimony, no money was spent except for absolute necessities, and the Empress and her daughters spent practically every waking hour working and praying for the soldiers. But society, when it was not otherwise amusing itself, was indulging in a new and madly exciting game of intrigue against the throne. To spread slanders about the Empress, to inflame the simple minds of workmen against the state was the most popular diversion of the aristocracy. A typical instance of this mania was related to me by my sister, who one morning was surprised by an unexpected visit from her sister-in-law, daughter of a very great lady of the aristocracy. Bursting into the room, this woman exclaimed delightedly: "What do you think we are doing now? Spreading stories through all the factories that the Empress is keeping the Emperor constantly drunk. Everybody believes it." I mention this story as typical because the woman involved afterwards became very prominent in the Grand Ducal cabal that forced the abdication, and she was also one of two women present in the Yusupoff Palace on the night of Rasputine's assassination.

Every possible circumstance, no matter how inconsequential, was eagerly seized as capital by these plotters. A former lady in waiting, Marie Vassilchikoff, long retired from Court and living on her Austrian estates, came to Petrograd, I know not how, and asked for an audience with the Empress. Since Russia was at war with Austria this audience could not be granted, nor did the Empress even remotely desire it. Yet as the story was circulated Marie Vassilchikoff was represented as having been sent for by the Empress to negotiate a separate peace with Austria, and that this treachery was frustrated only by the vigorous intervention of the Grand Duchess Serge.

These stories were spread not only by Court and society people, but were made into a regular propaganda in the army, especially among the higher command. The propaganda was chiefly in the hands of members of the Union of Zemstvos, its most successful agent being the infamous Goutchkoff, who now, it is gratifying to know, has earned the contempt of every Russian political group, even including the Bolshevists. Thus in a whirl of heartless gaiety and an organized campaign against the Sovereigns and against the Empire passed the winter of 1915, the dark prelude of darker years to come.

In the spring of that year, my health being still very precarious, their Majesties sent me in charge of a sanitary train filled with invalid soldiers and officers to the soft climate of the Crimea. With me went a sister of mercy and the sanitary-corps man Jouk, of whom I have spoken. On the same train journeyed also three members of the secret police, ostensibly to protect, but really, as I well understood, to spy upon me. Their presence the Empress, who came in the pouring rain to see the train off from the station, was powerless to forbid, as she herself was constantly under the surveillance of the dread Okhrana. Our train traveled slowly, taking five days from Petrograd to the Black Sea. But this we did not mind as we were very comfortable, the weather became beautiful, and our frequent stops at Moscow and towns farther south were full of interest. Our destination was Evpatoria on the eastern shore of the Black Sea, and here all of us were cordially received, M. Duvan, the head man of the city, giving me for a residence his own flower-hung villa overlooking the sea. Here I spent two peaceful months, finding the mud baths wonderfully restoring, and meeting some unusually interesting people. I am sure that few people outside of Russia have ever heard of the Karaim, a racial group among the most ancient in the world and of whom, even then, a bare ten thousand existed. They were not Jews, although they worshipped in synagogues, because they acknowledged Christ as God, or at least a special prophet of God. They were, and are, if they still exist, a strange mixture of pious Jews and early Christians, left-overs from the days of the decaying Roman Empire when Judaism and Christianity were trying to unite in one faith. The head of the Karaim in Evpatoria was a fine black-bearded patriarch named Gaham, and with him I formed an almost immediate friendship. Dressed in the long black robe of his office, he used to sit with me for hours reading and reciting the legends of his people, many reaching back into the dim twilight of civilization. I liked the patriarch, not only for his simplicity and his kindness to me, but for his evident love and loyalty to the Imperial Family, a loyalty shared by all the people of the Karaim.

A telegram from the Empress told me that she was

then leaving for the Stavka, from which she and the Emperor and the whole Imperial Family would proceed to the Crimea for an important military and naval review. Obeying her instructions I motored from Evpatoria to Sevastopol, through an enchanting landscape of hills and plains, the latter being literally carpeted with scarlet poppies. Arriving at Sevastopol, I had some difficulty in passing the guard, but the Empress's telegram, marked "Imperial," I had brought with me, and this proved the open sesame to the Emperor's special train. I lunched with the Empress and the Grand Duchesses, meeting the Emperor and Alexei when they came from the reviews at six o'clock. I spent that night in town, and the next day returned to Evpatoria, their Majesties promising to visit me within a few days. On May 16 they arrived and received a most enthusiastic welcome, not only from the townspeople but from the Tartars, who came in from the hills by thousands, from the people of the Karaim, and others as strange and as picturesque. The huge square before the cathedral was strewn with fragrant roses over which the Imperial Family walked to service. The next few hours were spent in a round of visits to churches, hospitals, and sanatoriums, and it was to a late luncheon at my villa that they finally arrived. After luncheon we walked and sat on the beach, but the gathering crowd became so large and so curious that the poor Emperor, who had looked forward to a sea bath and a swim, had to relinquish both. Alexei enjoyed the day, boy fashion, without regard to the crowds, playing on the beach and building a big sand fortress, which the schoolboys of the town next day surrounded by a high wall of stones to protect it from the ravages of the tide. We had tea in the garden, the Empress greatly enjoying the Oriental sweets sent her by the Tartars. In the evening I dined on the Imperial train and traveled with it a short distance on its way back to Petrograd.

In June I returned to Tsarskoe and resumed work in my beloved hospital training school. The weather was unusually hot but the Empress continued her constant duties in the hospitals and operating rooms. Often I accompanied her on her rounds, and it came to me as a painful shock that the surgeons and some of the wounded officers no longer regarded her, as before, with respect and veneration. Too often an officer would assume in her presence a careless and indifferent manner which even a professional nurse would have resented. The Empress never did. She must have noticed evidences of disrespect but no word of complaint ever passed her lips. When I ventured to suggest to her that it might be well to go less frequently to her hospital, she rewarded me with a look of reproach. Whatever other people did, whatever their attitude towards the War, Royalty knew its duty and would perform it faithfully to the end.

Both the Emperor and the Empress during all this rising tide of disaffection persisted in underestimating its importance. The Emperor especially treated the whole movement with the contempt which no doubt it merited but which as a national menace it was far too dangerous to ignore. I realized it keenly, but knowing how impossible it was to make their Majesties understand that everything that was said against me, against Rasputine, against the Ministers, was actually directed against themselves, I was obliged to keep my lips closed. My parents realized as well as I did what was going on. They had good reason, in fact, for my mother had received two most insulting letters, one from Princess Galatzine, sister of Mme. Rodzianko, whose husband was President of the Duma, and another from Mme. Timasheff, a woman of the highest aristocracy, letters which indicated a certain collusion between the writers. In them my mother was brutally informed that neither of the women desired any further acquaintanceship or association with her as she too undoubtedly belonged to the German-spy party. My parents at the time were living quietly in the little seaside town of Terioke, near Petrograd, and were studiously avoiding the vulgar orgies and intrigues of society.

In the midst of all these heart-breaking events I sought distraction in the enlargement and perfecting of my occupational hospital which was rapidly becoming overcrowded with invalids I bought an additional piece of land and arranged for four portable houses to be brought from Finland. Two of these arrived duly, and I spent hours of absorbing interest watching them being put together on the newly acquired land. All these days I was constantly being bothered by people who, perhaps believing that the money I was investing in hospitals was another proof of my power over the Imperial treasury, tormented me with petitions of every kind and description, but all of them alike in the selfishness of their character. With cold hatred in their eyes, but with hypocritical words on their lips, these people besought my good offices with their Majesties on behalf of their sons, husbands, and relatives, all of whom were alleged to be worthy of promotions and of lucrative positions under the State. One woman of good social position invaded my hospital one day and treated me to a disgraceful scene because I had assured her that I was powerless to further her ambition to see her husband appointed head of a certain Government. Naturally it happened that some petitioners were poor and needy, and these, to the best of my ability, but without any political influence whatever, I did endeavor to help. I know now, after witnessing true sympathy and kindness to prisoners and persecuted, like myself in later days, that I never did half what I might have done in the time of my prosperity. If better days come to Russia in my lifetime God help me to devote all that remains of my years to the poor and especially to prisoners. Now that I have tasted poverty, now that I have known the hopelessness of captivity, I know better than I did what can be done for the lowly and unfortunate.

A number of very disquieting events occurred to us during the summer. On very hot days it was the custom of the Empress and the children to drive through the woods and shaded roads to Pavlovsk, a few versts from Tsarskoe Selo. One stifling afternoon we started out as usual in two carriages, the Empress and myself leading the way. The horses were magnificent animals, apparently in the very pink of condition, but suddenly one of the horses uttered a piercing scream and dropped dead in his harness. The other horse plunged sidewise in terror and for a few minutes it was all the coachman could do to avoid an overturn. The Empress, pale, but as always courageous, got out of the carriage and helped me, who was still on crutches, to alight. The carriage of the children drove up, and getting in, we returned without further incident to the palace. Whatever caused the sudden death of that horse, or what was the object of that carriage accident—if indeed it was an accident—we never knew, but it left behind in my mind, and I think also in the mind of the Empress, a strangely sinister impression. The Empress nevertheless went steadfastly on with her hospital work, arranging in the convalescent wards concerts and entertainments for the pleasure of the wounded. The best singers, the most accomplished musicians, were secured for these concerts, and the men seemed appreciative of them. Yet over the head of the Empress Alexandra Feodorovna drifted darker and darker the shadow of impending doom. The things I dared not say to her began to reach her from others. In August came from the Crimea the head man of the Karaim, of whom I have spoken. From the first he made an agreeable impression on the Empress and the children, especially upon Alexei, who never tired of listening to his stories. But Gaham had not made the journey from the Crimea to relate legends and tales. He had previously been connected with the Ministry of Foreign Affairs, serving in Persia and the East, and his acute mind was still occupied with the foreign affairs of the Empire on which he kept himself well informed.

Determined, if possible, to force the Empress to

understand the gravity of the situation, he told her a number of extraordinary things which had come to his knowledge, among them an organized plot against the throne which was being carried on by near relatives of the Tsar in the seclusion of an allied foreign embassy in Petrograd. His story, involving, as it did, the ambassador of a friendly power, the trusted representative of an own cousin of the Emperor, seemed to the Empress too preposterous to be credited. Horrified, she ended the conversation, and a few days later she went, taking me with her, to visit the Emperor at the Stavka. What he had to comment on her report of an alleged ambassadorial plot against him I never knew, but I soon became aware that representatives of other foreign countries were undeniably hostile. At the Stavka were military commissions of practically every allied country, among them General Williams and his staff from Great Britain, General Janin from France, General Rikkel from Belgium, and high officers from Italy, Serbia, Rumania, Japan, and other countries, all accompanied by subordinate officers. One afternoon when the gardens were quite crowded by these men and men of our own army, and while the Empress was making her customary circle, I chanced to overhear a conversation among officers of the foreign military missions, in which the most slanderous words against her Majesty were uttered. "She has come again, it appears," said one of these men, "to see her husband and give him the latest orders of Rasputine." "The suite hate to hear her arrival announced," said another officer. "They know it means changes."

Worse things were said, but without waiting to listen I managed to make my way to the Empress, and that night inviting, as I was well aware, her irritation and disbelief, I related something of what I had overheard. I went further and reminded her of what we both knew, the increasing demoralization of the Emperor's staff. The Grand Dukes and the commanding officers were, as a matter of course, invited each day to lunch with the Emperor, but with insolence and audacity hitherto unheard of, many of the Emperor's near kinsmen declined these invitations. They gave the most trivial and transparent excuses for their absence—headaches, fatigue, previous engagements, alleged duties. The Empress listened to what I said, silent and distraught She knew, and I also knew, that nothing she could say to the Emperor would make the slightest impression. His eyes and ears were still closed to the gathering tempest.

General Alexieff, Chief of Staff, and undoubtedly a valuable officer, had, I soon learned, been drawn into the plot. The Emperor suspected him to be in correspondence with the traitor Goutchkoff, but when questioned General Alexieff denied this vehemently. He was soon, however, to prove his treachery to the Emperor. There was in attendance on his Majesty at the Stavka an old officer, General Ivanoff, a St. George Cross man, who formerly had held command of the Army of the South. This devoted and loyal old soldier General Alexieff knew he must get rid of, and this, had he been honest, he might have done by pleading age or decreased usefulness. Instead, he merely summoned General Ivanoff and informed him that to the regret of the whole staff he was removed. The Chief of Staff was not responsible for this, he declared, the order having come from the Empress and her accomplices, Rasputine and Mme. Virubova. What General Alexieff said to the Emperor on the subject I do not know, but when next the two met the Emperor turned his head aside. This sudden coldness on the part of the Emperor, whom old General Ivanoff loved dearly, made it impossible for him to seek an audience, and yet the general was valiantly determined not to leave the Stavka without presenting his case to the Sovereign. Calling on me that same day, he repeated to me, while tears rolled down his white beard, the lying words of General Alexieff against the Empress. Feeling it against reason and justice that the Emperor should remain in ignorance of this insult to his wife, I promised to speak to him about it, and this I did, but to little purpose. The Emperor's wrath against Alexieff was indeed kindled but he evidently felt that he could not, at that critical hour, dismiss an officer whose services were so urgently in demand. Afterwards, however, his manner towards old General Ivanoff became conspicuously kind.

We remained for some time after this at the Stavka, days to me of such sad remembrance that I can scarcely endure the task of recording them. The Empress and her suite, the Grand Duchesses, and myself lived on board the Imperial train, motor cars coming each day at one o'clock to take us to staff headquarters to luncheon. Headquarters were in an ancient villa of the Governor of the Province, a rather old-fashioned and uncomfortable place. Even the huge dining room where the Emperor and Empress, the staff and the officers of the foreign missions met each day was a dull and gloomy room. When the weather became very warm this dismal apartment was abandoned, and luncheon was served in a large tent in a shady part of the grounds overlooking the town and farther away still the flowing tide of the mighty Dnieper. The only really bright circumstance of the time was the growing health and strength of the Tsarevitch. He was developing marvelously through the summer, both in bodily vigor and in gaiety of spirits. With his tutors, M. Gilliard and Petroff, he romped and played as though illness were a thing to him unknown. With several of the allied officers, notably with the Belgian General Rikkel, he was also on the best of terms.

Every day after luncheon the maids came from the train with what gowns and other apparel we needed for the remaining functions of the day. There was little room in the house in which to change, but we managed to appropriate a few nooks and corners, and to make ourselves as presentable as possible in the circumstances. In the Emperor's scant hours of leisure he loved to walk with his family in the woods along the river brink, and sometimes when I saw the Empress sitting on the grass talking informally with the peasant women who crowded around her, I took comfort, believing then, as I still believe, that the great mass of the Russian people were to the end faithful to their Sovereigns. As for the suite, most of them became increasingly indifferent, bound up in their foolish personal affairs, diverting themselves with whispered gossip and laughter, apparently quite indifferent to the calamitous progress of the War. People to whom religion is still in these cynical days a real refuge will understand me when I tell them what comfort I found in an ancient convent in the neighborhood, and in the poor little church which adjoined it. The one treasure of this church was an old and highly revered image of Our Lady of Mogiloff and almost every day of that distressful summer I managed to spend a few minutes on my knees before her dark and mystic image. One day, feeling in my heart the imminence of a danger I dared not name even to myself, I took off my diamond earrings and laid them at the foot of the shrine where I had sought and received peace of mind. I hope my poor offering was received with grace by the saint, who of course did not need it, but whose helpless ones always do. A little later the monks presented me with a small replica of the image, and strangely enough this was the one ikon I was permitted to take with me when I was sent to the Fortress of Peter and Paul.

Of that unhappy summer of 1916 I have only one or two more incidents to relate. One of these was a visit to the Stavka of the Princess Paley, wife of Grand Duke Paul. Coming from Kiev, where the Empress Dowager and the Grand Duke Nicholai Michailovitch were in residence, it appeared ominous to me that they too, all of them, seemed to be inoculated with the delusion of the German spy and the Rasputine influence. Neither the Princess nor the Grand Duke were in the least tactful in the expression of their opinions on the subject. Another visitor to the Stavka was Rodzianko, who came to demand the instant dismissal of Protopopoff, Minister of the Interior, once his friend and confidant, but now accused by the President of the Duma of being a lunatic. The Emperor received Rodzianko coldly, and did not even invite him to lunch. At tea that afternoon the Emperor said that the interview had angered him intensely as he knew quite well that Rodzianko's representations and motives were wholly insincere. Almost everything at the Stavka was growing worse and worse, the Grand Dukes being more insolent than ever and continually annoying General Voyeikoff by ordering trains and motors for themselves without any regard to the requirements of the Emperor. It was with feelings of unspeakable relief that in November, 1916, we left the Stavka for Tsarskoe Selo In the Imperial train with us traveled young Grand Duke Dmitri Pavlovitch who even then was probably involved in a deadly plot against their Majesties. Yet this young man was able to keep up a pretense of friendship with the Empress, sitting beside her couch and entertaining her by the hour with amusing gossip and stories. Hearing the laughter the Emperor often opened his study door to listen and to join in the conversation. It was a merry journey home, yet within a few days after we arrived troubles again began to multiply. Entering the Empress's door one day, I found her in a passion of indignation and grief. As soon as she could speak she told me that the Emperor had sent her a letter from Nicholai Michailovitch, in which the Empress was specifically charged with the most mischievous political machinations. "Unless this is stopped," the letter concluded, "murders will certainly begin." [1]

Nicholai Michailovitch, it appears, had gone to the Stavka from the group in Kiev, with the express object of delivering this letter. Every member of the staff knew his errand and expected him to be ignominiously ejected from the Emperor's study. Nothing of the kind happened, and the Grand Duke stayed to luncheon in the most friendly manner. I do not know what he said to the Emperor, but I do know that the letter was laid on the Emperor's desk. Nothing was said or done to avenge this deadly insult to the wife of Nicholas II whom undoubtedly he loved dearer than his own life. The only explanation I can think of was the Emperor's complete absorption in the War, and in his unshaken conviction that the plotters' gossip was entirely harmless. He had the kind of mind which could concentrate on only one thing at a time, and at this period his whole heart and soul was with the fighting armies. I well remember scraps of conversation with him during those days which indicated that in the back of his mind were many plans for future internal reforms. He spoke of important social changes which must come after the War, social and constitutional reforms. "I will do everything necessary afterwards," he said in more than one of these conversations. "But I cannot act now. I cannot do more than one thing at a time."

---

[1] Previous to the War and the impending revolution the Empress had had very little to do with politics, but it is true that when affairs became desperate she did what she rightly could to advise her husband.

The Empress, I think, for all her sensitiveness to the abominable accusations brought against her, tried to preserve the same waiting state of mind. Most disagreeable incidents she kept to herself, yet one day she showed me a letter written directly to her by a Princess Vassilchikoff, a letter so insulting that the Emperor was aroused to order the Princess and her husband, a member of the Duma, to their country estates. This letter was written on small scraps of paper evidently torn from a cheap writing tablet. "At least," said the Empress with faint sarcasm, "she might have used the stationery of a lady when addressing her Sovereign."

What had taken possession of Petrograd society? I often asked myself. Was it a mob delusion, contagious, like certain diseases? Was it a madness born of the War similar to other strange hysterias which arose during some of the wars of the Middle Ages? That the delusion was confined to Petrograd and a few other towns frequented by the aristocracy was perfectly apparent. In the last days of 1916 the Empress with Olga, Tatiana, and General Racine paid a brief visit to Novgorod to inspect military hospitals and to pray in the monastery and church of Sofisky Sobor, one of the oldest churches in Russia. Her visit was opposed, quite senselessly, by Petrograd society, which accused her of going for some bad purpose, God knows what. But at Novgorod the people poured out in throngs to greet her with peals of bells, music, and cheers. Before leaving the city the Empress paid a visit to a very old woman who had spent forty helpless years in bed, still wearing the heavy chains of penitence which as a pilgrim she had, almost a lifetime before, assumed. As her Majesty entered the old woman's cell a feeble voice uttered these words: "Here comes the martyred Empress, Alexandra Feodorovna." What could this aged and bedridden recluse have known or guessed of events which were to come?

CHAPTER XI

IN preceding chapters I have mentioned the name of Rasputine, that strange and ill-starred being about whom almost nothing is known to the multitude but against whom such horrible accusations have been made that he is universally classed with such monsters of iniquity as Cain, Nero, and Judas Iscariot. Even H. G. Wells, in whose "Outline of History" Joan of Arc and Abraham Lincoln are disposed of in a line, sacrifices valuable space to state as an established fact that in 1917 the Russian Court was "dominated by a religious impostor, Rasputin, whose cult was one of unspeakable foulness, a reeking scandal in the face of the world." I have no desire in this book to attempt an exoneration of Rasputine, for I am not so ambitious as to believe that I can change the collective mind of the world on any point. In the interests of historical truth, however, I believe it to be my simple duty to record the plain tale of how and why Rasputine came to be a factor in the lives of Nicholas II and of Alexandra Feodorovna, his wife, and exactly to what extent he did, or rather, did not, dominate the Russian Court. Those who expect from me secret and sensational disclosures will, I fear, be disappointed, for Rasputine's every movement for years was known to the Russian police, and the most sensational fact of his whole career, his assassination, has been described by practically every writer of the events of the Russian Revolution.

I will first explain the exact status of the man, for this does not appear to be generally understood. He has been called a priest, more often still a monk, but the truth is he was not in holy orders at all. He belonged to a curious species of roving religious peasant which in Russia were called *Stranniki,* the nearest English translation of the word being pilgrims. These wandering peasants, common sights in the old Russia, were accustomed to travel from one end of the Empire to the other, often walking with heavy chains on their bodies to make their progress more painful and difficult. They went from church to church, shrine to shrine, monastery to monastery, praying, fasting, mortifying the flesh, and their prayers were, by a very considerable population, eagerly sought and devoutly believed in. Once in a while a *Strannik* appeared who, by virtue of his extreme piety, gift of speech, or strong personality, acquired more than local reputation. Churchmen of high rank, estate owners, and even members of the nobility invited these men to their houses, listened with interest to their discourses, and asked for their prayers. Such a *Strannik* was Gregory Rasputine, who from the humblest beginnings in a remote Siberian village became known all over the Empire as a man of almost superhuman endowment.

Of the type of Russians to whom the *Stranniki* made a genuine appeal the Emperor and Empress undoubtedly belonged. The Emperor, like several of his near ancestors, was a born mystic, and the soul of Alexandra Feodorovna, either from natural inclination or from close association with him whom she so dearly loved, leaned also towards mysticism.   By this I do not mean that the Emperor and the Empress were at all interested in spiritualism, table-tipping, or alleged materializations from the world beyond.   Far from it. In the earliest days of my acquaintance with the Empress, as far back as 1905, she gave me a special warning against these things, telling me that if I wished for her friendship never to have anything to do with so-called spiritism.   Both the Emperor and the Empress were profoundly interested in the religious life and expressions of the whole human race.   They read with sympathy and understanding the religious literature not only of Christendom but of India, Persia, and the countries of the Far East.   I remember in connection with the Empress's first warning against spiritism that she gave me a book, an obscure fourteenth-century missal called *"Les Amis des Dieu"* which, in spite of her warm recommendation, I found great difficulty in reading.   This interest in religion and the life of the spirit was actually what constituted what Mr. Wells calls the "crazy pietism" of Nicholas II.   It was simple Christianity lived and not merely subscribed to as a theory.   They believed that prophecy, in the Biblical sense of the word, still existed in certain highly gifted and spiritually minded persons.   They believed that it was possible outside the church and without the aid of regularly ordained bishops and priests to hold communion with God and with His Spirit.   Before I came to Court there was a Frenchman, Dr. Philippe, in whom they reposed the greatest confidence, believing him to be one in whom the gift of prophecy existed.   I never knew Dr. Philippe, hence I can speak of him only as a sort of a forerunner of Rasputine, because, as the Empress told me, his coming was foretold by Dr. Philippe. Very shortly before his death the French mystic told them that they would have another friend authorized to speak to them from God, and when Rasputine appeared he was accepted as that friend.

Rasputine, although very poor and humble and almost entirely illiterate, had acquired a great reputation as a preacher, and had especially attracted the attention of Bishop Theofan, a churchman of renown in Petrograd. Bishop Theofan introduced the *Strannik* to the wife of Grand Duke Nicholas, who immediately conceived a warm admiration for him, and began to speak to her friends of his marvelous piety and spiritual insight. At that time the Emperor was on very friendly terms with the Grand Duke Nicholas, or rather with his wife and her sister, two princesses of Montenegro who had married, not quite in conformity with the rules of the Orthodox Church, the brothers, Grand Dukes Nicholas and Peter. One of these sisters, Princess Melitza, Grand Duchess Peter, had something of a reputation as a mystic, and it was at her house that the Emperor and Empress met first Dr. Philippe and later Rasputine. In one of my first conversations with the Empress she told me this, and told me also how deeply the conversation of the Siberian peasant had interested both her husband and herself. In fact Rasputine, at that period, interested and impressed almost everyone with whom he came in contact. When the house of Stolypine was blown up by terrorist bombs and, among others, his beloved daughter was grievously wounded, it was Rasputine whom the famous statesman summoned to her bedside for prayer and supplication. I am aware that the public generally believes that it was I who introduced Rasputine into the Russian Court, but truth compels me to declare that he was well known to the Sovereigns and to most of the Court long before I ever saw him.

It was about a month before my marriage in 1907 that the Empress asked Grand Duchess Peter to make me acquainted with Rasputine. I had heard that the Grand Duchess was very clever and well read, and I was glad of the opportunity of meeting her in her palace on the English Quay in Petrograd. Interesting as I found her, I was nevertheless thrilled with excitement when a servant announced the arrival of Rasputine. Before his entrance the Grand Duchess said to me: "Do not be astonished if I greet him peasant fashion," that is, with three kisses on the cheek. She did so greet him and then she presented us to each other. I saw an elderly peasant, thin, with a pale face, long hair, an uncared-for beard, and the most extraordinary eyes, large, light, brilliant, and apparently capable of seeing into the very mind and soul of the person with whom he held converse. He wore a long peasant coat, black and rather shabby from hard wear and much travel. We talked and the Grand Duchess, speaking in French, bade me ask him to pray for some special desire of mine. Timidly I begged him to pray that God would permit me to spend my whole life serving their Majesties. To this he replied: "Your whole life will be thus spent." We parted then, but shortly afterwards, just before my wedding day, when my heart was in a tumult of doubt and anxiety, I wrote to the Grand Duchess Peter and asked her to seek Rasputine's counsel in my behalf. His word to me was that I would marry as I had planned but that I should not find happiness in my marriage. It will be seen how little I regarded him as a prophet at this time since I paid no attention to his warning. A full year after my marriage I saw Rasputine for the second time. It was on a train going from Petrograd to Tsarskoe Selo, he being on his way there to visit friends who were in no way connected with the Court.

But, asks the bewildered reader, when and how did Rasputine acquire the dreadful, almost unprintable reputation which classes him with the arch-fiend himself? To answer the question satisfactorily I should have to reveal at great length the strangely abnormal and hysterical mentality of the Russian people of that epoch. I shall try to do this as I go farther, but here I shall give, as a sort of illustration of the lunacy of the hour, a little experience of my own. It was on the first occasion after my arrest by Kerensky in the spring of 1917, when I was brought before the High Commission of Justice of the Provisional Government. Weak and ill from my long imprisonment in the gloomy Fortress of Peter and Paul, I found myself facing an imposing group of something like forty judges, all learned in the law and clothed in such dignity of office that I gazed at them in a kind of awe. In my distracted mind I asked myself what questions these grave magistrates would ask me, and in what profound language would their questions be clothed. My heart almost stopped beating while I waited for the words of the chief judge. And this is what was said, in a deep and solemn voice: "Tell me, who was it at Court that Rasputine called a flower?" Sheer amazement held me speechless, but even had I been given time I could not have answered the question because there was no such person. The judges whispered together for a moment and then the same man, handing me a piece of cardboard, demanded impressively: "What is the meaning of this secret card which was found in your house by the soldiers?"

I took the piece of cardboard and almost instantly recognized it as a menu card of the yacht *Standert*, dated 1908. On the reverse side were written the names of war vessels present at that date at a naval review held near Kronstadt, Russian vessels all, among which the position of the Imperial yacht was marked by a crown. I handed the menu card back to the judge saying merely: "Look at it, and look at the date." He looked at it and in some confusion muttered: "It is true." One more question those giant intellects found to ask me. "Is it a fact that the Empress could not live without you?" To which I replied as any sensible person would have done: "Why should a happy wife and mother be unable to live without a mere friend?" The inquiry was then hastily closed and I was ordered back to prison, to be watched more closely than ever, *because I would not answer to judgment.*

This is a perfectly fair sample of the madness and confusion of the Russian mind, or rather the Petrograd mind, before and after the Revolution. That this madness, this unreasoning mania for the destruction of all institutions might have something to justify itself

in the public mind, it was absolutely necessary to find
and to persecute individuals who typified, in popular
imagination, the things which were so bitterly hated
Rasputine, more than any one other individual in the
Empire, did typify old and unpopular institutions, and I
can readily see why some intelligent and fair-minded
persons thus accepted him.   Dillon, for example, in his
book, "The Eclipse of Russia," says: "It is my belief
that although his friends were influential Rasputine
was a symbol."

Russia, like eighteenth-century France, passed
through a period of acute insanity from which it is only
now beginning to emerge in remorse and pain.   This
insanity was by no means confined to the ranks of the
so-called Revolutionists.   It pervaded the Duma, the
highest ranks of society, Royalty itself, all as guilty of
Russia's ruin as the most blood-thirsty terrorist.   What
had happened in these dark years between 1917 and
1923 is simply the punishment of God for the sins of a
whole people.   When His avenging hand has so
plainly been laid upon all of the Russian people how
dare any of us lay the calamity entirely at the doors of
the Bolsheviki?   We Russians look on the appalling
condition of our once great country, we behold the
famishing millions on the Volga and in the Ukraine, we
count the fearful roll of the murdered, the imprisoned,
the exiled, and we cry weakly that the Tsar was guilty,
Rasputine was guilty, this man and that woman were
guilty, but never do we admit that we were all guilty,
guilty of blackest treason to our God, our Emperor,
our country.   Yet not until we cease to accuse others
and repent our own sins will the white dawn of God's

mercy rise over the starved and barren desert that was once mighty Russia.

Rasputine, it seems to be generally assumed, having been introduced to the Imperial Family, took up his residence in the palace of the Romanoffs and thereafter held in his hands the reins of government. Those who do not literally believe this are nevertheless persuaded that Rasputine lived very near their Majesties, saw them constantly, was consulted and obeyed by the Ministers, and with the aid and connivance of adoring women attached to the Court, ruled by fear and superstition the whole governing class of the Empire. If I denied that Rasputine ever lived at Court, ever had the smallest influence over governmental policies, ever ruled through adoring and superstitious women, I should not hope to be believed. I will then simply call attention to the fact that every move of Rasputine from the hour when he began to frequent the palaces of the Grand Dukes, especially from the day he met the Emperor and Empress in the drawing room of the Grand Duchess Melitza, to the midnight when he met his death in the Yusupoff Palace on the Moika Canal in Petrograd, is a matter of the most minute police record. The police know how many days of each year Rasputine spent in Petrograd and how much of his time was lived in Siberia. They know exactly how many times he called at the palace at Tsarskoe Selo, how long he stayed and who was present. They know when and under exactly the circumstances Rasputine came to my house, and who else came to the house at the same time. The police know more about Rasputine than all the journalists and the historians put together, and their records show that he spent most of his time in Siberia, and that when he visited Petrograd he lived in rather humble lodgings in an unfashionable street, 54 Gorochovaia. Rasputine never lived in the palace, seldom visited it, saw the Emperor less frequently than the Empress, and had among the women of the Court more enemies than. friends.

The English-speaking reader may doubt the completeness and the accuracy of police records, knowing that in his own country only criminals and people of the underworld are really watched by the police. To know what police surveillance can mean it is necessary to have known Russia before 1917. I do not speak of the Bolshevik police. It is fairly well known what they are, but after all their methods, if not their motives, are founded on the Okhrana of the old days.

To give an idea of the ever-open and searching eye of the old Russian police I will describe what the situation was in the Imperial palace itself. In connection with the palace, or any of the Imperial residences, the persons of the Emperor and his family, the police force was organized in three sections. There were the palace police, a Cossack *convoi,* and a regiment of Guards known as the *Svodny Polk.* Besides the ranking officers of these organizations there was, over them all, a palace commandant, in the latest days of the Empire, General Voyeikoff. It was impossible for anyone to approach the palace, much less to be received by one of their Majesties, without the fact being known to scores of these police guards. Every soldier, every guard, in uniform or out, kept a notebook in which he was obliged to write down for inspection by his superiors the movements of all persons who entered the palace and even those who passed its walls. Moreover, they were obliged to communicate by telephone with their superior officers every event, however trivial, of which they were witness. This vigilance was extended even to the persons of the Emperor and his family. If the Empress ordered her carriage for two o'clock in the afternoon, the lackey receiving the order immediately informed the nearest police guard of the fact. The guard telephoned the news to the palace commandant's office and from there the information went by telephone to the offices of the separate police organizations: "Her Majesty's carriage has been ordered for two o'clock." This meant that from the time the Empress and her companion, or her children, drove from the palace doors to the hour when they returned the roads were lined with police, ready with their notebooks to record every single incident of the drive. Should the Empress stop her carriage to speak to an acquaintance, that unhappy individual would afterwards be approached by a guard standing in the road or behind trees or shrubbery, who would demand: "What is your name, and for what reason had you conversation with her Majesty?" With all her heart the Empress detested this system of police espionage, but it was one of the Russian ironclad traditions which neither she nor the Emperor could alter or abolish.

If the Imperial Family was thus subject to police surveillance the reader can easily imagine how closely the ordinary citizen and especially citizens of eminence were watched. I would not venture to declare on my own unsupported authority that Rasputine rarely visited the palace, at first two or three times a year, and but little oftener at the last, but I can state that these facts are on record in the police annals of Petrograd and Tsarskoe Selo. In the year of his death, 1916, Rasputine saw the Emperor exactly twice. There is one unfortunate fact in connection with these visits. I write it regretfully but it is true, and I can see how that circumstance served with some people to put a false emphasis on the visits of Rasputine to the Imperial household. In spite of the well-known fact that every visit of Rasputine was necessarily a public appearance, in full limelight, as it were, the Emperor and Empress attempted to throw over his visits a certain veil of secrecy. They had done the same thing with Dr. Philippe, and I suppose from the same motives. Every human being craves a little personal privacy. In the most loving family circle who does not at times want to be alone with his thoughts or his prayers behind closed doors? Thus it was with their Majesties. Rasputine represented to them hopes and aspirations far removed from earthly power and glory, and from earthly pain and suffering. They knew that he was a simple peasant and that many people of rank in official circles thought it strange, some even thought it undignified, for their Majesties of great Russia to listen to the counsels of so lowly and ignorant a man. For this reason, I know of no other, the Emperor and Empress vainly tried to make the visits of Rasputine as inconspicuous as possible. He was admitted into a side entrance instead of the main doorway; he went upstairs by a small staircase; he was received in the private

apartments and never in the public drawing rooms. It
was the same in Tsarskoe Selo and in the Crimea, in
which latter place a day's visit served for a year's
gossip throughout the entire estate. More than once I
pointed out to the Empress the futility of the course
pursued. "You know that before he reaches the
palace, much less your boudoir, he has been written
down at least forty times," I reminded her. The
Empress always agreed. She knew that the police
were everywhere, inside and outside the palace, in
every corridor, at every door. She knew that there
could be no secrets in the palace, and the Emperor
knew it as well as she did, yet they persisted in trying
to shield Rasputine from the publicity they knew to be
inevitable for everyone.

It was generally in the evening that he was received,
not because the eternal police vigilance was relaxed at
that time, but because it was only in the evening that
the Emperor found leisure for his personal friends.
In the hour following dinner it sometimes happened
that little Alexei came downstairs in his blue night-
gown to talk with his father a few minutes before going
to bed. When on these occasions Rasputine was present, the boy and his parents and any intimate friend
who happened to be in the room would listen fascinated
while the *Strannik* talked of Siberia and its peasants,
of his wanderings through remote corners of Russia,
and of his sojourn in the Holy Lands. His speech was
simple, but strangely eloquent and uplifting. Their
Majesties talked gladly to him of whatever happened
to be on their minds, the ill health of their only son,
principally, and he seemed to know how to comfort and

to give them hope. They were always lighter of heart after his visits, and even had I conspired with him to gain their friendship the effort would have been quite useless and unnecessary. They liked him so well that when gossip or newspaper accusations of Rasputine's drunkenness and debauchery were brought to their attention they said only: "He is hated because we love him." And that ended the matter.

I will say for the Empress that although she had the fullest confidence in Rasputine's integrity she thought it worth while to make some inquiries into his private life in Siberia, where most of his time was spent. On two occasions she sent me, with others, to his distant village of Pokrovskoe to visit him. I wished then, and I do now, that she had selected someone wiser and more critical than myself. Of detective ability I possess not a trace. With me it is always, what I have seen I have seen. In company with Mme. Orloff, mother of General Orloff, and with two other women and our maids, I made the long journey to Siberia leaving the railroad at the little town of Toumean. Here Rasputine met us with a clumsy peasant cart drawn by two farm horses. In this springless vehicle we drove eighty versts across the steppes to the village where Rasputine dwelt with his old wife, his three children, and two aged spinsters who helped in the housework and in the care of the fields and the cattle. The household was almost Biblical in its bare simplicity, all the guests sleeping in an upper chamber on straw mattresses laid on the rough board floor Except for the beds the rooms were practically without furniture, although on the walls were ikons before which faint tapers burned. We ate our plain meals in the common room downstairs, and in the evening there usually came four peasant men, devoted friends of Rasputine, who were called "the brothers." Sitting around the table they sang prayers and psalms with rustic faith and fervor. Almost every day we went down to the river to watch Rasputine and the brothers, fishermen all, draw in their nets, and often we ate our dinner by the river, cooking fish over little campfires on the shore, sharing in common our raisins, bread, nuts, and perhaps a little pastry. The season being Lent we had no meat, no milk, nor butter.

On my return to Tsarskoe Selo I described this pastoral existence to the Empress, and I had to add to my observations only that the clergy of the village seemed to dislike Rasputine, while the majority of the villagers merely took him for granted as one they had long been accustomed to. In a later year I was again sent to Siberia, this time with Mme. Julia (Lili) Dehn, wife of a naval officer on the yacht *Standert,* and several others, and a man servant as my special assistant as I was then very lame from the railroad accident which I have described. This time we went by boat from Toumean to Tobolsk on the River Toura, to view the relics of the Metropolitan John of Tobolsk, a sainted man of the time of Peter the Great. While in Tobolsk we were entertained in the house of the Governor of the Department, the same house where in the first days of their Siberian exile the Imperial Family were lodged. It was a large, very well furnished house on the river, but one could see that in winter it must have been extremely cold. On our way back we stopped for two days at Pokrovskoe, visiting Rasputine and finding him exactly as before, the old wife and the serving maids still occupied with household tasks and with field labor. I may add that in both of these visits I went to the famous monastery of Verchotourie, on the Ural River, where are kept some deeply venerated relics of St. Simeon. In the forests surrounding the monastery are many tiny wooden huts in which dwell solitary monks or anchorites, and among these was a celebrated old monk known as Father Makari. This aged and pious monk apparently held Rasputine in higher respect than did the village clergy, and they talked together like equals and friends, while we listened silently but with deep interest.

The wave of popular opposition against Rasputine began, I should say, in the last two and a half years of his life. Long after it began, long after his name was reviled and execrated in the press and in society, his lodgings in Petrograd, where he began to spend longer and longer intervals, were constantly crowded with beggars and petitioners. These were people of all stations who believed that whether he were good or evil his influence at Court was limitless. Every kind of petty official, every sort of poverty-stricken aspirant and grafting politician, and, of course, a whole crew of revolutionary agents, spies, and secret police haunted the place, pressing on Rasputine papers and petitions to be presented to the Emperor. To do Rasputine strict justice, he was forever telling the petitioners that it would be no good at all for him to present their papers, but he did not seem to have strength of mind to refuse point-blank to receive them. Often in pity for those who were sick and poor, or as he thought deserving, he would send them to one or another of his rich and influential acquaintances with a note saying: "Please, dear friend, receive him." It is very sad to reflect that his recommendation was the worst possible introduction a poor wretch could bear with him.

One of the hardest tasks which the Empress imposed upon me was the taking of messages, usually about the health of Alexei, to these crowded lodgings of Rasputine. As often as I appeared the people overwhelmed me with demands for money, positions, advancement, pardons, and what not. It was of no use to assure the people that I neither possessed nor desired to possess the kind of influence they believed to be mine. It was equally useless to assure them that their petitions, if I took them, would not be read by the Empress, but would merely be referred to her secretary, Count Rostovseff. Sometimes I encountered a case of great distress which if possible I tried privately to relieve. One day I met on the staircase a very poor young student who asked me if I could help him to a warm coat. I knew where I could get such a coat and I sent it to the student Months afterwards when I was a prisoner in the fortress I received a note from this young man, telling me that he prayed daily for my safety and release. This almost unique instance of gratitude remains in my mind among memories much less agreeable of my visits to the lodgings of Rasputine.

CHAPTER XII

THERE is a photograph which, in the last days of the Empire, was published all over Russia, and was, I am informed, also published in western Europe and in America. It represents Rasputine sitting like an oracle in his lodgings, surrounded by ladies of the aristocracy. This photograph is supposed to illustratē the enormous hold which Rasputine possessed on the affections of the women of the Court. In plain language it is assumed to be a representation of Rasputine sitting in the midst of his harem. There has been no account published which, as far as I know, does not dwell on this phase of the Rasputine story, and there have been books published in which the most erotic letters, purporting to have been written him by the Empress herself and even by the innocent young Grand Duchesses, have been included, the publishers apparently never having inquired into their authenticity. Knowing that my evidence will be considered of little worth, I still have the temerity to state without any qualification whatsoever that these stories are without the slightest foundation. Rasputine had no harem at Court. In fact, I cannot remotely imagine a woman of education and refinement being attracted to him in a personal way. I never knew of one being so attracted, and although accusations of secret debauchery with women of the lower classes were made against him by agents of the Okhrana, the special inquiry instituted by the Commission of the Provisional Government failed to produce any evidence in support of the charges. The police were never able to bring forward a single woman of any class whom they could accuse with Rasputine.

The photograph, however, is authentic. I figure in it myself, therefore I am in a position to explain it. It shows a group of women and men who after attending early Mass sometimes gathered around Rasputine for religious discourse, for advice on all manner of things, and probably on the part of some for the gratification of idle curiosity. I do not know whether or not in western countries religion produces in the neurotic and shallow-minded a kind of emotional excitement which they mistake for faith, but in Russia there was a time when this was so. For the most part, however, it was really serious people, men and women, who went after Mass to listen to the discourses of Rasputine. He was, as I have said, an unlettered man, but he knew the Scriptures and his interpretations were so keen and so original that highly educated people, even learned churchmen, liked to listen to them. In matters of faith and doctrine he could never be confused or confounded. Moreover, his sympathy and his charity were so wide and tender that he attracted women of narrow lives whose small troubles might have been dismissed as trivial by ordinary confessors. For example, many lovelorn women (men too) used to go to those morning meetings to beg his prayers on their heart's behalf. He knew that unsatisfied love is a very real trouble, and he was always gentle and patient with such people, that is, if their souls were innocent. For irregular love affairs he had no patience whatever, and in this connection I remember an incident which illustrates this point, and also his remarkable powers of divination, or if you prefer, his keen intuition. A young married woman, harmless enough in her intentions, but rather frivolous nevertheless, came one morning to Rasputine's lodgings en route to a rendezvous with a handsome young officer who at the moment strongly attracted her. It was her idea to ask Rasputine's prayers in behalf of her special desire, but before she could say a word to him he gave her a keen glance and said: "I am going to relate to you a story. Once when I was traveling in Siberia I entered a small railroad station and beheld at a table a monk who recognized me and begged me to join him in a glass of tea. As I approached the table I saw him hastily conceal a bottle under the folds of his soutaine. He said: 'You are called a saint. Will you not help me to understand some of the troubled problems of my life?' I replied 'Ah! You call me a saint. But why do you at the time of asking me to help your troubled soul try to hide that bottle under your robe?'" The young woman turned deathly pale and without a word rose hastily and left the room.

This is only one of many similar incidents. Once at Kiev a Government functionary approached Rasputine and asked his prayers for one lying very ill. Rasputine's amazing eyes gazed into the eyes of the other and he said calmly: "I advise you to beseech not my prayers but those of Ste. Xenia." The functionary completely taken aback exclaimed: "How

THE THREE CHILDREN OF RASPUTINE BEFORE THEIR
HOUSE IN SIBERIA.

THE GUEST ROOM (THE ONLY LARGE ROOM) IN RAS-
PUTINE'S HOUSE IN SIBERIA.

could you know that her name was Xenia?" I could relate many other such instances which can, of course, be attributed to intuition, thought transference, anything you like. But of true predictions of future events made by Rasputine what explanation can be given? What of his mysterious powers over the sick?

In behalf of the suffering little Tsarevitch the Emperor and Empress constantly asked the prayers of Rasputine, and the incident which I shall now relate will appeal to any mother or father of a suffering child and will render less childlike the faith of the afflicted parents of the heir to the throne. One day during the War the Emperor left Tsarskoe Selo for general headquarters, taking with him as usual the Tsarevitch. The child seemed to be in good condition, but a few hours after leaving the palace he was taken with a nosebleed. This is ordinarily a harmless enough manifestation, but in one suffering from Alexei's incurable malady it was a very serious thing. The doctors tried every known remedy, but the hemorrhage became steadily worse until death by exhaustion and loss of blood was threatened. I was with the Empress when the telegram came announcing the return of the Emperor and the boy to Tsarskoe Selo, and I can never forget the anguish of mind with which the poor mother awaited the arrival of her sick, perhaps her dying child. Nor can I ever forget the waxen, gravelike pallor of the little pointed face as the boy with infinite care was borne into the palace and laid on his little white bed. Above the blood-soaked bandages his large blue eyes gazed at us with pathos unspeakable, and it seemed to all around the bed that the last hour of the unhappy child was at hand. The physicians kept up their ministrations, exhausting every means known to science to stop the incessant bleeding. In despair the Empress sent for Rasputine. He came into the room, made the sign of the cross over the bed and, looking intently at the almost moribund child, said quietly to the kneeling parents: "Don't be alarmed. Nothing will happen." Then he walked out of the room and out of the palace.

That was all. The child fell asleep, and the next day was so well that the Emperor left for his interrupted visit to the Stavka. Dr. Derevanko and Professor Fedoroff told me afterwards that they did not even attempt to explain the cure. It was simply a fact. For this and for other like services Rasputine never received any money from the Emperor or the Empress. Indeed he was never given any money by their Majesties except an occasional one-hundred-ruble note to pay cab fares and traveling expenses when he was sent for. In the last two years of his life the rent of his modest lodgings in Petrograd was paid. What money he had was received from petitioners who hoped through him to benefit in high quarters. Rasputine took this money, but he gave most of it to the poor, so that when he died his family was left practically penniless. That Rasputine, whatever his faults, was no mercenary is the simple truth. As far back as 1913 Kokovseff, Minister of Finance, who disliked and distrusted Rasputine, offered him 200,000 rubles if he would leave Petrograd and never return. Two hundred thousand rubles was a fortune beyond the dream of avarice to a Russian peasant, but Rasputine

declined it, saying that he was not to be bought by anybody. "If their Majesties wish me to leave Petrograd,"
he said, "I will go at once, and for no money at all."

I know of many cases of illness where the prayers of
Rasputine were asked, and had he been so minded he
might have demanded and been given vast sums of
money. But the fact is he often showed himself extremely reluctant to exert whatever strange power he
possessed. In some instances where sick children were
involved he would even object, saying: "If God takes
him now it is perhaps to save him from future sins."

This indifference to money on the part of Rasputine
was all the more conspicuous in a country where almost
every hand was stretched out for reward, graft, or
blackmail. The episode of one of Rasputine's bitterest enemies, the "mad" monk Illiador, is illuminating.
Illiador was a person altogether disreputable, an unfrocked monk, and in my opinion a man mentally as
well as morally irresponsible. He made friends with
certain ministers, among them Chvostoff, one of several
who, after the death of Stolypine, held for a time the
portfolio of Minister of the Interior. Between Chvostoff and Illiador was concocted a plot to assassinate
Rasputine. This was not successful because Illiador
made the mistake of sending his wife to Petrograd with
incriminating documents. But he was able to send a
woman to Siberia, and she dealt Rasputine a knife
wound from which he with difficulty recovered. This
was in 1914.

After Rasputine the object of Illiador's greatest
hatred was the Empress. His plot against Rasputine
failing, he wrote against the Empress one of the most

scurrilous and obscene books imaginable, but before attempting to publish it he sent her word that he would sell her the manuscript for sixty thousand rubles.   Publishers in America, he wrote, would pay him a much higher price for the book, but he was willing to sacrifice something to save a woman's reputation.   To this low blackmailer the indignant Empress returned no answer at all.   Illiador lives in Russia now, a great favorite with the Bolsheviki because of his bitter attacks on the clergy.   But whether or not they permitted him to retain his profits on the book against the Empress I do not know.

But what of Rasputine's political influence, his treason with the Germans?   The excuse for his murder was that he was leading the Emperor and Empress into the German net, persuading them to betray the Allies by making a separate peace.   If I knew or suspected this to be true I would not hesitate to record it here. I would not dare to suppress such important historical evidence, if I had it, because all that I am writing in this book is for the future, not the present; for history, not for the ephemeral journalism of the day.   Ministers, politicians, churchmen haunted the lodgings of Rasputine, and if any man ever had an opportunity to mingle in secret diplomacy he was that man.   As a matter of plain justice to him, I do not believe such matters ever interested him.   On two occasions of which I have knowledge he did give the Emperor political advice, and very shrewd advice, although it was received with irritation and resentment by his Majesty. One of these occasions was in 1912 when Grand Duke Nicholas, whose wife it will be remembered was a

Montenegran, tried his every power of persuasion to bring Russia into the Balkan Wars. Rasputine implored the Emperor not to listen to this counsel. Only enemies of Russia, he declared, wanted to involve their country in that struggle, the inevitable outcome of which would be disaster to the Empire and to the house of Romanoff.

Rasputine always dreaded war, predicting that it would surely bring ruin to Russia and the monarchy. At the beginning of the World War he was lying wounded by Illiador's assassin in Siberia, but he sent a long telegram to the Emperor begging him to preserve peace. The Emperor, believing intervention in Serbia a point of honor, tore up the telegram and for a time appeared rather cold towards Rasputine. But as the War progressed they became friends again, for after it became inevitable Rasputine wanted the War fought through to a victorious end. The last time the Emperor saw him, about a month before his assassination, he gave a signal proof of this. The meeting took place in my house, and I heard every word of the conversation. The Emperor was depressed and pessimistic. Owing to heavy storm and lack of transportation facilities there had been difficulty in getting foodstuffs into Petrograd, and even some army battalions were lacking certain necessities. Nature itself, said the Emperor, seemed to be working against Russia's success in the War, to which Rasputine replied strongly advising the Emperor never, on any account, to be tempted to give up the struggle. The country that held out the longest against adverse circumstances, he said, would certainly win the War.

As Rasputine was leaving the house the Emperor asked him, as usual, for his blessing, but Rasputine replied: "This time it is for you to bless me, not I you." Finally at parting he humbly begged the Emperor to do everything he could in behalf of the wounded and of war orphans, reminding him that all Russia was giving its nearest and dearest for his sake. Did Rasputine on this day have a premonition of the fate that was so soon to overtake him? I cannot answer that question. It is impossible for me to know with any certainty whether or not this strange man was actually gifted with the spirit of prophecy or whether his frequent forecastings of truth were simply fruits of a mind more than normally keen and observant. All I can do, all I have attempted to do, is to picture Rasputine as I knew him. I never once saw him otherwise than I have described. I knew that he was reputed to drink and to indulge in other reprehensible practices. I heard, I suppose, every wild tale that was told of him. But no one ever presented to the Imperial Family or to myself any evidence, any facts in support of these accusations. It is a matter of record, and this the historians of the future will stress, that this man was called a criminal, but that he was never meted out the common justice which is supposed to be the right of the most abandoned criminal. He was accused of nameless crimes and he was executed for those crimes. But he was denied even the rough justice of a trial by his self-appointed judges. Did "Tsarist" Russia ever do such a thing to a man caught red-handed in the murder of an Emperor?

I have added as an appendix to this book a document

which has been published in Russian and French, but which I believe appears here for the first time in English. It is the statement of Vladimir Michailovitch Roudneff, a judge of a superior court in Ekaterinoslav, one of a number of distinguished jurists appointed by Kerensky, when Minister of Justice in the Provisional Government, to a special High Commission of Inquiry and Investigation into the Acts of the Sovereigns and other prominent personages before the Revolution of 1917. Judge Roudneff, with great courage and honesty, made an effort to sift the evidence against Rasputine and to separate truth from mere rumor. That he was unable to treat the matter in a mood of perfect judicial calm, although he earnestly wished to do so, is proof enough of the madness of the Russian mind in that time of turmoil and bewilderment. Anyone at all familiar with rules of evidence will perceive how, with the best intentions, Judge Roudneff often offers opinion where facts alone are called for. A great many of his statements, if given in a court of justice, would in any civilized country be challenged and probably ruled out. However, the statement is valuable because it is the unique attempt of a justice-loving individual to escape from the mob mind of 1917 Russia and to present impartially the known facts about Rasputine. For his honesty in insisting that the facts be made public Judge Roudneff was ignominiously removed from the commission by its president, Judge Mouravieff. As far as I know and believe, none of the other members of the commission attempted to publish their findings.

I shall always feel that it was a great pity that Rasputine was not arrested, tried in the presence of his accusers and of all available witnesses, and if found guilty punished to the very limit of the law.   As it was he was merely lynched and the question of his guilt or innocence will ever remain unsolved.   Latest accounts certainly absolve the Empress of Russia from being his tool and his guilty partner, and death, whether by assassination or at the hand of public justice, has the same end, the righteous judgment of God, and from that perfect justice not the worst enemy of the man could bar the soul of Rasputine.

One thing more I deeply regret and that is that Judge Roudneff could not have tried Rasputine in person as he did try me.   I appeared before him no less than fifteen times and I always found him studious at getting at the truth, separating facts from hysterical gossip, all in the interests of justice and of historical records.   In his reports concerning me there are some errors, but not serious ones, some confusion of dates, but nothing important, and once or twice some trifling injustice for which I bear not the slightest malice. Judge Roudneff, for example, accuses me of loquacity, and in my testimony of jumping irrelevantly from one thought to another.   I cannot help wondering if even a learned judge, after weeks of imprisonment, accompanied by inhuman insults and bodily injuries, and for the first time given an opportunity for explanation and self-defense, would have spoken in quite a calm and normal manner.   However, I do not complain of anything Judge Roudneff says of me.   I am grateful to the only Russian in a position of authority who has had the chivalry to give me the benefit of a reasonable doubt.

All others, including members of the Romanoff family who have known me from my earliest childhood, who in youth danced and chatted with me at Court balls, who knew my mother and my father, with his long and honorable record, have assailed me without a shred of mercy. They have represented me as a common upstart, an outsider in society who managed through unworthy schemes to worm her way into the confidence of the Empress. They have represented me as an abandoned woman, a criminal, a would-be poisoner of the Tsarevitch. They have been so loud in their denunciations of one defenseless woman that they have succeeded in concealing the fact of their own participation in events for which the Sovereigns were brought to ruin. They have thrown a blind before their responsibility for bringing Rasputine to the Court of Russia. Never do they allow it to be remembered that it was the Grand Dukes Nicholas and Peter and their Montenegran wives, Stana and Melitza, who introduced the Emperor and Empress to the poor peasant pilgrim who, had he never been taken up by these aristocrats, might have lived out an obscure, and perhaps valuable, existence in far Siberia. It was easier for these powerful ones, these sheltered women, these noble gentlemen, to avoid explanation of their part in the Russian tragedy and to take refuge behind the skirts of a woman who, after the overthrow of the Imperial Family, had not a friend on earth to defend or to protect her.

CHAPTER XIII

TWO days after the return of the Empress from her visit to Novgorod, in the earliest hours of December 17 (December 31, Western Calendar) was struck the first blow of the "bloodless" Russian Revolution, the assassination of Rasputine. On the afternoon of December 16 (December 30) I was sent by the Empress on an errand, entirely non-political, to Rasputine's lodgings. I went, as always, reluctantly, because I knew the evil construction which would be placed on my errand by any of the conspirators who happened to see me. Yet, as in duty bound, I went. I stayed the shortest possible time, but in that brief interval I heard Rasputine say that he expected to pay a late evening visit to the Yusupoff Palace to meet Grand Duchess Irene, wife of Prince Felix Yusupoff. Although I knew that Felix had often visited Rasputine it struck me as odd that he should go to their house for the first time at such an unseemly hour. But to my question Rasputine replied that Felix did not wish his parents to know of his visit. As I was leaving the place Rasputine said a strange thing to me. "What more do you want?" he asked in a low voice. "Already you have received all." All that his prayers could give me? Did he mean that?

That evening in the Empress's boudoir I mentioned

this proposed midnight visit, and the Empress said in some surprise: "But there must be some mistake. Irene is in the Crimea, and neither of the older Yusupoffs are in town." Once again she repeated thoughtfully: "There is surely a mistake," and then we began to talk of other things. The next morning soon after breakfast I was called on the telephone by one of the daughters of Rasputine, both of whom were being educated in Petrograd. In some anxiety the young girl told me that her father had gone out the night before in the Yusupoff motor car and had not returned. I was startled, of course, and even a little frightened, but I did not then guess the real significance of her news. When I reached the palace I gave the message to the Empress, who listened with a grave face but with little comment. A few minutes later there came a telephone call from Protopopoff in Petrograd. The police, he said, had reported to him that some time after the last midnight a patrolman standing near the entrance of the Yusupoff Palace had been startled by the report of a pistol. Ringing the doorbell, he was met by a Duma member named Puritchkevitch who appeared to be in an advanced stage of intoxication. In answer to the policeman's inquiry as to whether there was trouble in the house the drunken Puritchkevitch said in a jocular tone that it was nothing, nothing at all, only they had just killed Rasputine. The policeman, probably a none too intelligent specimen, took it as a casual joke of one of the high-born. They were always joking about Rasputine. The man moved on, but somewhat later he decided that he ought to report the matter to headquarters, which he did, but even then his superiors appear to have been too incredulous to act at once.

Protopopoff's message, however, so disquieted the Empress that she asked me to summon another of her trusted friends, Mme. Dehn, whose name I have mentioned before. Mme. Dehn came and we talked over the mystery together, but still without conviction that Puritchkevitch's reckless statement contained any real truth. Later in the day, however, came a telephone message from Grand Duke Dmitri Pavlovitch, asking to be allowed to take tea with the Empress that afternoon at five. The message was conveyed to the Empress, who, pale and reflective, answered formally that she did not care just then to receive his Highness. Dmitri took the reply in bad grace, insisting that he must see the Empress as he had something special to tell her. Again the Empress refused, this time even more curtly. Almost immediately afterwards, almost as if the two men were in the same room, there came a telephone message from Felix Yusupoff asking if I would see him at tea, or later in the day if I so preferred. I answered that the Empress did not wish me to receive any visitors that day, whereupon Felix demanded an audience with the Empress that he might give her a true account of what had occurred. Her Majesty's reply was: "If Felix has anything to say let him write to me." Several times before the day ended telephone messages came from Felix to me, but none of these would the Empress allow me to answer.

Felix finally wrote a letter to the Empress. I cannot quote this letter verbatim, but I remember exactly its contents. By the honor of his house Prince Felix

Yusupoff swore to his Sovereign Empress that the rumor of Rasputine's visit to his home was without any foundation whatever. He had indeed seen Rasputine in the interests of Irene's health, but he had never decoyed the man to his palace, as charged. There had been a party there, on the night in question, just a few friends, including Dmitri, to celebrate the opening of Felix's new apartments. All, he confessed, became drunk, and some foolish and reckless things were said and done. By chance, on leaving the house, one of the guests had shot a dog in the courtyard. That was absolutely all. This letter was not answered, but was turned over to the Minister of Justice.

Thoroughly aroused, the Empress now ordered Protopopoff to make an investigation of the whole affair. She called into council also Minister of War Belaieff, a good man, afterwards murdered by the Bolsheviki. The police, at their commands, went to the deserted Yusupoff palace, first searching for and finding the body of the dog which Felix said they had shot. But the bullet hole in the dog's head had let out little blood, and when the men entered the palace they found it a veritable shambles of blood and disorder. Evidences of a terrific struggle were found in the downstairs study of Prince Felix, on the stairs leading to an upper room, and in the room itself. Then, indeed, the whole power of the police was invoked, and somebody was found to testify that in the dead of night a motor car without any lights was seen leaving the Yusupoff Palace and disappearing in the direction of the Neva. Winter nights in Russia are very dark, as everyone knows, and the car was soon swallowed up in the shadows. The river was next searched, and by a hole in the ice, not far from Krestovsky Island, the police found a man's golosh. By Protopopoff's orders divers immediately searched the hole in the ice, and from it was soon dragged the frozen body of Rasputine. Arms and legs were tightly bound with cords, but the unfortunate man had managed to work loose his right hand which was frozen in a last attempt to make the sign of the cross. The body was taken to the Chesma Hospital, where an autopsy was performed. Although there were bullet holes in the back and innumerable cuts and wounds all over the body, the lungs were full of water, proving that they had thrown him alive into the icy river, and that death had occurred by drowning.

As soon as the news became public all Petrograd burst into a wild orgy of rejoicing. The "beast" was slain, the "evil genius" had disappeared never to return. There was no limit to the wild hysteria of the hour. In the midst of these demonstrations came a telephone message from Protopopoff asking the Empress's advice as to an immediate burial place for the murdered man. Ultimately the body would be sent to his Siberian village, but in the present circumstances the Minister of the Interior thought a postponement of this advisable. The Empress agreed, and she replied that a temporary interment might be arranged at Tsarskoe Selo. On December 29 (January 12) the coffin, accompanied by a kind-hearted sister of mercy, arrived at Tsarskoe. That same day the Emperor came home from the front, and in the presence of the Imperial Family and myself the briefest of services were held. On the dead man's breast had been laid an ikon from Novgorod, signed on the reverse by the Empress and her daughters as a last token of respect. The coffin was not even buried in consecrated ground, but in a corner of the palace park, and as it was being lowered a few prayers were said by Father Alexander, priest of the Imperial chapel. This is a true account of the burial of Rasputine, about which so many fantastic tales have been embroidered.

The horror and shock caused by this lynching, for it can be called by no other name, completely shattered the nerves of the family. The Emperor was affected less by the deed itself than by the fact that it was the work of members of his own family. "Before all Russia," he exclaimed, "I am filled with shame that the hands of my kinsmen are stained with the blood of a simple peasant." Before this he had often shown disgust at the excesses of the Grand Dukes and their followers, but now he expressed himself as being entirely through with them all.

But Yusupoff and the others were by no means through with the Rasputine affair. Now that they had murdered and were applauded for the deed by all society, it seemed to them that they were in a position to claim full legal immunity. Grand Duke Alexander Michailovitch, the Emperor's brother-in-law, went to Dobrovolsky, Minister of Justice, and with a good deal of swagger told him that it was the will of the family—that is, of the Grand Dukes—that the whole matter should be quietly dropped. The next day, December 21 (January 5), Alexander Michailovitch drove with his oldest son to Tsarskoe Selo and, without the slightest assumption of deference or respect, en-

tered the Emperor's study, demanding, in the name of
the family, that no further investigation of the manner
of Rasputine's death be made.   In a voice that could
easily be heard in the corridor outside the Grand Duke
shouted that should the Emperor refuse this demand
the throne itself would fall.   The Emperor's answer
to this insolence was an order of banishment to their
estates of Nicholai Michailovitch, Felix, and Dmitri.
At this the wrath of the Grand Dukes knew no bounds..
A letter blazing with anger and impudence, signed by
the whole family, was rushed to the Emperor, but his
only comment was a single sentence written on the mar-
gin: "Nobody has a right to commit murder."   Following this came a cringing letter from Dmitri who,
like Felix, tried to lie himself out of all complicity in
the crime.   On his sacred honor, he declared he had
had nothing to do with it.   If the Emperor would only
consent to see him he promised to establish his innocence.   But the Emperor would not consent to see
Dmitri.   Pale and stern he moved through the rooms
or sat so darkly plunged in thought that none of us
ventured to disturb or even to speak to him.   Into this
troubled atmosphere a letter was brought to the Emperor by the Minister of the Interior, who had a right
to seize suspicious mail matter.   It was a letter written
by the Princess Yusupoff to the Grand Duchess Xenia,
sister of the Tsar and mother of Felix Yusupoff's wife.
It was a most indiscreet letter to be sent at such a time,
for it was a clear admission of the guilt of all the plotters.   Although as a mother (she wrote) she felt
deeply her son's position, she congratulated the Grand
Duchess Zenia on her husband's conduct in the affair.

THE EMPRESS AND YOUNG GRAND DUKE DMITRI, AFTER-
WARDS ONE OF RASPUTINE'S ASSASSINS.

MINISTER OF COURT COUNT FREDERICKS, THE EMPRESS IN HER RECLINING CHAIR, AND GRAND DUCHESS TATIANA TAKING TEA IN THE WOODS IN FINLAND, 1911.

Sandro, she said, had saved the whole situation, evidently meaning that his demand for immunity for all concerned would have to be granted. *She was only sorry that the principals had not been able to bring their enterprise to its desired end.* However, there remained only the task of confining *Her.* Before the affair was finally concluded, she feared, they might send Nicholai Nicholaievitch and Stana to their estates. How stupid to have sent away Nicholai Michailovitch!

This was by no means the end of letters and telegrams seized by the police and brought to the palace. Many were written by relatives and close friends, people of the highest rank, and they all revealed a depth of callousness and treachery undreamed of before by the unhappy Sovereigns. When the Empress read these communications and realized that her nearest and dearest connections were in the ranks of her enemies, her head sank on her breast, her eyes grew dark with sorrow, and her whole countenance seemed to wither and grow old. A few days later the Grand Duchess Serge sent her sister several sacred ikons from the shrine of Saratoff. The Empress, without even looking at them, ordered them sent back to the convent of the Grand Duchess in Moscow.

I should add that from the day of the assassination of Rasputine my mail was full of anonymous letters threatening me with death The Empress, perhaps more than any of us, instinctively aware of the endless ramifications of the Rasputine affair, commanded me in terms that admitted of no argument to leave my house and to take up residence in the palace. Sad as I was to leave the peace of my little home, I had no alternative than to obey, and with my maid I moved into two rooms in the Grand Ducal wing of the palace, occupied also by maids of honor and reached by the fourth large entrance to the palace. From that day, by command of their Majesties, every movement of mine was closely guarded. The soldier Jouk was assigned to my service and without him I never left the palace even to visit my hospital. When in the February following my only brother was married I was not allowed to attend the wedding.

Little by little, in spite of fears, the palace took on a certain air of tranquillity. In the evenings we sat in the mauve boudoir of the Empress; and as of old, the Emperor read aloud. At Christmas their Majesties saw that the customary trees and gifts were sent to the hospitals and that the usual presents were distributed to the servants. The children too had their Christmas celebration, but over us all hung a cloud of sorrow and of disillusionment. Never had the Emperor and Empress of Russia, rulers of nearly two hundred million souls, seemed so lonely or so helpless. Deserted and betrayed by their relatives, calumniated by men who, in the eyes of the outside world, seemed to represent the Russian people, they had no one left except a few faithful friends, and the Emperor's chosen ministers every one of whom was under the ban of popular obloquy. Most of them were accused of being the appointees of Rasputine, but this at least I am in a position to deny.

Sturmer, Minister of the Interior, and afterwards Prime Minister, was, according to Witte, recommended to the Tsar after the assassination of Pleve. The well-known fact that Sturmer was head of the nobility in the Government of Tver, that he was possessed of enormous estates, and that he had held several important positions at Court, ought to be sufficient proof that he needed no help from Rasputine or any other man. Sturmer was an old man, not brilliant perhaps, but certainly a man of high principles. He was arrested by the Provisional Government, and in the fortress suffered such frightful hardships that he died within a day after the Government, unable to fasten on him the slightest guilt, released him from prison. The Social Revolutionary Sokoloff, a just man, if wrong-headed, has declared publicly that had any Constitutional Assembly been held in Russia, the responsibility of Sturmer's death would have been laid upon Milukoff personally.

As for Protopopoff, he was appointed by the Emperor mainly on his record as a confidential agent of the Duma, and as a personal representative of Rodzianko, President of the Fourth Duma. After Protopopoff's return from an important foreign mission on behalf of the Duma he was presented to the Emperor at G. H. Q., and in a letter to the Empress a few days later, he expressed himself as delighted with the man. The appointment was made in one of those moments of impulse characteristic of Nicholas II, yet it must have been the result of some reflection, as it was the Emperor's expressed desire at this time to name a Minister of the Interior who could work in harmony with the Duma. Protopopoff, who, aside from his relations with Rodzianko, had for many years been a delegate from his own Zemstvo to the Union of Zemstvos, naturally appealed to the Emperor as an ideal popular candidate. No one could have been more astonished than he when, almost immediately after his appointment, Rodzianko and almost the entire majority party in the Duma joined in a clamor for Protopopoff's removal. The only charge I ever heard against him was that his mind had suddenly failed. Protopopoff, who was a man of high breeding, was nevertheless exceedingly nervous, and I always thought, somewhat weak-willed. He was not the infirm old man he has generally been represented, being about sixty-four years of age with white hair and mustache and young, bright black eyes. That he had plenty of physical and moral courage was proved by his conduct after the Revolution. Walking to the door of the council chamber of the Duma he announced himself thus: "I am Protopopoff. Arrest me if you like." He was arrested by orders of Rodzianko, but was released later, only to meet death by the bullets of the Bolsheviki. That Protopopoff was on friendly terms with Rasputine is true, but that Rasputine had anything to do with his appointment, or with his retention in office after the attack by the Duma, is simply absurd.

Maklakoff, Minister of the Interior before Protopopoff, was a former governor of Chernigoff. The Emperor met him in the course of a journey to the famous fête of Poltava, a jubilee of the wars of Peter the Great. The acquaintance was made in the leisure of a boat trip, and the Emperor, in another of his fits of impulsiveness, decided that he had found an ideal Minister of the Interior. Their friendship deepened with time, and the Emperor found great satisfaction in his new minister's reports, which he declared reflected his own point of view. Nothing against the administration of Maklakoff was ever even whispered until late in 1914, when Nicholai Nicholaievitch, as supreme commander of the Russian forces in the field, suddenly demanded his demission. Grand Duke Nicholas, it must be said, continually interfered with the affairs of the interior government, with which as military chief he had nothing whatever to do, but in the early days of the War the Emperor seemed to think it the part of wisdom to suffer this irregularity. Reluctantly he yielded to the request for Maklakoff's demission, saying to him with genuine regret: "They demand it, and at such a time I cannot stand against them."

In the place of Maklakoff was named Tcherbatkoff, a friend and protégé of Nicholai Nicholaievitch, a man whose former office had been head of the remount department of the State. Doubtless he knew a great deal about horses, but of the interior affairs of State he knew so little that even the influence of Grand Duke Nicholas was powerless to retain him in office longer than two months.

Tcherbatkoff was followed by Khvostoff who, previous to his appointment, was an entire stranger to Rasputine. Khvostoff had made a record as governor of Nizjni Novgorod, and afterwards as a vigorous anti-German orator in the Duma. He was also supposed to be a devoted friend of the Imperial Family. Soon after his appointment Khvostoff began sedulously to cultivate the friendship of Rasputine, and it is a matter of police record that this Minister of the Interior frequently played on Rasputine's unfortunate weakness for drink. Possibly he thought that by getting the poor man intoxicated he could worm from him the many Court secrets he was supposed to possess. Failing in this Khvostoff began, with the help of Chief of Police Belezky, a plot against Rasputine which nearly succeeded in the latter's assassination. This being discovered the demission of Khvostoff became imperative.

Soukhomlinoff, who when I knew him was an old man of seventy-five, was a former military governor of Kiev, and before his appointment as Minister of War, had been a great favorite of the Emperor. That he showed brilliant ability in the mobilization of the Russian Army in 1914 was admitted by the Allied Governments, and in fact no intrigue against him developed until some time after the beginning of the War. His principal enemies were Grand Duke Nicholas, General Polivanoff, and the notorious Goutchkoff. In my opinion their propaganda against him was instigated solely with the object of impairing the prestige of the Emperor. The crimes laid at the door of Soukhomlinoff were almost countless. He was accused of withholding ammunition from the armies, of harboring German spies in his house, and in general of being completely incapable of performing his duties of office. Of him the English historian Wilton says that time alone will prove whether the odium of the Russian war scandals rested on Soukhomlinoff or on Grand Duke Nicholas. At all events it was poor old Soukhomlinoff who was arrested, tried before a tribunal of the Provisional Government, and sentenced to life imprisonment. His young wife, who was arrested with him, occupied a cell next to mine in the Fortress of

Peter and Paul, and without regard to the charges brought against her, I had reason constantly to admire the courage and self-possession with which she bore the hardships of prison life. So great was her dignity and self-command that she became universally respected by the soldiers, and I am confident that this alone saved us both from far worse indignities than those which we were called upon to bear. In prison Mme. Soukhomlinoff managed to keep herself constantly occupied. She wrote and read whenever writing materials and books were procurable, and her clever fingers fashioned out of scraps of the miserable prison bread really beautiful sprays of flowers. For coloring matter she used the paint from a moldering blue stripe on the walls of her cell, and scraps of red paper in which tea was wrapped. After months of imprisonment, bravely endured, Mme. Soukhomlinoff was brought to trial before a court of the Provisional Government. Her examination was of the most searching character, but at its close she left the courtroom fully acquitted, to the applause of the numerous spectators. Taking advantage of an amnesty pronounced some time later Mme. Soukhomlinoff got her aged husband released from prison and saw him safely to Finland. It is rather an anticlimax to the story that after so many trials borne together the marriage of the Soukhomlinoffs was dissolved, Mme. Soukhomlinoff marrying a young Georgian officer with whom she later perished under the Bolshevist terror.

One more person of whom I can speak with knowledge was, although not a minister, falsely alleged to be an appointee of Rasputine. This was the Metro-

politan Pitirim, a man of impeccable honesty and very
liberal views regarding Church administration. The
Emperor met him in late 1914 on one of his visits to
the Caucasus, Pitirim then being Exarch of Georgia.
Not only the Emperor but his entire suite were enchanted by the charming manners, the piety, and learning of the Exarch, and when, a little later, the Empress
met the Emperor at Veronesh, he told her that he had
Pitirim in mind for Metropolitan of Petrograd. Almost immediately after his appointment the propa-
gandists began to connect his elevation with the
Rasputine influence, but the truth is that the two men
were never at any time on terms of more than formal
acquaintanceship. As for their Majesties, they liked
and respected Pitirim but he never was an intimate
member of their household. Practically all their conversations which I overheard concerned the state of
the Church in Georgia, which Pitirim insisted was
lower than in other parts of the Empire. The Church
of Georgia, Pitirim alleged, received too little support
from the State, although it deserved as much if not
more than others, because Georgian Christianity is
the oldest in all Russia. According to tradition this
Church was established by the Holy Virgin herself
who, after a shipwreck off Mount Athos, visited
Georgia, converted its chiefs and established the first
Christian temple. Pitirim was essentially a churchman, yet he always advocated a certain separation of
Church and State. That is, he desired the establishment of a parish system whereby the support of the
Church should be the responsibility of the people
rather than of the Imperial Government. Unworldly

to the last degree, he nevertheless came in for his full share of slander and abuse. After my arrest by the Provisional Government my mother visited Kerensky in my behalf, and was astounded when he brutally told her that one of the charges against me was that all my diamonds were gifts from Pitirim, the inference being that we were on unduly intimate terms.

Another high personage to whom I wish to pay the tribute of just appreciation is Count Fredericks, chief minister of the Court. This honorable gentleman had spent almost his entire life in the service of the Imperial Family, having first been attached to the person of Alexander III. Nicholas II and his family he served with ability, discretion, and rare devotion. In virtue of his office he had to deal personally with the affairs of the Grand Dukes, their complicated financial transactions, their morganatic marriages, and other confidential affairs. Everyone, except those of the Grand Dukes who with reason had earned his contempt, loved this charming man whom their Majesties usually spoke of as "our old man." Count Fredericks, in his turn, always called them *"mes enfants."* His house was to me for many years a second home, his daughters, the elder Mme. Voyeikoff, and the younger one, Emma, being among my dearest friends. Emma, who suffered a painful curvature of the spine, had the compensation of a rarely beautiful singing voice with which she often charmed the Emperor and Empress. Count Fredericks was arrested by the Provisional Government, but owing to his great age, was afterwards released.

The charge has often been brought against Nicholas

II that he surrounded himself with inferior men. The fact of the case is that in the beginning of his reign he chose as his chief advisers men of ability and integrity who had been friends of his father, Alexander III. Later he chose men who in his opinion were the best ones available, and it must be admitted that there were few men of first-class ability among whom he could choose. The events of the War and the Revolution prove this, for neither of these two terrible emergencies produced in Russia a single man of conspicuous merit. Not one real leader appeared then nor in the years which have since elapsed. Truly has a distinguished American writer pointed out that never could Bolshevism and its insane philosophy have taken such strong roots in Russia, had not the soil been previously so well prepared. Every Russian who really loved his country must admit the truth of this statement. Too many exiled Russians, however, still cling to the delusion that some outside influence was the cause of their country's downfall. Let them acknowledge the truth that it was Russians themselves, especially Russians of the privileged classes, who principally are responsible for the catastrophe. For years before the Revolution the national spirit was in a state of decline. Few men or women cherished ideals of duty for duty's sake. Patriotism was practically extinct. Family life was weakened, and in the last days, the morale of the whole people was lower than in almost any other country of the civilized world.

May the blood of the thousands of innocents who have perished in War and Revolution wipe out the sins of the old hard-hearted and decadent Russia.

May the millions still living, in exile and under Communist oppression, learn that only by repentance and by toleration of others' weaknesses can there be any possibility of a restoration of national life. Not by any outside help but by our own efforts, by loyal Russians coming together, not as political groups but as compatriots, can great Russia rise again out of her shame and desolation and become once more a nation among the nations of the earth.

CHAPTER XIV

FOR two months after the assassination of Rasputine the Emperor remained at Tsarskoe Selo, but he was by no means idle. In fact his whole heart and mind were occupied, not so much with the scandal that had reached its tragic climax in the Yusupoff Palace, but with the War which at that moment seemed to favor Russian arms. According to our advices the food shortage in Germany and in Turkey had become acute, and the Emperor believed that a vigorous spring offensive might bring the War to a speedy close. In his billiard room were spread out a large number of military maps which no one of the household, not even the Empress, was invited to inspect. The Emperor spent hours over these maps and his plan of a spring campaign, and when he left the billiard room he locked the door and put the key in his pocket. I had never seen him more completely the soldier, the commander in chief of a great army. All this time, from December, 1916, to February, 1917, the Russian front was comparatively quiet, furious snowstorms preventing the advance either of our own or the enemy's forces. Alas! The storms interfered also with railroad transport and Petrograd and Moscow were beginning to feel the pinch of hunger, a fact that gave their Majesties constant concern.

Meanwhile the Grand Duke Alexander Michailo-

vitch persisted in his demand for an interview with
the Empress, and as his letters to her failed of their
object he began to write to the Grand Duchess Olga.
The Empress, whose courage was great enough to
enable her to ignore any possible danger to herself,
decided to see the man and once for all let him have
his say. In this decision the Emperor concurred, but
he stipulated that he should be present in case the conversation should become unduly disagreeable. The
Emperor's aide-de-camp for the day happened to be a
spirited young officer, Lieutenant Linevitch, who after
luncheon on the day set for the audience, lingered in
the palace, apparently occupied in an amusing puzzle
game with Tatiana. Afterwards Linevitch told me
that so well did he know the extent of the Grand Ducal
cabal, and especially the character of Alexander
Michailovitch, that he had remained on purpose and
that his sword had been ready at any moment to
rescue the Empress from insult or from attempted assassination. As we expected the Grand Duke had
nothing new to say to the Empress, but merely reiter-
ated in more than usually violent terms the demand for
Protopopoff's dismissal and for a constitutional form
of government. The answer to these demands was as
usual—everything necessary after the War, no funda-
mentally dangerous changes while the Germans remained on our soil. The Grand Duke, purple with
anger, rushed out of the Empress's sitting room, but
instead of leaving the palace, as he was expected to do,
he entered the library, ordered pens and paper and
began to write a letter to the Emperor's brother,
Michail Alexandrovitch. No sooner had he begun his

epistle than he perceived standing respectfully in the room the aide-de-camp Linevitch, whom, after a more or less civil greeting, he tried to dismiss. "You may go now," he said, coldly polite, but the astute Linevitch replied with ceremony: "No, your Highness, I am on service today and as long as your Highness is here it is not permitted for me to leave." In a fury Alexander Michailovitch got up and left the palace.

Men like Linevitch and many others, as faithful as ever to their Majesties, saw the threatening tempest more clearly than those within palace walls could possibly see it. The day after the visit of Alexander Michailovitch I received a call from one of the finest of the Romanoff connections, Duke Alexander of Luchtenberg. Painfully agitated, the Duke told me that he wanted me to help him to induce the Emperor to take a remarkable, indeed an unprecedented step. At the time of his accession to the throne every member of the family, it is well known, must make a solemn vow of fealty to the Tsar, and the Duke of Luchtenberg now begged me to persuade the Emperor, through the Empress, to exact from all the family a renewal of this vow. For the lives and safety of the Imperial Family the Duke believed this to be absolutely essential. "None of them are loyal, not one," he said earnestly. "And if the Emperor values the lives of his wife and children he must force the Grand Dukes and their families to declare themselves." Quite staggered, I replied that it was impossible for me to make such a proposition to their Majesties, but I added that the Duke himself, as a member of the family, might with entire propriety do so, and thus the matter was decided. Of the details of the conversation between the Emperor and his kinsman I know nothing, but I know that the conversation took place, because later the Emperor remarked in my hearing that "Sandro" Luchtenberg, in the kindness of his heart, had made a great matter out of a trifle, and he added, "Of course I could not ask of my own family the thing he suggested."

As one more indication of the gathering storm there came to me at my hospital from Saratoff an old man so feeble and so deaf that he had to bring with him a woman relative who through long familiarity was able to act as an interpreter in his conversations. This old man represented an organization known as the Union of the Russian People, a large group devoted to the Empire and to the persons of their Majesties. With intense emotion he told me that his organization had incontestable proofs of most treacherous propaganda which was being circulated by the Union of Zemstvos and Towns, under the personal direction of Goutchkoff and Rodzianko. He had brought with him documentary proofs of his assertions and he implored me to help him lay his proofs before the Emperor. I communicated his message to the Emperor, but as he was that day importantly engaged he suggested that the Empress might receive him instead. This she consented to do, but after an hour's conversation she sent the old man away, touched by his devotion but unconvinced of the gravity of the situation as he presented it.

To relieve somewhat the dullness and gloom that had settled on the palace we organized in those early winter days of 1917 a series of chamber-music recitals, the performers being Rumanian musicians who had been playing very beautifully in the convalescent wards of the Tsarskoe Selo hospitals. At the request of the Empress I arranged for performances in my own apartments in the palace, inviting, with their Majesties' approval, the Duke of Luchtenberg, Mme. Dehn, Count Fredericks, his daughters, my sister and her husband, and a few other intimate friends. The concerts were delightful, greatly cheering us all, including the somewhat lonely young Grand Duchesses and the much harassed Emperor. But something in the music, perhaps its wild and mournful tzigane numbers, moved the Empress to the depths of her sensitive soul. Her beautiful eyes became more than ever filled with melancholy and her heart seemed heavy with premonitions of disaster.

Partly because of her increased melancholy and partly moved by just anger against the propagandist press in which our innocent concerts were described as "palace orgies," the Emperor for the first time was awakened to consciousness that the safety of his family was indeed threatened. At least he became aware of the fact that despite the dangerous unrest of the times, Tsarskoe Selo and even Petrograd remained practically ungarrisoned. The capital was guarded by only a few regiments of reserves, while Tsarskoe Selo, the residence of the Imperial Family, had no regiments at all outside its peace-time quota of soldier and Cossack guards. At the command of the Emperor several additional regiments which had served for some time at the front were ordered to Tsarskoe for rest and recuperation, and, although naturally nothing of this was mentioned in the order, to augment if necessary the inadequate military force at hand. The first order was given for a strong detachment of naval guards, but after these men were actually entrained for Tsarskoe they were stopped by a counter order from General Gourko, who in the illness of General Alexieff was in command at G. H. Q. This counter order being at once communicated to the Emperor, he exercised his supreme authority and the regiment once more started for Tsarskoe Selo. But the audacity of General Gourko had not yet reached its limit. When the military train reached the station at Tsarskoe it was met by a telegram from General Gourko to the officer in command, ordering the regiment back to the front. The bewildered officer for a few moments was at a loss what to do, but fortunately news of his dilemma was telephoned to the palace, and the regiment, under the peremptory command of the Emperor, left the train and went into garrison at Tsarskoe. The Emperor next commanded that one of his favorite regiments of Varsovie Lancers be sent to Tsarskoe, but instead General Gourko left headquarters for the palace, where a long interview between the Emperor and the commander took place. By arguments of which I have no knowledge the Emperor was persuaded that the Lancers could not, for the time being, be spared from their front-line position, and he recalled his order

However, it was clear that the Emperor was at last awake to the appalling menace of disaffection which was closing in like black cloud banks on every hand. The War was going badly, as every student of the times must remember. Brusiloff's brilliant offensive of the summer and autumn of 1916 had indeed made it plain that Russia was by no means out of the struggle, but although this famous drive had netted the Russians a gain of territory even larger than that which was yielded in the great Battle of the Somme, it had finally stopped leaving us with much lost territory still unredeemed. The Emperor knew this and it tormented his heart and soul. The intriguers knew it and resolved to use it as a weapon to get the Tsar away from his capital and from his family. It was on the 19th or 20th of February (Russian Calendar) that the Emperor's brother, Grand Duke Michail Alexandrovitch, visited the palace and told the Emperor that it was his immediate duty to return to the Stavka because of grave threats of mutiny in the army. Very reluctantly the Emperor consented to go. Mutiny in the army was a serious enough matter and demanded the presence of the commander in chief. But other things were at the same time occurring to cause keen anxiety. The Empress had acquainted me with the nature of these disquieting events, but because of the international character of the most serious I dislike even now to put them in writing. However, I am here repeating only what was then told me and I have no firsthand information to offer in verification of their truth. Their Majesties had been informed and finally from a source which they believed to be absolutely reliable, that the center of intrigue against the throne was not in any secret garret of disaffected workingmen but in the British Embassy, where the Ambassador, Sir George Buchanan, was personally aiding the Grand

Dukes to overthrow Nicholas II and to replace him by his cousin Grand Duke Cyril Vladimirovitch. Sir George Buchanan's main purpose, it was said, was not so much to further the ambitions of the Grand Dukes as it was to weaken Russia as a factor in the future peace conference. Unable fully to believe that an ambassador of one of the Allied Powers would dare to meddle maliciously in the internal affairs of the Empire, the Tsar had nevertheless decided to communicate his information in a personal letter to his cousin King George of England. The Empress, deeply indignant, advised a demand on King George for the Ambassador's recall, but the Emperor replied that he dared not, at such a critical time, make public his distrust of an Ally's representative. Whether or not the Emperor ever wrote his letter to King George I never knew, but that his anxiety and depression of spirits persisted I can well testify. On the evening of February 29, the day before the Emperor's departure, I gave a small dinner to some intimate friends among the officers of the Naval Guard, Mme. Dehn helping me in my duties as hostess. A note from the Empress summoned us all to spend the end of the evening in her sitting room, and as soon as I saw the Emperor I knew that he was seriously upset. During the tea hour he spoke little, and when I tried to catch his eye he turned his head aside. The Empress murmured in my ear that all his instincts warned him against leaving Tsarskoe Selo at that time, and as this coincided exactly with my own judgment I ventured to tell him, on saying good night, that I should hope to the last moment that he would not go away until the worst of the uncertainties in Petrograd were removed. At this he smiled, almost cheerfully, and said that I must not allow myself to be frightened by wild rumors and idle gossip. Go he must, but within ten days he expected to be able to return.

The next morning I went to the door and watched his motor car drive out of the palace grounds, the Empress and the children going with it as far as the station. As usual on such occasions, there was a display of flags, of guards standing at salute, and bells from the churches pealing their farewell. Everything appeared the same, yet in that hour the flags, the soldiers, the pealing bells were speeding the Tsar of all the Russias to his doom.

I felt ill that morning, ill physically as well as mentally, yet as in duty bound I went to my hospital, where a soldier in whose case I took a special interest was to undergo an operation which he dreaded and at which he had implored me to be present. While the anesthetic was being administered I stood beside the poor man holding his hand, but at the same time I realized that I was becoming feverish and that my headache was almost unbearably increasing. Returning to the palace, I lay down in my bedroom, after writing a line to the Empress excusing myself from tea. An hour later Tatiana came in, sympathetic as usual, but troubled because both Olga and Alexei were in bed with high temperatures and the doctors suspected that they might be coming down with measles. A week or two before some small cadets from the military school had spent the afternoon playing with Alexei, and one of these boys had a cough and such a flushed face that the Empress had called the attention of M. Gilliard to the child, fearing illness. The next day we heard that he was ill with measles, but because our minds were so troubled with many other things none of us thought much of the danger of contagion. As for me, even after Tatiana had told me that Olga and Alexei were suspected cases, it did not at once occur to me that I was going to be ill. Still my temperature went on rising and my headache was unrelieved. I lay in bed all the next day until the dinner hour when Mme. Dehn came in and I made a futile effort to get up and dress. Mme. Dehn made me lie down again, and looking me over carefully she said: "You look very badly to me. I think you will have to have the doctor." The next instant, so it seemed to me, the doctor was in the room and I heard him say: "Measles. A bad case." Then I drifted off into sleep or unconsciousness.

That same day Tatiana fell ill, and now the Empress had four of us on her hands. Putting on her nurse's uniform, she spent all the succeeding days between her children's rooms and mine. Half conscious, I felt gratefully her capable hands arranging my pillows, smoothing my burning forehead, and holding to my lips medicines and cooling drinks. Already, as I heard vaguely, Marie and Anastasie had begun to cough, but this news disturbed me only as a passing dream. I was conscious of the presence of my mother and father and of my younger sister, and still as in a kind of nightmare I understood that they and the Empress spoke in hurried whispers of riots and disorders in Petrograd. But of the first days of Revolution, the strikes in Petrograd and Moscow, the revolt of the mobs and the hesitancy of the half-disciplined reserves to restore order, I know nothing except what was afterwards related to me. I do know, however, that through it all the Empress of Russia was completely calm and courageous, and that when my sister, hurrying to the palace after witnessing the wild scenes in Petrograd, had cried out to the Empress that the end had come, her fears were quieted by brave and reassuring words.

It was the devoted old Grand Duke Paul, as the Empress afterwards told me, who brought her the first official tidings, and made her understand that that most calamitous of all blunders, a political revolution in the midst of world war, had been accomplished. Even then she lost none of her marvelous courage. She did not call upon the Ministers or upon the Allied Ambassadors to protect her and her children. With dignity, unmoved she witnessed day by day the cowardly desertion of men who for years had lived at Court and who had enjoyed the faith and friendship of the Imperial Family. One by one they went, General Racine, Count Apraxine, officers and men of the bodyguard, servants the oldest and the most trusted, all with smooth excuses and apologies which translated meant only *sauve qui peut.*

One night came the noise of rioting and the sharp staccato of machine guns apparently approaching nearer and nearer the palace. It was about eleven o'clock and the Empress was sitting for a few minutes' rest on the edge of my bed. Getting up hastily and wrapping herself in a white shawl, she beckoned

Marie, the last of the children on her feet, and went out of the palace into the icy air to face whatever threatened. The Naval Guard and the Konvoi Cossacks still remained on duty, although even then they were preparing to desert. It is altogether possible that they would have gone over to the rioters that night had it not been for the unexpected appearance of the Empress and her daughter. From one guard to another they passed, the stately woman and the courageous young girl, undaunted both in the face of deadly danger, speaking words of encouragement, and most of all of simple faith and confidence. This alone held the men at their posts during that dreadful night and prevented the rioters from attacking the palace. The next day the guards disappeared. The Naval Guards, led by Grand Duke Cyril Vladimirovitch,[1] marched with red flags to the Duma and presented themselves to Rodzianko as joyful revolutionists. The very men who in the previous midnight had hailed the Empress with the traditional greeting, *"Zdravie Jelaim Vashie Imperatorskoe Velichestvo!"* Health and long life to your Majesty! So loud had been their greeting that the Empress, not wishing me to know that she had left the palace, sent a servant to tell me that the Guards were waiting to meet the Emperor.

There was now in or about the palace practically no one to defend the Imperial Family in case the mob decided to attack. Still the Empress remained calm, saying only that she hoped no blood would have to be

[1] This is the same Cyril Vladimirovitch who has recently proclaimed himself "Head of the Romanoff Family and Guardian of the Throne."

shed in their defense. A telegram from the Emperor revealed that the crisis had become known to him, for he implored the Empress to join him with the children at headquarters. At the same hour came an astounding message to the Empress from Rodzianko, now head of the Provisional Government, notifying her that she and her whole family must vacate the palace at once. Her answer to both messages was that she could not leave because all five of the children were dangerously ill. Rodzianko's reply to this appeal of an anguished mother was: "When the house is on fire it is time for everything to be thrown out " Desperately the Empress consulted doctors and nurses. Could the children possibly be moved? Could Anna? What was to be done in case the Provisional Government proved altogether pitiless?

Into this soul-racking dilemma of the mother came to the wife of the Emperor the terrible news of his abdication. I could not be with her in that hour of woe, nor did I even see her until the following morning. It was my parents who broke the news to me, almost too ill and too cloudy of mind to comprehend it. Mme. Dehn, who was with the Empress on the evening when Grand Duke Paul arrived with the fatal tidings, has described the scene when the broken-hearted Empress left the Grand Duke and returned to her own room.

"Her face was distorted with agony, her eyes were full of tears. She tottered rather than walked, and I rushed forward and supported her until she reached the writing table between the windows. She leaned heavily against it, and taking my hands in hers she said brokenly: *'Abdiqué!'*

"I could hardly believe my ears. I waited for her next words. They were scarcely audible. At last [still speaking in French, for Mme. Dehn spoke no English] 'Poor darling —alone there and suffering—My God! What he must have suffered!'"

In that hour of supreme agony there was not a word spoken of the loss of a throne. Alexandra Feodorovna's whole heart was with her husband, her sole fears that he might be in danger and that their boy might be taken from them. At once she began to send frantic telegrams to the Emperor begging him to come home as soon as possible. With the refinement of cruelty which marked the whole conduct of the Provisional Government in those days these telegrams were returned to the Empress marked in blue pencil: "Address of person mentioned unknown."

Not even this insolence nor all her fears broke the sublime courage of the Empress. When next morning she entered my sickroom and saw by my tear-drenched face that I knew what had happened her only visible emotion was a slight irritation that other lips than her own had brought me the news. "They should have known that I preferred to tell you myself," she said. It was only when gone her rounds of the palace and was alone in her own bedroom that she finally gave way to her grief. "Mama cried terribly," little Grand Duchess Marie told me. "I cried too, but not more than I could help, for poor Mama's sake." Never in my life, I am certain, shall I behold such proud fortitude as was shown all through those days of wreck and disaster by the Empress and her children. Not one single word of bitterness or resentment passed their lips. "You know, Annia," said the Empress gently, "all is finished for our Russia. But we must not blame the people or the soldiers for what has happened." Too well we knew on whose shoulders the burden of responsibility really rested.

By this time Olga and Alexei were decidedly better, but Tatiana and Anastasie were still very ill and Marie was in the first serious stage of the disease. The Empress in her hospital uniform moved tirelessly from one bed to another. Perceiving that from my floor of the palace practically every servant had fled, even my nurses and my once devoted Jouk having yielded to the general panic, she found people to move my bed upstairs to the old nursery of the Emperor. We were now almost alone in the palace. My father's resignation having been demanded and of course given, my parents were detained in Petrograd.

Days passed and still no word came from the Emperor. The Empress's endurance had almost reached its breaking point when there came to the palace a young woman, the wife of an obscure officer, who threw herself at the feet of the Empress and begged to be allowed the dangerous task of getting a letter through to the Emperor. Gratefully indeed did the Empress accept the offer, and within an hour the brave woman was on her way to Mogiloff. How she managed to reach headquarters, how she passed the cordon of soldiers and finally succeeded in delivering to the captive Emperor his wife's letter we never knew, but all honor to this heroic woman, she did it.

The palace was now full of Revolutionary soldiers, quite drunk with their new liberty. Their heavy boots tramped through all the rooms and corridors, and groups of dirty, unshaven men were constantly pushing their way into the nurseries bawling out hoarsely: "Show us Alexei!" For it was the heir who most of all aroused the interest and curiosity of the mob. Meanwhile, behind closed doors and anxiously awaiting the arrival of the Emperor, the Empress and her few faithful friends were at work forestalling the coming of Kerensky by burning and destroying letters and diaries, intimate personal records too precious to be allowed to fall into the ruthless hands of enemies.

CHAPTER XV

IN anxiety almost unbearable we waited until the morning of March 9 (Russian) the arrival of the Emperor. I was still confined to my bed and Dr. Botkine was making me his first visit of the day when my door flew open and Mme. Dehn, pale with excitement, rushed to my bedside exclaiming breathlessly "He has come!" As soon as she could command words she described the arrival of the Emperor, not as of yore attended, but guarded like a prisoner by armed soldiers. The Empress was with Alexei when the motor cars drove into the palace grounds, and Mme. Dehn told how she sprang to her feet overjoyed and ran like a schoolgirl down the stairs and through the long corridors to meet her husband. For a time at least the happiness of reunion blotted out the suspense of the past and the gloomy uncertainty of the future. But afterwards, alone, behind their own closed doors, the emotion of the betrayed and deserted Emperor completely overcame his self-control and he sobbed like a child on the breast of his wife. It was four o'clock in the afternoon before she could come to me, and when she came I read in her white, drawn face the whole story of the ordeal through which she had passed. With prideful composure she related the events of the day. I tried to match her in courage but I am afraid I failed. I, who in all the twelve years of

my life in the palace had but three times seen tears
in the eyes of the Emperor, was entirely overwhelmed
at her recital.

"He will not break down a second time," she said
with a brave smile. "He is walking in the garden now.
Come to the window and see." She helped me to the
window and herself pulled aside the curtain. Never,
never while I live shall I forget what we saw, we two,
clinging together in shame and sorrow for our disgraced country. Below in the garden of the palace
which had been his home for twenty years stood the
man who until a few days before had been Tsar of
all the Russias. With him was his faithful friend
Prince Dolgorouky, and surrounding them were six
soldiers, say rather six hooligans, armed with rifles.
With their fists and with the butts of their guns they
pushed the Emperor this way and that as though he
were some wretched vagrant they were baiting in a
country road. "You can't go there, Gospodin
Polkovnik (Mr. Colonel)." "We don't permit you to
walk in that direction, Gospodin Polkovnik." "Stand
back when you are commanded, Gospodin Polkovnik."
The Emperor, apparently unmoved, looked from one
of these coarse brutes to another and with great dignity
turned and walked back towards the palace. I had
been a very sick woman, and I was now hardly fit
to stand on my feet. The light went out suddenly and
I fainted. But the Empress did not faint. She got
me back to my bed, fetched cold water, and when I
awoke it was to feel her cool hand bathing my head.
From her calm and detached manner no one could have
guessed that the scene we had just witnessed was part

also of her own tragedy. Before leaving me she said as to a child: "If you will promise to be very good and not cry he shall come to see you this evening."

After dinner they came, the Emperor and Empress with our friend Lili Dehn. The two women sat down at a table with their needlework leaving the Emperor free to sit by my bed and talk to me privately. I have tried to show Nicholas II as a human person, with human emotions, and I have no desire now to represent him, in the hour of his humiliation, as other than a man feeling keenly and acutely the bitterness of his position. I had been unable until the day of his return to realize with any degree of clarity the full extent of his calamity. It was to me almost unbelievable that his enemies, who had so long plotted and schemed for his overthrow, had at last succeeded. It was beyond reason that the Emperor, the finest and best of the whole Romanoff family, should be allowed to fall under the feet of his decadent, treacherous kinsmen and subjects. But the Emperor, his eyes hard and glistening, told me that it was indeed true. And he added: "If all Russia came to me now on their knees I would never return."

With tears in his voice he spoke of the men, his most trusted relations and friends, who had turned against him and caused his downfall. He read me telegrams from Brusiloff, Alexieff, and other of his generals, others from members of the family, including a message from Nicholai Nicholaievitch, in which the writers "on their knees" begged his Imperial Majesty, for the salvation of Russia, to abdicate In whose favor did they wish him to abdicate? The weak and ineffectual Duma? The great untaught masses of the people? No, to their own blind and self-seeking oligarchy, which, under a regent of its own choosing, would rule the boy Alexei and through him the people and the uncounted wealth of Russia. But this at least the Emperor could and did prevent. Both his heart and his mind forbade him to abdicate in favor of the Tsarevitch. "My boy I will not give to them," he said feelingly. "Let them get some one else, Michail, if he thinks he is strong enough."

I regret that I cannot remember every word the Emperor told me of the scenes in his train when the deputation from the Duma came to demand his abdication. I was trying too hard to obey the Empress's injunction to "be good and not cry." But I remember his telling me how arrogant and vain the deputies, especially Goutchkoff and Shoulgin, showed themselves. On their departure the Emperor's first words were addressed to the two tall Cossacks who stood guard at his door. "It is time now for you to tear my initials from your shoulder straps," he told them. The Cossacks saluted and one of them said: "Please your Imperial Majesty, please allow us to kill them." But the Emperor replied: "It is too late to do that now."

Of his mother, who hurried from Kiev, accompanied by Grand Duke Alexander Michailovitch, to see him, he said that he was vastly comforted to have her near him, but that the sight of the Grand Duke was unendurable. Driving away from the train with the Empress Dowager, the Emperor had been much moved to see the people along the whole distance of two versts fall on their knees to bid him farewell. There was a group of schoolgirls from the institute at Mogiloff who forced their way past the guards and surrounded their Sovereign, begging his handkerchief, his autograph on bits of paper, the buttons from his uniform, anything for a last souvenir. The Emperor's face grew sharply lined when he spoke of those brave girls and the kneeling people. "Why did you not appeal to them?" I asked. "Why did you not appeal to the soldiers?" But the Emperor answered gently: "The people knew themselves powerless, and as for appealing to the soldiers, how could I? Already I had heard threats of murdering my family." His wife and children, he said, were all on earth he had left to live for now. Their happiness and well-being were all his soul desired. As for the Empress, more than himself the real object of malice, only over his body should any hand be raised to injure her. Giving way once more for a brief moment to his grief the Emperor murmured half to himself: "But there is no justice, no justice on earth." Then as if in apology he said: "It has shaken me badly, as you see. For the first few days I was so little myself that I could not even write my diary."

As we talked it came over me for the first time in full force that all was indeed finished for Russia. The army was disrupted, the nation fallen. I could foresee, to some extent at least, the horrors we should have to meet, but in a kind of desperate hope I asked the Emperor if he did not think that the riots and strikes would now be put down. He shook his head. "Not for two years at least," he predicted. But what did he think was to become of him, of the Empress and the children? He did not know, but there was one prayer he should not be too proud to make to his enemies, and that was that they should not send him out of Russia. "Let me live here in my own country, as the humblest and most obscure proprietor, tilling the land and earning the poorest living," he exclaimed. "Send us to any distant corner of Russia, but only let us stay."

This was the only time I ever saw the Emperor in the least degree unmanned, or overcome with the bitterness of grief which I knew must have filled his spirit. After that first day in the palace gardens he gave his jailers no opportunity of insulting him. With Prince Dolgorouky he walked out daily but only along near pathways to the palace doors. The snow was heavy on the ground and the two men vigorously exercised themselves shoveling it from paths and roadways. Often the Emperor would look up from this strenuous work to wave a hand to those of us who were watching from the windows. In the solitude of my sick chamber I tormented myself with thoughts of what might be in store for the Emperor and the beloved family whose happiness and well-being were more to him than the most exalted throne. They were all prisoners of the Duma now, and what dark and hapless fate was the ruthless, irresponsible Duma preparing for them? Not a comforting question to haunt the mind of one ill in body and soul. From my first waking moment on I lived in anticipation of the daily visit of the Empress. She who had all at stake still kept her wonderful courage alive. She came in tall and stately, a smile on her gentle, melancholy face, bringing me the news of the nurseries, messages from the children, making me work, doing everything possible to cheer and to lighten my mind. In the evening the Emperor usually came, wheeling his wife in her invalid's chair, for by night her strength had all but gone. They stayed with me for an hour and then went on to say good night to the suite in the drawing room. Sadly diminished in numbers was that suite, but unchanged in fealty and affection for fallen majesty. Among those devoted friends who appeared almost like the survivors of a shipwreck were Count Benkendorff, brother of the former Russian ambassador to Great Britain, and his wife, who had boldly arrived at the palace when it was first surrounded by mutinous soldiers; two maids of honor, Baroness Buxhoevden and Countess Hendrikoff; the faithful Miss Schneider ("Trina"), Mme. Dehn, Count Fredericks, General Voyeikoff and the Hussar officer, General Groten. The two devoted aides-de-camp, Lieutenant Linevitch and Count Zamirsky, who had flown to the palace to be near the Empress after the abdication, had been forced to leave, or they too would have remained to the end. Of the household M. Gilliard and Mr. Gibbs, the French and English tutors of Alexei, had elected to remain. Madeleine, and several other personal attendants, including three nurses, also stayed. "In good times we served the family," said these honest souls, "never will we forsake them now."

Not once, after the very first of our conversations, and not at any time I believe to others in the palace did the Emperor or the Empress make the smallest complaint of their captivity. They seemed to suffer for

Russia rather than for themselves, for they knew, and said so, that the army, suddenly in the midst of war released from all discipline, would soon cease to fight efficiently, or perhaps to obey orders at all. This of course the world knows is precisely what did happen. The Emperor, I must admit, sometimes betrayed a gruesome kind of humor over the fantastic blunders of the self-styled statesmen who were so rapidly making general shipwreck of their revolution. In every way they showed their weakness and bewilderment. Whether or not they feared to trust old officers of the Empire with the custody of the Imperial Family I cannot be sure, but the men they sent to Tsarskoe were a constant source of ironic mirth to the suite. Most of these men were young, raw, underbred, and inexperienced, the best of them being junior officers promoted since 1914. One day one of the guard officers, just to show how democratic Russia had become, swaggered up to the Emperor and offered to shake hands with him. Unfortunately, as he afterwards told me, the Emperor was so busy shoveling snow that he could not take advantage of the man's condescension.

The newly appointed commandant of the palace was a young man named Paul Kotzebou, before the War an officer of the lancers, but for some piece of misconduct cashiered from the service. I had long known Kotzebou and aside from his doubtful army record I was not sorry to see him in the palace, for I knew that if weak of character he was at least kind of heart. Kind indeed he proved himself, for he visited my sickroom in friendly fashion, risked arrest by consenting to smuggle letters to my parents in Petrograd, and

was the first to warn me that the Provisional Government was contemplating my arrest. Many of the old
friends and advisers of the Emperor were already in
prison, but the proposal to arrest a woman whose sole
crime had been devotion to the Empress and her children gave us all an uncomfortable, premonitory shock.
The distress of the Empress was greater almost than
her pride. The mercy she would have scorned to ask
for herself she was ready to beg for me, and she did
most earnestly implore Kotzebou to intercede in my
behalf. "What possible good will it do them to arrest one helpless woman?" she urged. "Parting with
her would be like losing one of my own children."
Kotzebou, whatever his feelings, could only reply:
"If I could, Madame—but there is nothing I can do,
nothing."

The Emperor alone refused to believe my arrest at
all probable, but the others were badly frightened at
the prospect. The sister of mercy who had worked
in my hospital and was taking care of me, almost
went on her knees to the Emperor and Empress.
"Now is the time to show your real love for Anna
Alexandrovna," she cried. "Take her into the rooms
of your own children and never let anybody touch her."
Cooler counsel came from Count Benkendorff, who advised the Emperor and Empress not to oppose my
arrest if it were ordered. The only result of opposition, he pointed out, would be more arrests and
perhaps increased hardship for the Empress. "I do
not think they will detain her, unless it is in one of the
rooms of the Tauride," he said, meaning that I might
only be isolated for a time in the palace where the

Duma held its sessions. Count Benkendorff was later to learn what kind of justice was being prepared by the criminal lunatics who were at Russia's throat.

One morning towards the 20th of March I had a hurried note from the Empress, the contents of which were enough to make me forget all my own troubles Marie, who had been very ill and who now she feared was dying, was calling constantly for me. The servant who brought the note told me that Anastasie also was in a critical condition, lungs and ears being in a sad state of inflammation. Oxygen alone was keeping the children alive. Kotzebou was calling on me at the time, and as I sat up in bed wildly demanding to be dressed, he begged me not to leave my room. "They are only waiting until you are well enough to be arrested," he assured me. But though I feared arrest I feared still more letting the child I loved die with one single wish unfulfilled, and as soon as I could be sufficiently clothed it was Kotzebou himself who wheeled my chair through the long corridors to the nurseries It was the first time in weeks that I had seen the children and our meeting was full of tears. We wept in each other's arms and then without wasting any time I went on into Marie's room. The child indeed seemed to be at the point of death, but when she saw me the suffering in her eyes turned to something like joy. Her weak hands fluttered on the bedclothes and with a feeble cry, "Annia, Annia," she began to weep. Long I sat beside her holding her hot and wasted body in my arms, and when I left her she was asleep. Shaken though I was with that experience, I had one more agony to bear. When my chair was being wheeled back along the corridor I passed the open door of Alexei's room, and this is what I saw. Lying sprawled in a chair was the sailor Derevanko, for many years the personal attendant of the Tsarevitch, and on whom the family had bestowed every kindness, every material benefit. Bitten by the mania of revolution, this man was now displaying his gratitude for all their favors. Insolently he bawled at the boy whom he had formerly loved and cherished, to bring him this or that, to perform any menial service his mean lackey's brain could think of. Dazed and apparently only half conscious of what he was being forced to do, the child moved about trying to obey. It was too much to bear. Hiding my face in my hands, I begged them to take me away from the sickening spectacle.

The next day, my last in the palace, I went again to the children, and for a few hours at least was a little bit happy. The Emperor and Empress had luncheon served in the nurseries, and we were all able to eat in some comfort because both Marie and Anastasie were showing signs of improvement. Still we were troubled because Kotzebou, as a reward for his too kindly treatment of the captives, had that morning been removed from the palace, and the doctors when they came brought with them newspapers, fair samples of the new "free" press of Russia, bristling with frightful stories, especially about me. For the first time I began to realize, with a sick heart, what an arrest might mean, what grotesque charges I might be called upon to face. For the first time, in these newspapers I read the amazing tale of how I had conspired with Dr.

Badmieff to poison the Emperor and the Tsarevitch. Dr. Badmieff, that half mad old Siberian root and herb doctor, who never in his life had been admitted to the palace as a physician or even as a friend! It was too absurd to resent. Even the Empress who at first had shown anger, burst into mocking laughter. "Here, Annia," she cried, "keep this story for your collection."

The next day I was arrested. I awoke in a morning of storm and howling wind and in my soul a feeling of dread and foreboding. Immediately after my coffee I wrote a note to the Empress asking her not to wait until afternoon to see me. Her reply was kind and cheering, but she was busy in the nurseries and could not leave until after the arrival of the doctors. With luncheon came Lili Dehn, and scarcely had we finished the meal when we were aware of great noise and confusion in the corridor outside. An icy hand seemed to seize my heart. "They are coming," I whispered, and Mme. Dehn, springing from her chair cried: "Impossible. No— no—" and panic-struck fled the room. The door flew open to admit a frightened servant with a note from the Empress. "Kerensky is going through our rooms. Do not be frightened. God is with us." Hardly had the man retired when again the door opened and another frightened servant, a palace messenger in a feathered cap, announced in a drowned voice the arrival of Kerensky. In a moment the room seemed to fill up with men and walking arrogantly before them I beheld a small, clean-shaven, theatrical person whose essentially weak face was disguised in a Napoleonic frown. Standing over me in

his characteristic attitude, right hand thrust into the
bosom of his jacket, the man boomed out: "I am the
Minister of Justice. You are to dress and go at once
to Petrograd." I answered not a word but lay still
on my pillows looking him straight in the face. This
seemed to disconcert him somewhat for he turned to
one of his officers and said nervously: "Ask the
doctors if she is fit to go. Otherwise she must be arrested and isolated in the palace." Count Benkendorff, who stood in the back of the room near the door,
volunteered to see the doctor, and when he returned
it was with the message that Dr. Botkine gave them
permission to take me. Afterwards I learned that the
Empress reproached the doctor bitterly, saying over
and over through her tears: "How can you? How
can you? You who have children of your own." But
Dr. Botkine was by this time a victim of craven fear,
and he was incapable of refusing any request of the
Provisional Government.

They gave me time to dress warmly, and I had a
moment in which to reply briefly to a note from the
Emperor and Empress, in which they enclosed small
pictures of Christ and the Virgin, signed with their
Majesties' initials, N. and A. When at last I was
ready to go it suddenly surged over me that this might
be the end of my long association with these dearly
loved friends, my Sovereigns, whose intimate lives I
had shared for twelve years. Ready to fall on my
knees before him if necessary I made a final appeal
to Colonel Korovitchinko, the new commandant of
the palace, begging him to let me see them for one
moment, just long enough to say good-bye. Colonel

Korovitchinko, who afterwards died a cruel death at the hands of the Bolsheviki, at first refused, but moved by my tears he relented a little. The Emperor, he said, was outside and could not be summoned, but he would exert his authority far enough to send me under guard to say good-bye to the Empress. Under escort of two officers I was taken to the apartment of Mlle. Schneider, and very soon the pale Empress was wheeled into the room by her devoted attendant Volkov. We had time for only one long embrace and the hurried exchange of two rings. Then Tatiana, who came with her mother, embraced me, weeping, and as she too begged for a last memory gift I gave her the only thing I had to give, my wedding ring. Then the soldiers tore us apart but I saw that the man who gave the order did it with tears in his eyes. The last I remember was the white hand of the Empress pointing upward and her voice: "There we are always together." Volkov, weeping, cried out courageously: "Anna Alexandrovna, God will surely help."

They carried me downstairs to the motor, for I could neither walk nor stand, even with the help of my crutches. At the door stood several soldiers and Court servants, visibly distressed, but by this time I felt nothing, heard nothing. I was turned to stone. When I was lifted into the car I was startled to see there another woman, like myself swathed in wraps and veils. It was Lili Dehn, whose arrest had not before this day even been threatened. Dazed as I was, it was some comfort to hear her whisper that we were to travel to Petrograd together. I recovered myself a little, enough at least to recognize the frightened face of the servant who closed the door of the car. Killed a few months later, this good man had been for a long time a sailor on the Imperial yacht. "Take care of their Majesties," I managed to say to him. Then the motor car shot forward, and I left the palace at Tsarskoe Selo forever. Both Lili and I pressed our faces to the glass in a last effort to see those beloved we were leaving behind, and through the mist and rain we could just discern a group of white-clad figures crowded close to the nursery windows to see us go. In a moment of time the picture was blotted out and we saw only the wet landscape, the storm-bent trees, the rapidly creeping twilight. In another few moments we were at the station, the dear, familiar station of Tsarskoe, where so many, many times I had waited to greet or to say a short farewell to the Emperor and Empress. Ready for us was one of the small Imperial trains, now the special train of Kerensky. Our guards hurried us into a carriage, and the train immediately began to move. At the same time our carriage was invaded by Kerensky and a group of soldiers. Without even a pretense of decent politeness the new Minister of Justice began to shout at us: "Give your family names," and because we did not speak quickly enough the little man became insulted. "You will learn that when *I* ask a question you must answer promptly." We gave our names and Kerensky, turning triumphantly to the soldiers, ejaculated: "Well! Are you convinced now?" Apparently some of the men had expressed doubts as to whether they had bagged the right criminals. Sick and half fainting, I sank back into the cushions and

closed my eyes on their departing figures. Lili bent
over me with her salts bottle and soon I was able to
sit up with some show of courage. It was the first
time I had left the house since my illness and I was
still very weak.

Arrived in Petrograd, Kerensky paraded us before
his officers like barbarian captives of some Roman
emperor, but this did not affect us seriously. Our
eyes were busy gazing at the changed aspect of Petrograd, soldiers swanking around the streets proud of
their slovenly appearance, the badge of their new
freedom; mobs of people running aimlessly about, or
pausing to listen to street-corner orators; and everywhere on walls and buildings masses of dirty red flags.
An old-fashioned coach belong to the Imperial stables
had been sent for us and still closely guarded we drove
to the Ministry of Justice. There we climbed a long
and very steep staircase—how I did it on my crutches
I do not yet understand—and were shown into a room
on the third floor, empty even of a wooden chair.
Silently we stood and waited, and after a time men
came in carrying two sofas. On one of these Lili sat
down and on the other I lay prone. Again we waited,
no one near us save the unkempt soldier who guarded
the door. The evening lengthened and finally
Kerensky honored us with another brief visit. He did
not look at me at all but asked Lili if they had built
us a fire. It was an unnecessary question, for he must
have felt the icy chill of the room. A few minutes
later, however, a servant did build a fire in the tiled
stove, and another brought in a tray with eggs and
tea. Left alone with the unkempt soldier, the man

suddenly amazed us by breaking into a volley of speech in which he cursed most eloquently the new order of things.   Nothing good would come of it, nothing, was his opinion.   Somewhat reassured because we had a guard who was not at heart a Revolutionist, we lay down, but the night brought to neither of us any anodyne of sleep and rest.

CHAPTER XVI

MORNING dawned cold and gray, and so exhausted was I with sleeplessness and the discomfort of a hard bed without linen or blankets, that Lili was alarmed and when the tea arrived she begged the soldier who brought it to have a doctor sent me. But Kerensky replied that the doctor was engaged with War Minister Goutchkoff and could not be approached at present. Within a short time I was to be removed to a hospital, and as for Mme. Dehn, she might expect good news soon. As a matter of fact Mme. Dehn was released from custody the next day. Feeling confident that she would be let go, I gave her what jewels I had brought with me, asking her to turn them over to my mother. In return Lili gave me a few necessaries, including a pair of stockings for which later I was extremely grateful because the prison stockings were so coarse and heavy that they hurt my injured leg.

About three o'clock in the afternoon Colonel Peretz, who afterwards wrote a book on the Revolution, came into the room with a group of young boys, former cadets of the military academy, now commissioned officers of the new army. "Say good-bye to your friend and come along," I was ordered, and after a quick embrace I parted with Mme. Dehn, my last link with the past, and followed the men downstairs, where a large motor car was waiting. We all got in, the men's rifles considerably reducing the carrying capacity of the seats. As we drove off the colonel began a long and insulting monologue to which I tried not to listen. "Ah! You and your Grichka (Gregory)," I heard him saying, "what a monument you both deserve for helping us to bring about the Revolution." But all that I wanted to learn from him was my destination, and as if in answer to the unspoken question he said: "All night we were discussing the most appropriate lodgings for you, and we decided on the Troubetskoy Bastion in the fortress." At this point we passed a church and, after the invariable custom, I made the sign of the cross. Colonel Peretz flamed into anger at this. "Don't dare cross yourself," he cried with emphasis on the last word. "Rather pray for the souls of the martyrs of the Revolution." Then as I made no response he exclaimed: "Why don't you answer when I speak to you?" I replied coldly that I had nothing whatever to say to him, whereupon be began to revile the Emperor and Empress in coarsest terms, ending with the words: "No doubt they are in hysterics over what has happened to them." Then I did speak. "If you knew with what dignity they are enduring what has happened you would not dare say what you have said." After which the monologue was for a moment or two halted.

Turning into the Liteiny, a street in which many barracks and ministries are located, the car stopped and Colonel Peretz dispatched one of the cadet officers on an errand into a Government building. On his return the colonel delayed matters long enough to make a bombastic speech on the great services to the Revolution performed by the cadets, and again we drove on. Realizing that we were not proceeding in the direction of the Fortress of Peter and Paul, I allowed my feminine curiosity to get the better of my pride and I asked whither we were bound. "To the Duma first," was the grim answer. "To the fortress afterwards." Arrived at the Tauride Palace we alighted at what is known as the Ministers' Pavilion and immediately went into the building. What a sight! Crowding the rooms and the corridors, men and women of all ages and conditions, prisoners of the Provisional Government! Looking about, I saw many people of my own class, among them Mme. Soukhomlinoff who for all her manner betrayed might have been a guest rather than a prisoner. We exchanged cheerful greetings and she introduced the two women beside her, Mme. Polouboiarenoff and Mme. Riman, wife of a well-known general. Mme. Polouboiarenoff, of whom I had heard as a brilliant writer on a conservative newspaper (murdered for this later by the Bolsheviki), was quite self-possessed, but Mme. Riman's face was wet with constantly flowing tears. A young girl student, a typical Revolutionist who seemed to be in some kind of authority, passed us in a hurry, pausing to say to Mme. Riman: "What are you crying about? You are going to be set free while these two"—Mme. Soukhomlinoff and myself—"are going to the fortress." Poor Mme. Riman was crying because her husband was already in prison, but the revolutionary student could not be expected to sympathize with that.

It really is easier to be calm over one's own than over another's fate, as I learned when I found myself, with Mme. Soukhomlinoff, once more in a motor car bound for that mysterious prison on the left bank of the Neva, directly opposite the Winter Palace, the Fortress of Peter and Paul. As we left the Tauride the girl student, who after all had some natural feelings, asked me for my father's telephone number that she might notify my parents where I had been sent. "No need to bother about that," broke in the chivalrous Colonel Peretz. "The newspapers will have a full report." "All the better," I rejoined, "for then many more will pray for me."

Rolling into the vast enclosure of the fortress, we stopped at the entrance of the Troubetskoy Bastion. A group of soldiers, dirty and wolfish of demeanor, rushed to meet us. "Now I am bringing you two very desperate political prisoners," shouted the colonel, as the men closed around us. But a stout Cossack, much more human than the rest, assumed authority saying that he was that day acting in place of the governor of the fortress. Preceded by this man, we traversed a long series of narrow, winding stone passages, so dark that I could see only a few feet ahead. Suddenly I was halted, hinges creaked, and I was roughly pushed into a pitch-dark cell the door of which was instantly bolted behind me.

No one who has not been a prisoner can possibly know the sickening sensation which possessed me, standing there in that dark hole, afraid to take a step forward, unable to touch with my groping hands either walls or furniture. My heart leaped and pounded in

my breast and I clung desperately to my crutches lest
I should fall into that unfathomed darkness. A few
minutes of wild terror and then as my eyes grew accustomed to the dark I saw ahead of me a narrow iron
cot towards which I moved with infinite caution. In
my progress towards the bed my feet sank into pools
of stagnant water which covered the floor, and soon I
perceived that the walls of the cell were also dripping
with moisture. The tiny window, high in the farthest
wall, admitted little air, and the whole place was foul
with dampness and the odor of years. It reeked with
even worse smells as I quickly discovered, for close
to the bed was an uncovered toilet connected with
archaic plumbing. The bed was hard and lumpy and
I do not think that the thin mattress had ever been
cleaned or aired. However, that mattress was not to
afflict me long. Within a few minutes my cell door
was thrown open and several uniformed men entered.
At their head was a black-bearded ruffian who told me
that he was Koutzmine, representative of the Minister
of Justice, and was authorized to arrange the régime
of all prisoners. At his orders the soldiers tore from
under me the ill-smelling mattress and the hard little
pillow, leaving me only a rough bed of planks. Under
his orders they tore off my rings and jerked loose a
gold chain from which were suspended several precious
relics. They hurt me and I cried out in protest, whereupon the soldiers spat at me, struck me with their
fists and left, noisily clanging the iron door behind
them. Wrapping my cloak around me, I crouched
down on the bed shivering from head to foot and filled
with such an agony of loathing and disgust and deso-

lation that I thought I should die. Not a particle of food was brought me that day, and nothing broke the monotony of the dragging hours save now and again when the small grating in the door of my cell was pushed aside and a gaping soldier looked in. Then came night, hardly darker than the day, but more silent. Weak with hunger, spent with pain I clutched my aching head with my hands and asked God if He had forgotten me. At that moment of extreme misery I was startled and at the same time strangely comforted by a sudden low but distinct rapping on the other side of the wall. Instinctively I knew that it was Mme. Soukhomlinoff who was trying to speak to me in the only language prisoners have. I rapped back, almost happily, for I felt that with a friend so near I was not entirely deserted.

I must have slept after that, for the next thing I remember was a man entering the cell with a pot of hot water and a small piece of black bread which he placed on an iron shelf near the bed. "As soon as your money arrives you can have tea," he announced briefly. Tea would have been a priceless blessing in that cold place, but I was so thirsty that I drank every drop of the hot water and was thankful. I suppose I ate the black bread too, bad as it was, for I was very hungry.

How to describe the days that followed, slow-paced, monotonous, yet each one filled with its special meed of suffering? On one of the first days a grim woman came in and stripped me of my underclothes, substituting coarse and unclean garments marked with the number of my cell, which was 70. No prison dress seemed to be provided, so I was allowed to keep my own. But in the process of undressing the woman discovered a slender gold bracelet which I had worn day and night for many years and which was locked on my arm. She called Koutzmine and his guard of soldiers and they, indignant that they had overlooked a single article of value, began to force the bracelet over my hand. As the little circlet was not intended to go over my hand their efforts caused me such pain that I screamed in spite of myself. Touched, or perhaps merely annoyed at this, Koutzmine suggested to the soldiers that if I would promise not to give the bracelet to anyone I might be allowed to keep it. But his suggestion met with no sympathy and the bracelet was finally forced over my bruised hand.

The awful food and the still more awful solitude were daily afflictions, and I think they were really the worst of all. Twice a day a soldier brought in a nauseous dish, a kind of soup made of the bones and skin of fish, none too fresh. Sometimes, if the soldier happened to be in an especially vicious mood, he spat in the soup before giving it to me, and more than once I found small pieces of glass among the bones. Yet so ravenous was my hunger that I actually swallowed enough of the vile stuff to keep myself alive. Only by holding my nose with my fingers was I able to get a few spoonfuls down my throat. What was left I was careful to pour into the filthy toilet, for I had been told that unless I ate what was given me I would be left to starve. Hot water and black bread continued to be doled out in small quantities, but there was never any tea. No food was allowed to be given the prisoners even when it was brought to the fortress by relatives and friends. Neither was any kind of occupation given the wretched captives. We were not even allowed to clean our own cells, a soldier coming in once a week to wipe up the wet and slimy floors. When I begged the privilege of doing this myself the soldier replied: "A prisoner who works is not a prisoner at all." It is true that when he has absolutely nothing to do he is worse than a prisoner, he is a living corpse.

Actual death being too merciful for political prisoners, we were taken out, one by one, for ten minutes every day. The exercise ground was a small grassy court where a few shrubs and trees gave promise of green leaves later on. No words can describe the relief, the blessed joy that those few moments of light and air and the sight of the blue sky brought to my heart. It seemed to me that I lived only for those moments. Of course the walled court was well guarded by armed soldiers and never once did their fierce eyes ever leave me. Still it was a bit of God's beautiful world, a breath of His sweet air, and I breathed it deep into my soul, keeping it there for hope and comfort until the next day came. In the center of the court was a small and dingy bath house where, on Fridays and Saturdays, the prisoners were treated to a sort of a bath. On those days we were not permitted to walk, but I for one did not complain of this. Any respite from the gravelike existence of the cells was a blessing. It was still very cold and when I lay down for the night I never removed my clothes. I had two woolen handkerchiefs, or rather, head kerchiefs, and one of these I tied over my head and the other I wrapped around my shoulders for warmth. Usually I slept until about four o'clock when the bells of a church hard by broke into my slumbers. After that I tried to doze, but very soon came the tramp of boots on the stones of the corridors and the crash of wood which the soldiers brought in each day for their stoves. I always woke up shivering and my first move was towards a corner of my cell where the stones were dry and a little warm from the stove outside. Here I huddled and shook until the hot water and the black bread were thrust in. I had never fully recovered from my illness and the cold and damp brought on first a pleurisy and afterwards a racking cough. I was so weak that sometimes in crossing from the bed to what I called the warm corner I slipped and fell and lay on the wet floor unable to rise. The soldier who thus found me, if he were of the half decent sort, would pick me up and throw me on the plank bed. Otherwise he would merely kick me.

For the first two weeks I spent in the Troubetskoy Bastion the only attendants were men. The soldiers had the keys to the cells and the complete freedom of the corridors. The first lot were men of the 3rd Rifle Regiment of Petrograd, but within a few days some of them were shifted and their places were taken by a miscellaneous force from one of the most unruly of the mutinous reserves. Riots and fights between the two bands became an almost daily occurrence and the nerves of the prisoners were tortured by the yells and blows of the battle. My only comfort, aside from the ten minutes' respite of the exercise ground, was in the wall-tapping between my cell and Mme. Soukhomlinoff's. This had developed into a regular code and we managed to carry on, by alternately long and short taps, quite lucid conversations. Once to our fright the Governor of the bastion, Chkoni, caught us at this forbidden game and threatened us, if it happened again, with the dark cell, a place of unknown horrors, as we knew, for we had listened to the groans and cries of the former police chief Belezky while he suffered there. After the warning of Chkoni Mme. Soukhomlinoff and I communicated with each other only in the middle of the night when the snores of the soldiers in the corridors guaranteed a degree of safety. Without these cautiously tapped-out conversations I really do not know how I should have lived and kept sane.

The cough which had been afflicting me grew worse rather than better and the only relief that was offered me was a primitive kind of cupping which did the cough no good but covered my chest with black and blue bruises. Finally, at the request of the sanitary soldier who had done the cupping, the prison doctor was sent for. This man, whose name was Serebrianikoff, was one of the most dreadful persons I ever came in contact with. He had a red, malicious face, his clothes and person were revoltingly dirty, and to increase their effect he wore on his bulging waistcoat a huge red bow, emblem of his revolutionary ardor. When he came into my cell he literally tore the clothes from my back in a pretended examination, then turning to the soldiers in the doorway he shouted: "This woman is the worst of the whole lot; an absolute idiot from a life of vice." Slapping me on one cheek and then on the other, he began to ask me questions which I cannot repeat here of my alleged orgies with Rasputine, with Nicholas and "Alice" as he called the Empress. Even the soldiers looked disgusted and I shuddered away from him sick with repulsion. That night I was so far gone physically and mentally that I could not answer Mme. Soukhomlinoff when she tapped on the wall. All I could do was to cough and shiver and in an incoherent, half mad fashion pray: "My God, my God, hast Thou forsaken me?"

The next morning the soldier who brought my hot water and bread thought me dying and insisted in sending again for the unspeakable Serebrianikoff, although I begged him not to. "Send a woman, I implore you," I whispered. But there was no woman to send, and the prison doctor came instead. Declaring that I was merely shamming, this brute again struck me in the face and left saying: "I'll punish you for this. There'll be no exercise for you for two weeks after you think yourself well enough to go out." He kept his word, and for two weeks after I ceased to be acutely ill I remained all day in my cell weeping for the clean air and a sight of the blue sky. Little trickles of pale sunlight were beginning to steal through my barred windows, the cold was less intense and I knew that outside, in the world of freedom, the spring had come.

One little bit of good news came at this time. Women wardresses had been appointed to look after the special needs of the women prisoners. Two attendants from a women's prison were the first to arrive, but they were so shocked at the conditions they found in the fortress that they refused to stay. They were replaced by others, one a saucy young person whose sole energies went into flirtations with the soldiers, and an older woman with melancholy dark eyes and the best and kindest of hearts. I cannot tell her name because if she is still alive and in Russia she must be in the employ of the Bolsheviki. I will call her simply the Woman. Her kindness to me I can never repay, but at least I shall never forget it, especially since I knew that every kind act she did was at her own personal risk. The Woman was on duty only until nine o'clock at night and was never allowed to enter my cell alone. Yet she often managed cleverly to follow slowly when she and the guard left the cell, and she frequently dropped on the floor behind her little pieces of sausage, chocolate, or bread nearly white. In the cell we dared not talk, but when she took me to the bath house we exchanged whispered conversations, and through her I got a little news of the exciting events of the time. The Provisional Government was tottering and the star of Kerensky was rising rapidly. The Imperial Family were still at Tsarskoe Selo, prisoners but alive, and that knowledge gave me a new impulse to live.

I must record one especially kind act my new friend did in my behalf. Easter Sunday came, and sitting on my hard bed I ventured to sing softly a verse or two of a well-remembered Easter hymn. On the Good Friday preceding we had been allowed to leave our cells one by one under guard and to confess to a good old priest, whose distress at our sorry plight so moved him that he heard our confessions with great tears in his eyes. Earnestly this old priest had begged Kerensky to allow him to visit prisoners in their cells and do what he could for their comfort, but Kerensky curtly refused.

I was thinking of him on this Easter morning. The soldiers had been running through the corridors calling to one another, perhaps in jest, perhaps as a matter of habit, the Russian greeting: "Kristos Voskrese," Christ is risen, to which the response is: "Voistino Voskrese," He is risen indeed. I could see that the soldiers had plates of the sugary cheese which everybody eats at Easter and which some of the prisoners received. Not I, because I was considered too wicked, too vile. Nevertheless, because of the trickle of sunshine that stole through the bars of my window, and because the old priest had really given me great comfort, I began to sing. Instantly the soldiers outside commanded me rudely to keep silent. It was too much. I laid my head down on the rags that formed my pillow and began to cry miserably. Then my hand strayed under the pillow, touching something. It was a little red Easter egg left there by the Woman, to make me feel that even in that place I was not entirely friendless. Never did a gift come as such a joyful surprise. I hugged it to my heart, kissed it and thanked God.

I was not forsaken. Indeed the worst was already passed for me, for the next day I was told that on every Friday after I was to receive a visit from my parents, whom I had feared I was never to see again on earth.

CHAPTER XVII

VISITORS in prison! Who but one who has spent days and nights of anguished loneliness behind bolted doors can possibly imagine the joy of such anticipation? I looked forward, almost as toward freedom itself, to the first Friday when I should see my beloved parents. I pictured myself running forward to embrace them, I could see my father's kind and loving smile, my mother's blue eyes full of happy tears. How we would sit, hand in hand, and talk over all that had happened since our parting! They would bring me news, messages, perhaps even letters from those other captives in Tsarskoe Selo. I should hear that the children were well again and the Empress's deepest anxieties were removed.

Alas! the harsh reality of my foolish dreams. When the day came I limped, between armed soldiers, through the long, gray corridors to the visitors' room, and there at the end of a long wooden table which divided us like an impassable gulf I saw my mother. There was no embrace allowed, not even a touch of hands. My mother tried to smile, tried to look at me with the love I craved, but in spite of herself her face paled and an expression of horror congealed her features. I stood there before her white with the pasty whiteness of prison, my uncombed, unkempt hair hanging about my shoulders, my dress dirty and wrinkled and an unhealed cut ploughing a bloody furrow across my forehead. To the question she dared not ask I touched the ugly wound and told her it was nothing, nothing. I could have told her that a soldier named Izotov, in a fit of animal temper, had knocked me against the edge of the cell door, and that the cut had received absolutely no attention since. Had we been alone I should have wept the whole story out on her breast, but we were not alone. Standing over us like inquisitors were the Procureur of Petrograd and the terrible Chkoni, governor of the Troubetskoy Bastion, and afterwards governor of the fortress itself. Ten minutes only were allowed us, and at the end of eight fleeting minutes Chkoni, watch in hand, roared out: "Two minutes left. Finish your talk." But we had no talk. Sobs choked our words, the few commonplace words that in such circumstances can be spoken. We could only bid each other be brave and trust in God's mercy. We could but gaze and gaze at each other through streaming tears. Then they separated us.

When the next Friday came I resolved to make myself a little more presentable. I had no mirror but I begged the Woman to loan me a small, cracked fragment. They had taken away all my toilet articles and every single hairpin, but the Woman gave me two hairpins of her own and, combing my hair with my fingers I arranged it more or less neatly. Every day I washed and cared for the cut on my forehead and when the visiting hour at last arrived I fancied that I looked rather more like myself. This time the precious ten minutes were spent with my father, and because he had been prepared in advance for the wretched object his daughter had become our brief interview was less emotional than that of the preceding Friday. Brave and erect my father held himself before those brutal jailers, and my heart glowed with love and pride to see him. We managed to exchange a few sentences and my father told me that he had obtained permission to send me money to buy tea and a few other comforts. He told me that he and my mother had waited three hours to see me and because it had been ruled that they could not both be admitted on the same day that my mother was standing close to the door of the next room just to catch the faint sound of my voice. These words roused Chkoni to a perfect fury. "So!" He fairly yelled. "But I'll spoil that game," and rushing out he slammed the door between the two rooms. My father flushed crimson but he spoke no word nor, of course, did I. A single protest might have meant punishment for me, and for us all no more visits.

I saw my father only three times, my mother a little oftener, as her health was the better of the two. The money my father sent me did not reach me except in very minute sums. By far the greater part of it was kept by the jailers, and gambled away. Not satisfied with that, the men warned my father that nothing except payment to the prison heads would save me from death, or worse still from assault by the soldiers. My father had long ago been deprived of his income, but he and my mother sold some valuables and gave it to the blackmailers who wanted it only for more gambling. Their sacrifice gave my parents a little

peace of mind, but it did not save me from three of
the most horrible nights I spent in the fortress. On
each of these nights my cell was invaded by drunken
soldiers who threatened me with unspeakable things.
On the first occasion I simply groveled on the wet floor
and prayed the man, in the name of his mother and
mine, to let me alone, and, drunk as he was, my words
actually penetrated his dark soul and shamed it. The
next men were less drunk but were far more bestial.
At the sight of them I threw myself against the wall
and pounded frantically, screaming at the top of my
lungs. Mme. Soukhomlinoff heard and understood.
She screamed too, frightfully, and with all her might
shook the heavy door of her cell. This brought the
guard and once-more I was saved. The third time I
was so paralyzed with fright that I could not scream.
I simply fell on my knees, holding up my little ikon,
and begged like a trapped animal. The man hesitated
a moment, spat on me contemptuously, and left. The
next day, half dead with shame and fear, I managed
to tell the Woman all that had passed. Indignantly
she went to the Governor of the fortress, and after
that even I, "the worst woman in prison," was spared
the ultimate insult.

Although we could not know it, things were gradually changing for the better in the fortress. A little
physical improvement was apparent. The cold had
lessened and in our short walks in the prison yard we
could see that lovely spring, with its fresh green leaves
and springing flowers, had come to stay. I remember
one day seeing in the grass a little yellow flower. It
may have been a buttercup or a dandelion or some-

thing else we ordinarily call weeds, but to my eyes it was an exquisite thing. Audaciously I stooped and picked it, hiding it quickly in the bosom of my dress. The next visiting day I showed it to my father and dropped it on the table. On leaving the room he contrived to get hold of it and after his death in 1918 I found it, carefully preserved among his private papers. I never picked another flower in that prison yard, although once I tried. But this time a guard caught me, and struck the flower from my hand with the end of his rifle.

Things were improving under the surface, but aside from the welcome change in the weather conditions seemed for a time no better. In the cell adjoining that of Mme. Soukhomlinoff was my old friend General Voyeikoff, who was tortured almost as pitilessly as myself. My heart ached for him. In cell 69 was for some time the police detective Manouiloff, but when he was removed to another prison the writer Kolichko was placed in the cell. Kolichko, poor wretch, was so overcome by his arrest and imprisonment that during the first nights he sobbed so long and bitterly that I found it impossible to sleep. I was so unhappy that I began to pray for death, and once I even resolved to end my life. I had no weapon but a rusty needle which I had picked up and carefully concealed, but I had heard somewhere that there was a spot at the base of the brain which if punctured ever so little would cause death. Before seeking that spot I felt that I must say adieu to my brave little friend Mme. Soukhomlinoff, and so softly I rapped out a farewell message on the wall. Her quick mind instantly divined my intention and without losing any time she sent for the Woman and my rusty needle was taken away from me.

It began to be sultry in the Troubetskoy Bastion and the air in the cells became thick and foul. My small window, which looked out on a narrow court and a high wall, admitted little light and no breeze at all. I used to climb painfully up on the iron shelf which did duty for a table and pressing my face close to the bars I breathed in all the air possible. Instead of seeking the warm corner of my cell I now sat for hours together with my body against the wettest and coldest stones. My despondency increased every day, and I almost ceased to pray or to believe that the universe held any God to whom the prayers of captives could ascend. Yet all the time God was sending me help.

One day a soldier came to my cell and roughly bade me get up and go with two guards for examination. Not knowing exactly what that meant, I rose from my cot and followed the men to a room in the fortress where the High Commission of Inquiry appointed by Kerensky was then in session. Bewildered by the sudden transition from the bastion to a room full of comfortable furniture, and almost blinded by the brilliant light and sunshine, I had all I could do to answer their few inconsequential questions. I have described this first examination in another chapter, and I shall not repeat it here. It was so foolish that afterwards in my hot and ill-smelling cell I actually found myself laughing, and it had been a long time since I had laughed. Judge Roudneff, the only one of the com-

mission who showed himself fair-minded or even
capable of just judgment, was present at the inquiry,
but I do not think he said a word. Afterwards he was
charged with full responsibility of my case, and I appeared before him no less than fifteen times. At the
close of the first of these personal interviews I thanked
Judge Roudneff warmly. Astonished, he asked: "For
what do you thank me?" And I answered: "For the
happiness of four whole hours of sitting in a room
with a window, and through it a glimpse of green
trees." He did not reply except with a kind and sympathetic look, but I knew that his heart was touched,
and that he received a new conception of what life
meant to a prisoner.

Better things still were to come. Without our being
aware of it the revolutionary mania had begun to sub-
side a little and those men among our guards who had
once been clean and decent were now getting back to
their normal state of mind. Poor soldiers! Never
let me forget that they were not to blame for the tor-
ments they inflicted on me and other prisoners. It was
not they who invented the black calumnies that made
me seem a creature undeserving of mercy or any
clemency. It was not they who fashioned the cross
on which I was crucified. The soldiers did only what
they were incited to do by men and women far above
them, people who conspired to crush me that they
might crush the Empress. The soldiers I forgive, but
I cannot yet forgive those others. The fate of the
Imperial Family, the ruin of Russia, is on their souls.
For what they did they have never shown any penitence, but those rough soldiers in the fortress re-

pented and did what they could in atonement. One
of the head guards was a man, handsome in a rustic
sort of fashion, who at first had treated me with great
insolence. One morning this man opened my door,
hesitated for a moment, and then said in a low voice:
"I am very sorry for you. Please take this," and
vanished. "This" was an apple and a small piece of
white bread. Another morning the soldier who
brought my breakfast spoke in a grumbling aside but
loudly enough for me to hear: "What idiocy to keep a
poor sick woman in this place." One night the window
in my cell door was pushed aside and in a trembling
voice someone begged me to give him my hand. Tears
fell on it while the unseen friend told me that he was
a boy from Samara, and that it broke his heart to see
women caged like beasts in such holes. He must have
had a good mother, that boy. Perhaps they all had,
for it became almost a habit for men passing through
my corridor to slip me bits of bread, sausage, or sugar.

The most wonderful piece of good fortune came
through the soldier in charge of the prison library.
This man visited my cell one day, and after giving me
a keen look which I could not understand he laid the
library catalogue on my cot and went out. I had little
interest in the dull books at our disposal, but when one
sits hours in utter idleness he makes occupation out of
almost nothing. I opened the catalogue and turned
the leaves. To my astonishment out fell a folded
paper. Cautiously I opened it and read these words:
"Dear Anushka, I am sorry for you. If you have five
rubles I can get a letter to your mother." For a long
time after the incriminating paper had been destroyed

I sat trembling in doubt and foreboding. I had barely five rubles, and if I gave them would they be gambled away? Was the letter a trap? Was it merely an effort to get me into trouble? I did not know, but on a bit of blank paper left in the catalogue I wrote with my stub of a pencil: "I have suffered so much already that I cannot believe that you wish to do me any more harm." Folding the five rubles and the paper into a tiny note, I tucked it into the catalogue and waited. After a while the librarian returned, and this time I read in his silent gaze that he was asking for my confidence. The next day he came back and again left the catalogue on my bed. This time I seized it eagerly and shook its leaves. A letter from my mother dropped out, a short letter, for she had been given only a few minutes to write, but I read and reread it until I knew every word by heart.

Then began a smuggled correspondence with my father and mother, they gladly giving money to the men who risked their own liberty by carrying the letters back and forth. The letters reached me in prison books, in the sheets of my bed, under the tin basin which held my food, and once even in a soldier's sock dropped carelessly on the floor. In this sock was concealed a note from Lili Dehn, free now and in correspondence with the family at Tsarskoe Selo. There was a slip of paper enclosed with a tiny white flower glued to it, and in the Empress's handwriting: "God keep you." Another precious souvenir of the Empress sent me by my mother was a little moonstone ring long ago given me at Tsarskoe. Tearing a rag from the lining of my coat, I made a bag for this jewel, and begging a safety pin from the Woman, I pinned it inside my dress. The poor librarian. This was the last favor he ever did me, for falling under the suspicion of the Governor, he was abruptly discharged. The letters, however, had done me so much good that I was in every way better and more cheerful. I felt in touch with the world again. I knew in a general way what was going on, and though not all the news was pleasant it gave me a sense of being alive and not altogether hopeless. I knew now what tireless efforts were being made in my behalf, and I felt that in the end something must come of them. My parents had done everything humanly possible to move Kerensky but without any definite success. The first appointment with him was made through his secretary Chalpern, and although my parents were naturally exactly on time Kerensky kept them waiting for two hours. When at last they were received my parents were told that the Empress Alexandra Feodorovna, Rasputine, and Viroubova were responsible for the Revolution and would have to suffer for it. My parents had heard this before, but it was new to them to hear from Kerensky that he knew that I had had a great many diamonds from the Archbishop Pitirim and for that and other reasons nothing could be done for me. Later he softened a little and ended the interview by promising that my whole affair would be investigated. My parents then contrived an interview with the minister of Justice, Pereverzeff. They made two appointments in fact, for the first one Pereverzeff deliberately broke, going out for the day while my parents sat waiting in an ante-room. The next time my mother went to the Ministry she was received and was civilly treated. Pereverzeff also promised that a fair investigation would be made. By this time the Special Commission of Inquiry was sitting and my mother managed to see the president, Mouravieff. She took with her a letter from his brother to me before the abdication of the Emperor. In this letter I was warned of plots against me and was advised to leave the palace. I had replied to this letter, and my mother had a copy of my reply. I had written that I would never leave the Empress. My conscience was clean before God and man and I would remain to the end where God had placed me. I was astonished that a soldier should advise me to run away from a battlefield. Mouravieff who at first had been very harsh, changed after reading the letters. He even asked my mother to allow him to read them to the commission. They were significant, he said. As soon as my case had been referred to Judge Roudneff he called my parents to the Winter Palace, where he had his office, and talked with them, asking a great many questions, for nearly four hours. In this examination, for it was really that, my father and mother were allowed for the first time to defend me, to make explanations of obscure charges, to tell my life story to the man who was to judge me. No one else gave them such an opportunity, not even the Georgian deputy Cheidze, then very prominent in the Petrograd Soviet. Cheidze was kind and said that he would do anything in his power to help me to get justice, but I do not think he ever did anything. Members of the Provisional Government, Rodzianko and

Lvoff, to whom, while they were still in power, my parents had written begging to be received, never even replied to the letters.

One day, sitting in my cell and remembering what had been written me in the smuggled letters, another wonderful thing happened. In the noon meal of fish soup which I must eat or starve I found a large piece of really decent meat. I ate it greedily, of course, and the next day I ate another piece which had mysteriously arrived. I took the first opportunity to ask the Woman where the food came from, and she told me that it was a cook, a poor man whose duty it was to carry food to our bastion. He too pitied me, she said, and she thought he might be willing to run almost any risk for me. So almost at once I was again in correspondence with my parents. This cook did more than carry letters, the brave man. He brought me food, chocolates, clean clothes, linen, stockings, and even a fresh frock. Growing bolder, he ventured regularly to take away my soiled linen and to replace it with clean things. All during those months in the fortress I had washed my linen and stockings in cold water, without soap, and in the night had hung them up in the warm corner on a hook improvised from a broken hairpin. Of course they were never clean, nor even, when I put them on, very dry, and now they were stiff with dirt. Can anyone imagine what it was to me to feel a clean, soft, smooth chemise against my skin?

I am sure the cook could never have done so much for me had not the guards closed their eyes to his activities. They were nearly all friendly now, and used to talk with me through the window in my door.

In spring a number of pigeons flocked around the fortress and their constant sobbing voices got on my nerves. I spoke of this to one soldier who expressed surprise. "I was shut up here once," he said, "under the old Government, and I didn't find the birds bad at all. I used to feed them through the window." "You had a window in your cell," I exclaimed. "Then it couldn't have been as bad as this." And he assured me that it wasn't as bad under the Autocracy as under the beneficent Provisional Government and the Soviet. The prisoners had much better food and they could exercise two hours a day in the open.

Another prisoner of the Tsar's government, a non-commissioned officer named Diki, who had been very harsh to me in the beginning, now showed me kindness. Instead of robbing me, as of old, of every little privilege, he began to allow me an extra five minutes or so in the courtyard, he, too, saying that in the old days prisoners were better treated. Another of the guards in the courtyards, a man whom I had bitterly hated, and with cause, told the Woman that he wanted to speak to me. Afterwards while walking he approached me and I looked into his coarse face, deeply pitted with smallpox, and listened in fear at what he might have to say. Stammeringly he told me that he had just returned from a leave spent in his home in the Government of Saratoff. Visiting his sister's house, he was amazed to see, hanging under the ikon in the corner of the room, a photograph of me. "What!" he had exclaimed. "Do you have that shameless woman's picture in your house?" Whereupon his brother-in-law retorted: "Never dare to speak against her who was like a mother to me for two years in Tsarskoe. I was in her own hospital in the end, and it was like Heaven." The brother-in-law had charged the guard with all kinds of messages to me, telling him that they prayed for me daily in his family and hoped for my release. "Forgive me for being unjust to you," said the poor soldier, and offered me his hand. This was the first news I had of my hospital, and I learned with joy that the Provisional Government had not closed it. Later I heard that the Government had not only carried on my work but had added five new buildings. None of my nurses or orderlies had left, though their openly expressed faith in me might easily have secured their dismissal. Some of the invalids had petitioned the Duma for my release, and another group, indignant because a revolutionary newspaper declined to publish their letter refuting the usual slanders about me, wanted to leave the hospital long enough to blow up the office building! They were good at heart, those misguided Russian soldiers, those poor ignorant children. I know them, and whatever they have been forced to do in these years of horror, I still believe them sound and good of soul. In the last days of my imprisonment in Peter and Paul the guards did not even lock my cell door. They used to linger and talk, and sometimes they brought paper and pencils that I might make sketches of them to take home. I was rather clever with a pencil in those days.

CHAPTER XVIII

THE prison had changed, and except for an occasional riot or a fight between two drinking soldiers, it was almost peaceful. For now there was a man attached to the fortress, a man so brave and kind, and above all so commanding that terrors fled before him—Dr. Ivan Manouchine. The gratitude and respect with which I write his name cannot be expressed in words. It was on the 23rd of April, the name day of the Empress, ever a day of memories to me, that this good man came into the house of pain where lay the prisoners of the Provisional Government. A few weeks before this the soldiers, gradually recovering from their first revolutionary blood lust, had begun to revolt against the needless brutality of the prison doctor, Serebrianikoff, and had finally sent in to the all powerful Kerensky a request for his demission. In those days Kerensky, whose ambition to be at the head of the government was maturing, made a special point of granting soldiers' petitions, and he really consented to replace Serebrianikoff with a physician of reputation. From the point of view of the Duma Dr. Manouchine was entirely a safe man to be appointed. He was a republican in politics, and he conformed to the popular superstition of "dark forces" surrounding the court. But what the Duma did not know about Dr. Manouchine was that he had a heart of gold and a mind that was ruled not by any political party but by principles of right and justice.

When the new prison doctor first came into my cell, accompanied by the retiring man looking frightened and ill at ease, I was lying on my cot in a mood of unusual rebellion. In a quiet, professional voice he asked me how I felt, and when he examined my poor chest and saw it black and blue and swollen from the clumsy cupping it had received, he frowned with displeasure. He gave some quick directions for my relief and in a gentle tone assured me that he intended to visit the bastion every day. It was the first time in many long weeks that I had been spoken to by the type of man we call a gentleman, and after the door closed behind him something in my frozen heart seemed to melt like icicles in the sun. Almost with the faith of childhood I fell on my knees and prayed, and after that I lay down and slept for several hours.

Every day soon after the booming of the noonday gun he came and every one among us stood up as close as possible to the cell doors, waiting to catch the first sound of his voice as he came down the corridor. At every door he stopped and asked the health of the prisoner. To him they were not prisoners but patients, and he treated them with all the skill and, above all, the courtesy he would have accorded the richest and most powerful of his patients. He examined our food and pronounced it entirely unsuited to our needs. He did not stop there, but in the end succeeded in greatly improving the ration and supplementing it for the sick with milk and eggs. How he did it in the Russia of those days I cannot imagine. I only know that Dr. Manouchine had a will of steel, and against that will and the staunch uprightness of his character malice and fanaticism broke like waves against a rock.   Little by little Dr. Manouchine instituted other reforms.   The prisoners now received at least a part of the money furnished by their friends outside, and once a week the non-commissioned officer Diki went through the prison answering requests for such necessities as soap, tooth powder, and paper on which petitions to the Governor of the fortress might be written.   Often when a prisoner lacked money to pay for these things the doctor supplied it out of .his own pocket.

Meanwhile my examinations under the stern but just commissioner Roudneff were going on.   Weary under the long and apparently pointless inquisition, I asked Dr. Manouchine one day how much longer he thought they intended to torment me.   His reply was grave. "Not long, I think.   But before it is over you may have to undergo a still more trying ordeal."   A few day later he came to my cell alone; that is, he resolutely closed the door between us and his usual escort of soldiers, and told me in his kindest manner that the Special Commission of Inquiry had almost concluded that the charges against me were without foundation. One more proof, however, was necessary, a physician's sworn statement that the hideous accusations of vice made by enemies of the Emperor and Empress and their closest friends were false.   Would I, for my own sake, for the sake of the Imperial Family, submit to a medical examination?   Without at all knowing what was implied I gave an instant but rather frightened

consent to any examination he thought necessary. . . .
It was a terrible ordeal for a woman to live through.
Most of the questions asked me were of a nature which
appalled me, and yet were beyond my understanding.
I cannot here repeat even the least of them. I can only
say that they opened up to me an abyss of wickedness
and sin which I had not dreamed existed in the human
soul. . . . At the end of an hour—or many hours—
of trial, I lay on my bed, hands clasped over my eyes,
spent, exhausted, utterly incapable of speech. Up to
the very end Dr. Manouchine's manner had been that
of a physician, but now that it was over it was a friend
beyond anything human and sympathetic who laid his
hand on my quivering shoulder and said: "This clears
you absolutely. They will take my word for it."

Towards the end of May, a hot and wearying season, the fortress was visited by the head of the Provisional Government's Commission of Inquiry, a pom-
pous man, yet in his cautious way, rather kindly. Pausing before my cell, he told me that no crime had been
fastened upon me and that I might hope soon to be
transferred to a better place. Hope gave me new life
momentarily, but as the days dragged on my hope gave
way to bitter unbelief. My health always since my
arrest indifferent, now began to decline and I could see
that the doctor was seriously concerned for me. He
came to the prison only four times a week now, and
what ages seemed to elapse between his visits. All I
had left of courage his voice and ministrations gave
me.

One hot June day I was aroused from my sick
lethargy by the tramping of heavy boots on the stones

of the corridor. The heavy cell door swung open and I saw a crowd of strange men, several of whom unceremoniously invaded my cell and began an examination of my poor effects. Frightened, I watched them as they disdainfully picked up and threw aside the few rags a prisoner is allowed, but my fears were allayed when I saw in the background the tall figure of the doctor. "Do not be afraid, Anna Alexandrovna," he said. "This is only a committee of revision of prisoners." Later I heard him say to the committee: "This woman may have only a few days to live. If you are willing you may take on yourselves the responsibility of her death. As a physician I refuse to do so."

The next day he whispered to me that he was confident that I would be taken away, but that my release might be delayed a little because of renewed riots among the prison guards. He did not know where I was to be taken, and I feared it would be the Women's Prison, which the Woman had told me was almost as bad as the Troubetskoy Bastion. But soon I was relieved of that nightmare, for the doctor came again bringing me the good news that I should probably be taken to the House of Detention in a pleasant neighborhood on the other side of the river. In groups the friendly soldiers came to say good-bye and to assure me that even should the mutinous guards oppose my going they would see to it that I got safely way. Days went by, sleepless nights, and still no order of release arrived. I became almost hysterical with suspense. I gave way to dreadful fits of weeping until even the doctor grew stern and bade me control myself. I felt like a mouse under the teasing claws of a cat, and control was difficult even after I learned that the doctor had persuaded some members of the central committee of the Petrograd Soviet to visit the fortress and to reason with the mutinous guards.

Almost the last day of June, at six in the evening, I was standing barefooted and half dressed against the cool, wet wall of my cell thinking of my mother who, the·day before, had visited me. Her face was brighter than usual and she had said to me: "The next time we meet it may be in better circumstances" At the moment my door opened and the hated Chkoni appeared. "Well," he said, with his usual sneer, "did you have hysterics after seeing your mother?" "Certainly not," I replied coldly. "No?" he commented, "I thought you might because to-morrow or the next day they may take you away." I fell against the wall too overcome to speak, too blind to see the hands of the guard pressing my limp hand in congratulation. To-morrow or next day! The words repeated themselves in my brain countless times. But I was not even to wait until to-morrow, though Chkoni evidently wished me to think so. I heard the voice of the younger and less familiar wardress: "Dress yourself quickly. The doctor is bringing a deputation from the Soviet." I had nothing to put on except my ragged shoes and a torn gray woolen jacket, but these I rapidly seized while the wardress picked up and made a bundle of my small belongings. On the opposite wall I heard brave Mme. Soukhomlinoff rapping out a farewell message to which I responded as well as I could. Then the deputation arrived, and the doctor. There was some confused talk. . . . I cannot remember a word. . . .

I felt myself picked up and carried down the winding corridors. The great door of the bastion rolled open and we passed out into the cool, delicious evening air. There was a motor car into which I was lifted, another car into which the doctor climbed, there were soldiers, some friendly, some seemingly determined that the cars should not leave the courtyard. I remember very little until we drove out of the gates and over the Troizky Bridge. The wind, the brilliant twilight, the sight of water and the blue sky, blinded me so that I had to cover my face with both hands.

Within a short time the cars stopped at the Detention House in the Fourshkatskaia Ulitza, and I was carried into the office of the commissioner. He was an officer, rather short in stature, but dignified and efficient. Offering me his hand, he asked me if I would be seated while he made out the necessary papers. I had time to see that the House of Detention promised to be quite different from a prison. Indeed the soldiers of this house would not even permit the entrance of the fortress guards who had come with me. As if he divined that I was too weak to walk upstairs the commissioner gave orders that I was to be carried. It was into a large, light, clean room that they took me, and at my exclamation of joy at sight of windows the soldiers laughed heartily. But the doctor silenced them. "Go," he said, "see that her parents are telephoned, and send a woman to bathe and dress her." His own arms lifted me from the chair on which I half sat, half lay. On a bed softer and cooler than even existed in my memory he laid me, said good night, and gently left the room.

CHAPTER XIX

I SPENT a happy and peaceful month in the Detention House, the only disturbing event being the so-called July Revolution, the first serious attempt of Lenine's party to seize the government. The Soviet already transcended in power the old Provisional Government, most of whose original members had by this time disappeared from politics. Kerensky was premier, nominally, but only because a remnant of the Russian Army still resisted the separate peace propaganda and remained on duty at the front.

Persons in the Detention House were prisoners in the sense that they were under guard and were not allowed to leave the house. The guards were complacent, though, and visiting between the rooms was permitted. I soon found that I was the only woman in the place, and that some of the men there had suffered greater tortures than I. There were between eighty and ninety officers, almost the last remnant of the garrison of Kronstadt where in the first days of the Revolution the soldiers went quite mad and murdered, in ways too horrible to relate, a great many officers, and even young naval cadets against whom they could have had no possible grudge. The officers in the Detention House were in a sad state of body and mind. We talked together sometimes in the dining room, and learning that they longed for the consolation of Holy

263

Communion, I remembered that my hospital in Tsarskoe Selo possessed a movable altar and holy vessels. With the consent of Nadjaroff, commandant of the Detention House, the altar and my own priest were brought from Tsarskoe and the sacred ceremony was twice celebrated, the last time on July 29, my birthday.

I ought to say of the commandant Nadjaroff that he was an excellent man, kind to the prisoners, and conscientious in his work. The poor man had one fatal weakness, gambling. So strong a hold had this vice on an otherwise good man that when his money ran short he was not above borrowing and even begging from the prisoners and their friends. It seems almost too bad to record this blot on the character of a man who was kind and courteous to me, but I am trying to give the psychology as well as to portray the events of the Russian Revolution, and I must emphasize the fact that it was the weakness and self-indulgence of the people themselves that made the Revolution and its frightful aftermath possible.

From my first day in the Detention House I began to recover my health and my self-control. My windows were not barred, and through the open casement I feasted my eyes on the beauty of grass and trees, on the familiar little church of Sts. Kosma and Damian which stood almost opposite, and, strangest of all to me, of people walking or driving through the streets below. It took a few days for me to get used to a normal state of life, and at first, when night grew near, I was seized with such nervousness that they had to let a maid sleep in the room with me. As the fresh air and sunshine began to bring color to my face and I felt strength returning to my limbs I forgot my fears, and became something like the woman I had been before I was caged like a beast in the Fortress of Peter and Paul. Visitors were admitted both morning and afternoon, and I had the happiness of talking privately with my father and mother and with friends who still remained faithful. They brought me clothes, toilet articles, books, flowers, writing materials, and, best of all, news of what had happened during the months of my imprisonment. I learned of the rapid disintegration of the army under the weak and ineffectual Provisional Government, the tottering state of Kerensky's régime, and the threatening domination of the Soviets. What was in store for Russia no one knew, happily for Russians. Of the fall of the Soviets and the rise of Bolshevism no one yet had any premonition. The radical element was already in control, and there was a great deal of threatening talk of shooting the Emperor. However, the Imperial Family was still alive and in Tsarskoe Selo, which was as much as I had dared to hope.

Of the events of the July Revolution, the forerunner of the Bolshevist triumph of November, 1917, I know rather less than others who were at full liberty during that terrible week. It was about the 18th of the month, a brilliant summer day, when I was startled by long-continued shouting and bellowing of soldiers in a caserne not far from the house. In great excitement the men were running in and out of the yard calling on the *tovarishi* to arm themselves and join the uprising. As if by magic the streets filled with rough-looking people, singing wild songs, waving their arms, and forming processions behind huge scarlet banners on which I could read such inscriptions as "Down with the War!" "Down with the Provisional Government!" An endless line of these paraders passed and repassed, dirty, disorderly soldiers, equally dirty factory workers, yelling like crazed animals. Once in a while a gray motor truck would dash through the street, laden with shouting men and boys, rifles, and machine guns. In the distance we could hear shots and the ripping noise of the machine guns.

Of course we were all horribly frightened, especially the officers from Kronstadt, who knew that in case of invasion not one of them would be left alive. We were all advised to leave our rooms and take refuge in the corridors, as at any time the rioters might begin firing through the windows. But we were not out of danger even there because many of the guards openly sympathized with the rioters, and the head guard was so jubilant over the course of events that he went around boasting that he was quite prepared to surrender the house and all its inmates at the first demand of the Revolutionists. Some of the guards were better than this man, and one of them, a wearer of the St. George cross, said that in case of trouble he would try to get me to his sister's house, where I would be perfectly safe. For two nights nobody slept or even undressed. In the room next to mine was lodged old General Belaieff, former War Minister, whom imprisonment had left a sad wreck. He, like the other officers, fully expected death, and I found myself in the novel rôle of a cool and collected comforter. I, who

GRAND DUCHESSES OLGA, TATIANA, ANASTASIE, AND MARIE, PRISONERS AT TSARSKOE SELO, 1917.

ANNA VIROUBOVA.

A Photograph Taken Shortly after Her Release from the Fortress of
Peter and Paul, Petrograd.

had lately been afraid to sleep in a room by myself, now went from one old soldier to another urging them to keep up hope. The days passed, and the firing came no nearer, and within a week troops summoned from the front took possession of the city.

My examination under the High Commissioner Roudneff not being entirely finished, he came once or twice to the Detention House bringing with him on one occasion Korinsky, Procurator of Petrograd, a courteous gentleman, who at parting expressed a hope that I would soon be free. A few days later, August 5, if I remember correctly, M. Korinsky himself telephoned that if my parents would call at his office they would be given my warrant of release. Alas, my parents happened to be in Terioke that day, but too impatient to wait until the morrow I telephoned my uncle Lachkereff, who immediately hastened to the Procurator's office for the coveted warrant. Trembling with excitement, I stood at my window with several of my good friends waiting the result of his errand. At six o'clock we heard a drosky driven at great speed over the cobbles, and as it came in sight we saw my uncle standing up and wildly waving the papers in his hand. "Free!" he called out. "Anna Alexandrovna, you are free!" The rest is confusion in my mind. There were laughter and sobs. People kissed and embraced me. I was in the drosky driving through Petrograd streets. I was in my uncle's house. The tea table was spread. It was like a dream.

After prison one gets used to freedom by slow degrees. It seems strange at first to be allowed to move about freely, to go to church, to walk, to drive, to go wherever one desires, through woods, along leafy country roads. Not that I was entirely free to go where I liked. I could not safely go to Tsarskoe Selo, even to my own house, which after my arrest had been taken over by the police, and not only ransacked for evidence against me, but looted of every valuable. It was my faithful old servant Berchik who gave me the details of the search. He, honest soul, who had been forty-five years in the service of my family, was offered ten thousand rubles if he would testify against the Empress and myself. On his indignant refusal the police arrested him, while they tore up the carpets and even the floors of my rooms, demanding of Berchik the whereabouts of secret passages to the palace, the private telegraph and telephone wires to Berlin, my hidden writing desks, and all sorts of nonsense. Especially were they anxious to discover my wine cellar, and when they found that I possessed none they were angry indeed. They took possession of all the letters and papers they could find, and at the end of the search ordered my cook to prepare them an elaborate supper. Then they left taking with them the silverware.

If I could not visit Tsarskoe and those whom I loved and longed to see, I could at least, and I did, hear from the Empress. Just before the family were sent to their exile one of the maids smuggled out a letter which reached me safely and which I quote here, suppressing only the most intimate and affectionate passages.

"I cannot write much," the letter began, "my heart is too full. I love you, we love you, thank you, bless you, kiss the wound on your forehead. . . . I cannot find words. . . . I know what will be your anguish with this great distance between us. They do not tell us where we go (we shall learn only on the tiain), nor for how long, but we think it is where you were last" (Tobolsk). "Beloved, the misery of leaving! Everything packed up, empty rooms, such pain, the home of twenty-three years. Yet you have suffered far more. Farewell. Somehow let me know you received this. We prayed long before the Virgin of Znomenia, and I remembered the last time it was on your bed My heart and soul are torn to go so far from home and from you To be for months without news is terrible. But God is merciful. He won't forsake you, and will bring us together again in sunny times. I fully believe it."

With the letter the Empress sent me a box of my jewels which she had carefully guarded, and I heard a fairly full account of how the summer had been spent. For a time she and the Emperor had been kept apart, being allowed to speak to each other only at table and in the presence of guards. Revolutionary agents tried every possible means of incriminating the Empress, whom they hated even more than the Emperor, but finally failing in their efforts they allowed the family to be together once more. The day after they were sent to Siberia the maid visited me again with the story of their departure. Kerensky personally arranged every detail, and intruded his presence for hours together on the unhappy family. Under his orders everything was made ready for a midnight journey but actually they did not leave the palace until six o'clock in the morning. All night the prisoners sat in their traveling clothes and wraps in the round hall of the palace. At five a courageous servant brought them fresh tea, which gave them a little comfort, especially

Alexei, who stood the night badly. They drove away from the palace with perfect serenity as if going on a holiday to Finland or the Crimea. Even the Revolutionary newspapers, with grudging admiration, had to admit this.

A day or two later Mr. Gibbs, Alexei's English tutor, came to see me, and he told me that although he was not permitted to accompany the Imperial Family with the other tutors, M. Gilliard and M. Petroff, he intended to follow them to Tobolsk. He took a photograph of me for the Empress, who was anxious to see for herself if the long imprisonment had impaired my health. As a matter of fact I was not very well just then, as I had something very like jaundice, so I am afraid my photograph was none too reassuring. At this time I was staying in the home of my sister's husband who was attached to the British Military Commission in Petrograd. It was a cool and comfortable apartment, and I should have been contented to stay on indefinitely. But one day my brother-in-law, in deep embarrassment, showed me a letter from his sister, who was expected on a visit. This lady expressed herself unwilling to live under the same roof with a person as notorious as myself, and I, equally unwilling to associate with her, moved back to my uncle's hospitable home. But even there I found no serenity. I had been acquitted of all the crimes charged against me by the Provisional Government, [1] but now the Government of Kerensky found new accusations to make of me. This time I was a counter-Revolutionist, and as papers served on me in the

[1] See Appendix B.

middle of the night of August 24 (Russian) ordered, I had to leave for an unknown destination within twenty-four hours. As I was without money and was really in need of a physician's care, my relatives began at once to petition every authority for a delay of at least twenty-four hours more. This was finally allowed, but two soldiers were immediately placed before my door and I was a prisoner in my uncle's apartment. Meanwhile my parents and friends continued to make every preparation for my comfort in exile, and two of my hospital staff, the director and a nurse, volunteered to go with me. The night before I left my poor parents stayed with me, none of us going to bed. Very early on a rainy morning two motor cars filled with police came for us. They were kind enough to let my parents accompany me almost to the Finnish side, and they explained that they had come so early because they feared street demonstrations.

At the station we found a miscellaneous company of alleged counter-Revolutionists including a few old acquaintances. Among these was former detective Manouiloff, a tall officer named Groten, the editor, Tanchevsky, and the curious little Siberian doctor Badmieff, with his equally curious wife and child and a young maid named Erika whom I came to know very well. Badmieff was the herb doctor who, it will be remembered, was supposed to purvey the deadly poisons which I was alleged to feed to the Tsarevitch. He was a small, round, shriveled man, excessively old— over a hundred, they said—and in appearance resembled a quaint carved Buddha out of an antiquarian shop. He had the smallest, blackest eyes imaginable, set in a face yellow and wrinkled, and his long, scraggly beard was as white as cotton. His wife, many years his junior, and his funny little child, Aida, were as Mongolian in appearance as himself. The maid, Erika, a girl of about eighteen, was not uncomely with her bright eyes and short, curly hair. All the "counter-Revolutionists" were herded together in one carriage, the one farthest from the engine, and in charge of us was a Jewish official of the Kerensky Government. At Terioke I parted with my father and mother, the train moving on quickly to the Finnish town of Belieovstrov. Here we were met by an enormous crowd of soldiers and working people, all hostile, demanding to see the dangerous counter-Revolutionists. Especially they demanded to see me, but I shrank back in my seat, fearing every moment that the shower of stones against the carriage would break the windows. But quickly the conductor's whistle was blown and the train moved beyond the reach of the mob.

Worse was to come. When we reached Rikimeaki we found waiting us a larger and a still more furious crowd. Our carriage was unfastened from the train and the mob rushed in yelling that we must all be given up and killed. "Give us the Grand Dukes!" they shouted. "Give us Gourko!" I sat with my face buried in the shoulder of my nursing sister fearing that my end had come. My fears were not imaginary, for several ruffians pitched on me shouting that they had found Gourko in women's clothes. Frantically the sister explained that I was not General Gourko but only a woman ill and lame. Refusing to believe her, they demanded that I be stripped, and I have no doubt that this would have happened had not a motor car opportunely dashed up carrying a sailor deputation from the Helsingfors Soviet. These men pushed their way into the carriage, and without ceremony booted the invaders out. One man, a tall, slender youth named Antonoff, made a speech at the top of his voice, commanding the mob to disperse and to leave things in the hands of the Soviet. So authoritatively did he speak that the crowd obeyed him and allowed our carriage to be attached to another train bound for Helsingfors. Antonoff remained with us, and in the friendliest fashion sat down beside me and bade me to be of good cheer. He did not know why we had been sent away from Petrograd, but the Soviet at Helsingfors, of which he was a member, had received a telegram, he thought directly from Kerensky, saying that we were being sent on, and when we arrived were to be placed under arrest. Doubtless there would be explanations, and after that we would surely be released. To my mind the thing seemed not quite so simple. Kerensky had sent us from Petrograd, but not to be imprisoned in Helsingfors. What he desired was that the mobs, notified of our arrival from his office, would kill us before we ever reached Helsingfors at all. No doubt he hoped at the same time to dispose of General Gourko and the Grand Dukes left in Petrograd. But Gourko was too clever for Kerensky, and made good his escape to Archangel, where he took refuge with the British Occupational Force. As for the Grand Dukes, they were, for some reason, at this time left undisturbed by the Revolutionists.

It was night when we reached Helsingfors and we found the station practically deserted. The main body of the prisoners were taken away into the darkness, but Antonoff said that I and the nurse should spend the night in a hospital adjoining the station. We climbed several flights of steep stairs and passed through wards crowded with blue-gowned sick soldiers and sailors, not one of whom offered us the slightest rudeness. A skilled Finnish nurse undressed me and put me to bed, but unhappily not for long. Scarcely had I composed myself to sleep when the door opened, the lights flashed up, and Antonoff, red and very angry, entered the room. He had gone to the Soviet authorities, confident that he could persuade them to let me remain in the hospital, at least until word came from Petrograd of our exact status. But they refused his request and ordered him to take me at once to the ship on which the other prisoners were confined. There being no appeal I dressed and limped down the long stairs to the street where a dense mob had assembled, shouting, threatening, crowding dangerously around the motor car. It is a horrible thing to hear a mob shrieking for one's blood. One feels like a cornered hare in the face of yelping hounds. With the strength of desperation I clung to the arm of Antonoff, who for all I knew might yield suddenly and throw me to the crowd. Unworthy thought, for the man held me firmly, all the time demanding that the people give room and let us reach the car. When they saw me in the car their fury seemed to redouble. "Daughter of the Romanoffs," they yelled, "how dare she ride in a motor car? Let her get out and walk." Standing up in the car Antonoff repeated his commands that the mob disperse, and slowly at first and then more rapidly we got away. We reached the distant water front, and I was taken from the car to a ship. Picture my astonishment when I found myself standing on the deck of the *Polar Star,* the light and beautiful yacht on which I had so often sailed in Finnish waters with the Imperial Family. With all the Imperial property the *Polar Star* had been confiscated by the Provisional Government, and it was but another sign of the changing times that the yacht had later been taken away from the Provisional Government and was now the property of the Soviets, being the *Zentrobalt,* or headquarters of the Baltic fleet.

From the deck I was hurried past the open door of the main dining salon, once a place of ceremony and good living, now a dingy, disordered apartment where crowds of illiterate workmen gathered to dispose of the rest of Russia's ruined fleet and the future of our unhappy country.[2] At least a hundred of these men were in the salon when I passed it first, and during the five days I spent on the yacht their voices seemed to go on in endless orations, ceaseless wrangling, twenty-four hours at a stretch. It was like nothing I can describe, like an ill-disciplined lunatic asylum. I was herded with the other "counter-Revolutionists" 'far below decks in what I conjectured had been the stokers' quarters. The stifling little cabins were filthy, like all the rest of the yacht, and they simply swarmed with vermin. It was so dark that night and day the electric lights burned, and I was thankful for that because

[2] Finland had not then separated from the old Russian Empire.

somehow the bright light seemed to be a kind of protection against the swarm of grimacing, obscene sailors who infested the place, amusing themselves with discussions as to when and how we were likely to be killed. During the whole of the first night Antonoff stood guard over us and warned the sailors that no murder could be done without authority from the Soviet. Over and over again they suggested that he leave the place, but he always replied firmly that he was responsible for the prisoners and could not go. Finally towards morning the sailors left, and afterwards we learned that their blood lust towards us was not merely simulated. They had gone directly from the yacht to the *Petropavlovsk,* the flagship of the fleet, and had killed every one of the old officers left on board.

Antonoff left us early in the morning, left us expecting to return, but he never did return nor did we ever see or hear of him again. Such sudden disappearances were common enough even in those early days of the Russian Revolution, before murder became the fine art into which it has since developed. Five days we remained on the *Polar Star,* very miserable in our vermin-infested quarters below decks, but mercifully allowed part of each day in the open air. They might have allowed us longer time on deck had it not been for the hostile crowds that constantly thronged the quays. My time was spent in the shelter of the deckhouse near the main salon, a spot where in the old days the Empress and I loved to sit with our books and work. Here five years before, when the Empress Dowager visited the yacht, I had taken a photograph of her with her arm around the shoulders of the Emperor, both smiling and happy in the sparkling light of the fjord. Every corner of the yacht had been exquisitely clean and white in those days. Dirty as the yacht's present crew appeared, I cannot say they starved their prisoners or were cruel to them. We had soup, meat, bread, and tea, luxurious fare compared to Peter and Paul. Our worst condition was suspense of mind as to our ultimate fate. At every change of guard we begged news from Petrograd, but always we received the same answer. The Kerensky Government gave no reason or justification for our arrest. Two of the sailors were especially friendly to me because, as they explained, they came from Rojdestino, our family estate near Moscow. "If we had known that you were going to be brought here," they said, "we might have done something. But now it is too late." That night I found in my cabin a tiny note, ill-spelled and badly written, warning me that all of us were about to be transferred to the Fortress of Sveaborg in the Bay of Helsingfors. "We are so sorry," the note concluded. Although it was unsigned, I knew the note must have been sent in kindness by one of the men from my old home. But at the prospect of another imprisonment my heart turned sick with dread.

Next evening came Ostrovsky, head of the Helsingfors Okhrana, accompanied by several members of the main committee of the Soviet. Ostrovsky was a very young man, scarcely eighteen I should judge, but he had fierce eyes and all the assurance of a born leader. Turning to my nurse, to Mme. Badmieff, Erika the maid, and her little Mongolian charge Aida, he said roughly that they were free but that all the rest would be taken at once to the fortress. In a sudden panic of alarm I threw myself into the arms of my nursing sister and begged her to accompany me. But she too was fear-stricken and drew back while all the men laughed heartlessly. "What's the difference?" asked Ostrovsky brutally. "You're all going to be shot anyhow." At which the dauntless Erika, putting Aida into her mother's arms, came over to me and tucking her hand under my arms said: "I'm not afraid. I'm going wherever the doctor goes and I'll stand by you both." I gave the trembling nurse a small box containing all the trinkets I had brought with me, gave her messages to my father and mother, and followed my fellow unfortunates to the deck, down a slippery gangplank to waiting motor boats on which we traveled the half hour's journey from the yacht to the fortress.

CHAPTER XX

SVEABORG before the War was one of three principal naval stations of the Russian Empire, the other two being Kronstadt and Reval. Sveaborg occupies a number of small islands in the Bay of Helsingfors. The bay itself, shaped like a rather narrow half moon, is so enclosed by these wooded islands that in winter the salt water freezes solidly. In summer the islands are green and lovely and a few of them, not under military control, are used by the Finns as pleasure resorts. Even in the darkness and in the unfortuitous circumstances of our arrival I could see that the main island might be a very attractive place. Up a steep hill we panted, past a white church surrounded with trees, and at last reached the place of our confinement, a long, dingy, one-storied stronghold. A young officer and several very dirty soldiers took our records, and Erika and I were pushed into a small cell with two wooden bunks covered with dust and alas, nothing else. The place smelled as only old prisons do smell, and the only air came in through a small window high in one of the walls. Wrapping ourselves in our coats, we lay down on the hard planks and tried to sleep. In the early dawn we got up, our backs aching and our throats choked with dust, but the irrepressible Erika laughed so heartily and sneezed so comically that I found it impossible to lament our surroundings. The place was a dreadful hole just the same, no proper toilet facilities at hand, and of course no opportunity of washing, to say nothing of bathing. We had to pay for our food at the rate of about ten rubles a day, at that time no small amount of money. The food was not very bad except that Stepan, the commissary, used to wipe our plates with a disgustingly dirty towel which he wore around his neck, the same towel being used in a laudable attempt to wipe the dust from our bunks.

Climbing on the bunks, we had a view through the window of a new building going up, the workmen being women as well as men. At the same time we got a glimpse of the detective Manouiloff who, ever pessimistic, held up three fingers as an expression of his belief that we had only that many days to live. We, however, ventured the guess that we would not remain at Sveaborg more than a month. It was a mere hazard but it turned out a fortunate one. We remained just about a month. It was a queer life we lived during that month, surrounded by tipsy and irresponsible men whose officers seemed to fear them too much to insist upon discipline. The officers, especially one fine young man, did everything they dared to make us comfortable. After the first ten days our plank beds were furnished with green leather cushions which might have made sleep a comfort if they had not persisted in slipping from under us about as soon as we dozed off. Somewhat later, a week perhaps before our liberation, these cushions were replaced by real mattresses stuffed with seaweed, wonderfully luxurious by comparison with the bare boards. The prisoners were exercised every day in the open under Sveaborg guards and the gaze of a crowd of Finnish Bolshevists. These people seemed at first immensely diverted by the pomposity of the Siberian doctor Badmieff who, in his long white robe, tall cap, and white gloves was certainly a curious spectacle. Soon they tired of him and turned their stolid, expressionless eyes on the other prisoners with what intentions we could only conjecture. Badmieff continued to be a center of interest in the prison. Erika, his faithful disciple, demanded the privilege of attending him, and this was granted. Every day he sat cross-legged like the Buddha he so much resembled, dictating endless medical treatises to Erika. In the evenings he used to put his lamp on the floor at the foot of his bunk, strew around it flowers and leaves brought from outside, burn some kind of ill-smelling herbs for incense, and generally create what I assumed to be the occult atmosphere of his beloved Thibet. Erika, scantily clad, always attended these séances and gradually they appeared to hypnotize the sailors, who thought highly of the doctor's professional powers. Indeed towards the end I often heard them swearing that whoever left the fortress, they would at least keep their highly esteemed *tovarish* Badmieff and his Siberian-Thibetan lore.

In sad contrast to the condition of Dr. Badmieff was that of the poor editor, Glinka Janchevsky, who being without money was treated with the utmost contempt. Housed in a wretched cell covered with obscene drawings, the miserable man spent most of his time lying on his wooden bed wrapped up, head and all, in his overcoat. He used to creep to our cell door with a glass of hot water in his hand begging for a pinch of tea and, if we had it, a little sugar. Every day he used to ask pathetically: "When do you think we shall be let go?" Like all journalists, he was famished for news, and whenever I got hold of a stray newspaper I used to read it to him from the first column to the last.

The vacillating conduct of the Bolshevist sailors toward the prisoners of Kerensky I can only ascribe to the increasingly bitter conflict going on between the weak Provisional Government and the Bolsheviki. The sailors hated us because we were "bourgeois," but they spared us because Kerensky desired our destruction. The officers good-naturedly brought me flowers from outside, an occasional newspaper, and even letters from people in Helsingfors who knew my history and pitied my fate. Sometimes I was even invited to tea with the officers, and twice I was taken out of prison, ostensibly for examination, but really to attend services at the little white church on the island. The guards were rough and kind by turns, sometimes uttering horrible threats against all the prisoners, sometimes bringing me a handful of the wild flowers they knew I loved to have near me. Discipline was lax, and we never knew from one day to another what might befall. For example, the padlock to my cell got lost and for several nights the door was left unlocked. One can imagine how I slept! On one of these unguarded nights the cell was invaded by a group of drunken and lustful men. Erika and I fought them, screaming at the top of our lungs, until a few sober and better-minded sailors came to the rescue. A day or two later, when a rumor spread that we were all to be hanged, I among the first, I for one felt less terror than relief. Anything, even hanging, seemed better than this lunatic prison where the guards drank, played cards, and wrangled all night, and where the men's attitude towards Erika and myself, the only women, was by turns dangerously savage and dangerously friendly.

Besides the Kerensky prisoners the fortress sheltered eight or nine prisoners charged with crimes ranging from theft to murder. Some of these whom we encountered in the exercise yard looked like very decent men, shining perhaps by contrast with the rowdy Revolutionists I had seen in the course of two imprisonments. For these unfortunates and for the guards we bought cigarettes, thus establishing more cordial relations. Nobody knew or could guess what was going to happen to us. One day appeared the president of the Helsingfors Soviet, a black-eyed Jew named Sheiman, who assured us that we were to be sent back to Petrograd, and that we might as well have our things ready by nine o'clock that night. Nothing happened that night, nor did we, for some reason, expect anything. The next day Sheiman came again with his bodyguard of soldiers and sailors, and told us that his Soviet refused for a time to release us. It appeared that telegrams had arrived from Kerensky and from Cheidze, the Georgian leader in the Petrograd Soviet, urgently demanding our return. The Helsingfors Soviet might have obliged Cheidze, but they would not honor any demand of Kerensky's, so there we were. The Provisional Government and the Petrograd Soviet sent over several deputies, Kaplan, a small, black-bearded man, who smilingly told us that there was no possible hope for us; Sokoloff, the famous, or rather infamous, author in the first instance of Order No. 1 which was principally responsible for the break-up of the army; and Joffe, the little Jew, who, a few years later, became influential enough to be included among the delegates to the Genoa Conference. After their visit, I don't know why, prison discipline became still further relaxed. We had visitors and the attention of physicians if we needed it. We were informed that henceforth we would not be regarded as prisoners at all, but only as persons temporarily detained. Two hours a day after this we were allowed in the open air, and I became very friendly with the Finnish women carpenters at work on the new building on our island. These good souls brought me bottles of delicious milk, and one day the building foreman, a Moscow Russian, invited me to his house to tea, and here I, a poor prisoner, was treated with such deference that I was actually embarrassed. Not one of the family would eat with me or even sit down in my presence.

At this time Erika and I were given a more commodious cell furnished with the seaweed mattresses of which I have spoken. But to our horror we found the walls covered with the most frightful scrawls and pictures. The sailor guards, however, brought water and sponges and with many apologies washed off the disgusting records as well as they could. I was thankful for this a few days later when all unexpectedly I received a visit from my dear mother. It had been some days after our parting at the frontier before she and my father learned that I was in prison. Immediately they had gone to Helsingfors to appeal to General Stachovitch, the Governor of Finland. But he advised them to avoid trouble for themselves, perhaps for me also, by going quietly back to Petrograd. My parents gave him money for me, which I never received, and despite the Governor's advice they stayed on in Helsingfors in faint hope of seeing me. Dr. Manouchine, my mother told me, had returned from a long visit in the Caucasus and was doing what he could to get me released. My mother also gave me news of the last struggle to maintain the army, the conflict between Korniloff and Kerensky, ending, as everyone knows, in the death of Korniloff. These two were about equally hated by the Sveaborg sailors who would gladly have murdered them both. They had begun to speak with unbounded admiration of Lenine and Trotzky, especially of Lenine, who they declared was the coming saviour of Russia.

Bolshevism was in the air, and for a moment it assumed a really benevolent aspect. I remember a deputation of Kronstadt Bolshevists who came to Sveaborg to inspect us and to review our entire case. Some of these men were very civil to me, asking many questions about the Imperial Family and the life of the Court. At parting one said to me naïvely: "You are quite different from what I thought you'd be, and I shall tell the comrades so." The very next day another deputation came and, characteristic of the confused state of the public mind, these men were as brutal as the others had been kind. They stormed down the prison corridors roaring: "Where is Viroubova? Show us Viroubova!" I cowered in my cell, but when the guard came and admonished me, for my own safety, to show myself to the men I gathered courage to speak to

them.   Totally unprepared to see the terrible Viroubova merely a crippled woman in a shabby frock, the
men suddenly quieted down and made civil response to
my words.   "We didn't know that you were ill," said
one of the men as they prepared to move on.

Although we did not know it at the time, our fate
really hung on the outcome of a Congress of Soviets
which was then being held in Petrograd, and to which
both Sheiman and Ostrovsky were delegates.   Sheiman returned to Helsingfors and visiting my cell told
me that both Trotzky and Lounacharsky were insistent
on the release of Kerensky's prisoners.   That evening,
he said, would be held a secret session of the executives
of the Helsingfors Soviet at which he would urge the
recommendation of Trotzky and Lounacharsky.   If
the executives agreed the question would then be referred to the entire Soviet, made up principally of
sailors of the old Baltic fleet.   That evening I was
invited to tea in the officers' quarters, and while sitting
there the telephone rang.   "It is for you," said the
officer who answered the call.   I picked up the receiver
and heard Sheiman's voice saying briefly: "The executive has voted unanimously for the release of the
prisoners."

There was little sleep for me that night, but tired as
I was by morning, I greeted happily the unkempt cook
and his messy breakfast plate.   All day I waited with
the dumb patience only prisoners know, and at early
evening I was rewarded by the appearance of Sheiman
and Ostrovsky.   "Put on your coat and follow me,"
said Sheiman.   "I have resolved to take you, on my

own responsibility, to the hospital." To my nursing sister, who had spent the afternoon with me, he gave orders to go to Helsingfors and wait for further directions. At the prison gate Sheiman signed the necessary papers, and hurrying me past two gaping Bolshevist soldiers, he led the way down a bypath to the water. Boarding a small motor launch manned by a single sailor, we started off at high speed for Helsingfors. There was one bad moment when we approached a low bridge occupied by a strong guard, but at Sheiman's directions, uttered in a short whisper, I lay down flat in the launch and we passed unchallenged. The first stars were shining in the clear autumn sky as we reached the military quay of the town. We ran in under the lee of a huge warship and stepped ashore. There was a motor car waiting and the chauffeur, who evidently knew his business, started his engine without a word or even a turn of his head.

Sheiman spoke only one sentence. "Tovarish Nicholai, drive to—" naming a street and number. At once we were off, my head fairly swimming at the sight of electric lights, shaded streets, and people walking up and down. Turning into a quiet street we left the car, all three of us shaking hands with the discreet driver. Bidding Ostrovsky find my nurse and my small luggage, Sheiman conducted me to the door of the hospital where a nice clean Finnish nurse took me in charge and put me to bed in one of the freshest, airiest, most comfortable rooms I have ever occupied. "Take good care of this lady," were the last words of the President of the Helsingfors Soviet, "and let no one intrude on her." His words and the assured smile of the nurse were good soporifics and I fell almost instantly into a deep sleep.

Two days later, September 30 (Russian), Sheiman came to see me with the news that Trotzky had ordered all the Kerensky prisoners back to Petrograd, and that he, Sheiman, had personally seen to it that my nurse and my aunt, who was at that time in Helsingfors, were to accompany me. Sheiman himself, and also Ostrovsky, who was unfortunately very drunk, went with us in the train which left Helsingfors that same night about half past ten. It was an unpleasant journey, the prisoners being in a state of wild excitement, and many of the red-badged officers more or less tipsy. With my aunt and the nurse I sat in a corner of a dirty compartment praying for the day to come. At nine in the morning we reached Petrograd, and Sheiman, still solicitous of my welfare, escorted the three of us to the Smolny Institute, once an aristocratic school for girls, now the headquarters of the Petrograd Soviet. Here I had the happiness once more to embrace my mother, who, with relatives of other prisoners, waited our arrival. Many Soviet authorities were in the place, among others Kameneff, a small red-bearded man, and his wife, a sister of the renowned Trotzky. Both of the Kameneffs were extremely kind to us, seeing that my companions and I had tea and food, and expressing the hope that I should soon be out of trouble. Kameneff telephoned Kerensky's headquarters asking leave to send us home, but as it was a holiday nobody answered the call. "Well, go home anyhow," said Kameneff, leaving the telephone, but Sokolov stopped

us long enough to make us understand that the prisoners all had to appear the next day before the High
Commission in the Winter Palace. I never saw the
Kameneffs again even to thank them for their kindness,
but I read in the Kerensky newspapers that I was on
terms of intimacy with them and was therefore a Bolshevist. It was even stated that I was a close friend
of the afterwards notorious woman commissar Kolan-
tai, whom I have never seen, and that Trotzky was a
familiar visitor in my house.

Thus ended my second term of imprisonment. First
I was arrested as a German spy and intrigant, next as a
counter-Revolutionary. Now I was accused of being
a Bolshevist and the name of Trotzky instead of Rasputine was linked with mine. Hardly knowing what
next was in store for me, I reported at once to the High
Commission. Here I was told that their inquiries concerning me were finished, and that I had better see the
Minister of the Interior. At this ministry I was informed that I was in no immediate danger but that I
would remain under police surveillance. I asked why,
but got no satisfactory answer. Later I learned that
the tottering Provisional Government wanted to send
me and all the "counter-Revolutionists" to Archangel,
but this move Dr. Manouchine, who was still very
influential, was determined to prevent.

From my uncle's house, where I had first taken
refuge, I moved to a discreet lodging in the heart of the
city and from this place I never once in daylight ventured out. This was in late October, 1917, and the
Bolshevist revolution had begun in deadly earnest.
Day after day I sat listening to the sound of rifle shots

and the putter of machine guns, the pounding of armored cars over the stone pavements, and the tramp, tramp, tramp of soldiers. Russia was getting ready for the long promised constitutional convention which turned out to be a Communist *coup d'état*. Once in a while the husband of my landlady, a naval man, came to my lodgings, and it was he who gave me news of the arrest of the Provisional Government, the siege of the Winter Palace, and the ignominious collapse of Kerensky while women soldiers fought and died to hide his flight! The scenes in the streets, as they were described to me, were appalling, and soon it was decided that my retreat was too near the center of hostilities to be at all safe. About the end of October I was taken by night to a distant quarter of the town to the tiny apartment of an old woman, formerly a masseuse in my hospital. Here came our old servant Berchik, keen to protect me from danger, and here we stayed for a month, when my mother found me a still safer lodging on the sixth floor of a house in the Fourtchkatskaia, a cozy little apartment whose windows gave a pleasant view of roofs and church steeples. There for eight months I lived like a recluse, once in a great while venturing to go to church, well guarded by Berchik and the nurse. The Bolshevik Government seemed successfully established, and its policy of blood and terror and extermination was well under way. Yet in my hidden retreat it seemed to me that, for a time at least, I was forgotten, and my troubles were all over.

CHAPTER XXI

PARADOXICAL though it may appear, the last months of 1917 and the winter of 1918, spent in a hidden lodging in turbulent Petrograd, were more peaceful than any period I had known since the Revolution began. I knew that the city and the country were in the hands of fanatic Bolshevists and that under their ruthless theory of government no human life was at all secure. Food and fuel were scarce and dear, and there was no doubt that things were destined to grow worse long before they could, in any imaginable circumstances, grow better. The wreck of the army was complete, and while the war still waged in western Europe we, who had had so much to do with defiance of German militarism, were completely out of the final struggle. The peace of my soul was partly born of ignorance, I suppose, the ignorance of events shared by everyone not immediately in contact with the world catastrophe. I was free, I lived in a comfortable apartment, my dear father and mother came daily to see me, and two of my faithful old servants lived with me and were ready to protect me from all enemies.

Also, because the mind cannot fully realize the worst, I believed that the Russian chaos was a temporary manifestation. I thought I saw signs of a reaction in favor of the exiled Emperor. In this I was certainly encouraged by two of the oldest and most prominent Revolutionists known to the outside world,

Bourtseff, a leader among the old Social Revolutionaries, and the novelist Gorky. It was in December,
1917, if I remember correctly, that I learned that
Gorky was anxious to meet me, and as I preferred to
keep my small corner of safety as free from visitors as
possible, I made an appointment with the novelist in
his own home, a modest apartment on the Petrograd
side of the Neva, not far from the fortress. Gorky,
whose gaunt feautures are familiar to all readers, is
said to be a sufferer from tuberculosis, but as he has
lived many years since the first rumors of this disease
were circulated, there may be some reason to doubt
his affliction. That he is a sick man none can doubt,
for his high cheek bones seem almost to pierce his
colorless skin and his darkly luminous eyes are deeply
sunken in his head. For two hours of this first interview I sat in conversation with Gorky, strange creature, who at times seems to be heart and soul a Bolshevist and at other times openly expresses his loathing and disgust of their insane and destructive policies.
To me Gorky was gentle and sympathetic, and what he
said about the Emperor and Empress filled my heart
with encouragement and hope. They were, he declared, the poor scapegoats of the Revolution, martyrs
to the fanaticism of the time. He had examined with
care the private apartments of the palace and he saw
clearly that these unhappy ones were not even what
are called aristocrats, but merely a bourgeois family
devoted to each other and to their children, as well as
to their ideals of righteous living. He expressed himself as bitterly disappointed in the Revolution and in
the character of the Russian proletariat. Earnestly he

advised me to live as quietly as possible, never reminding the Bolshevist authorities or any strangers of
my existence. My duty, he told me, was to live and
to devote myself to writing the true story of the lives
of the Emperor and Empress. "You owe this to
Russia," he said, "for what you can write may help to
bring peace between the Emperor and the people."

Twice afterwards I saw and talked with Gorky,
showing him a few pages of my reminiscences. He
urged me to go on writing, suppressing nothing of the
truth, and he even offered to help me with my work.
But writing in Russia was at that time too dangerous
a trade to be followed with any degree of confidence,
and it was not until I was safely beyond the frontiers
that I dared begin writing freely and at length. I
wish to say, however, that it was principally due to
Gorky's encouragement and to the encouragement of
an American literary friend, Rheta Childe Dorr, that I
ventured to attempt authorship, or rather that I under-
took to present to the world, as they really were, my
Sovereigns and my best beloved friends. My casual
acquaintanceship with Gorky was naturally seized upon
by certain foreign journalists as evidence that I had
gone over to the Bolsheviki, and much abuse and scorn
were hurled against me. How little those writers knew
of Gorky and his half-hearted support of the Lenine
policies! He held an important office under the Communists, it is true, and his wife, a former actress, was
in the commissariat of theatricals and entertainments.
But no man in Bolshevist Russia has ever been permitted more freedom of thought and speech than
Gorky. He has done things which would have brought

almost any other man to torture and death. I know, for example, that he sheltered under his roof at least one of the Romanoffs, and that the man was finally assisted by him across the Finnish frontier. Gorky interested himself also in the fate of several of the Grand Dukes, Nicholai Michailovitch, Paul and George, who were arrested and later shot to death in Peter and Paul. Gorky did everything in his power to save these men, in whom personally he had no interest whatever. He simply believed their murder to be unjustified, and it is said that he actually induced Lenine to sign an order for their release and deportation, but the order was signed too late, and the men were brutally executed.

At Christmas, 1917, I had a great happiness, nothing less than letters and a parcel of food from the exiles in Tobolsk. There were two parcels in fact, one containing flour, sugar, macaroni, and sausage, wonderful luxuries, and the other a pair of stockings knit by the Empress's own hands, a warm scarf, and some pretty Christmas cards illuminated in her well-remembered style. I made myself a tiny Christmas tree decorated with bits of tinsel and holly berries and hung with these precious tokens of affection and remembrance. Nor was this the only Christmas joy vouchsafed me after a year of sorrow and suffering. Under the escort of my good old servant Berchik I ventured to attend mass in the big church near the Nicholai station, a church built to commemorate the three hundredth anniversary of the Romanoff succession. After the service an old monk approached me and invited me to accompany him into the *réfectoire* of his monastery. I followed him, a little unwillingly, for one never knew what might happen. Entering I saw, to my astonishment, about two hundred factory women who almost filled the bare and lofty room. The old monk introduced me to the women, and to my bewilderment their leader came forward bowing, and holding in her outstretched hands a clean white towel on which reposed a silver ikon. It was an image of Our Lady of Unexpected Joy, and the kind woman told me that she and her fellow workers felt that after all that I had unjustly suffered in the fortress I ought to have from those who sympathized with me an expression of confidence and good-will. She added that were I again in trouble I might feel myself free to take refuge in the lodgings of any one of them. Overcome with emotion, I could utter only a few stammering words of thanks. I kissed the good woman heartily, and all who could approached and embraced me. Knowing that I longed for more tangible expressions of gratitude, the good old monk pressed into my hands a number of sacred pictures and these I gave away, as long as they lasted, to my new friends. No words can tell how deeply I felt the kindness of these working women who, out of their scanty wages, bought a silver ikon to give to a woman of whom they knew nothing except that she had, as they believed, been persecuted for others' sake.

I needed the assurance that in the cruel world around me there were those who wished me well, for in the first months of the new year came one of the bitterest sorrows of my life, the death of my deeply loved and revered father. He died very suddenly, and without any pain, on January 25, 1918, leaving the world bereft of one of the kindest, most gifted, and sympathetic men of his generation in Russia. I have described my father as a musician and a composer, as well as a lifelong friend and functionary of the Imperial Family. His years of service as keeper of the privy purse might have made him a rich man, but so utterly honest was he that he accepted nothing except his moderate salary and he died leaving almost nothing, nothing but an unfading memory and the deep affection of my friends, including scores of poor students whose musical education and advancement he had furthered. At his funeral his own compositions were sung by volunteer choirs of his musician friends, and these followed his coffin in long procession the length of the Nevski Prospekt to the cemetery of the Alexandra Nevskaia Lavra, a monastic burial place where many of our greatest lie in everlasting repose. My mother came to live with me in my obscure lodgings, and together we faced our desolate future.

One thing alone lightened the darkness of those days. This was a correspondence daringly undertaken with my beloved friends in Siberia. Even now, and at this distance from Russia I cannot divulge the names of those brave and devoted ones who smuggled the letters and parcels to and from the house in Tobolsk, and got them to me and to the small group of faithful men and women in Petrograd. The two chiefly concerned, a man and a woman, of course lived in constant peril of discovery and death. Yet they gladly risked their lives that their Sovereigns might have the happiness of private communication with their friends. At this time their Majesties were permitted to write and receive a few letters, but every line was read by their jailers, and their list of correspondents was rigidly censored. Even in the letters smuggled out from Tobolsk the utmost precautions had to be observed, and the reader can see with what veiled and discreet phrases the sentences are couched.

I give these letters exactly as they were written, suppressing only certain messages of affection too intimate to make public. Most of the letters were written by the Empress, but one at least came from the Emperor, and a number are from the children. To me these letters are infinitely precious, not only as personal messages, but as proofs of the dauntless courage and deep religious faith of these martyrs of the Russian Revolution. Their patriotism and their love of country never faltered for a single moment, nor did they ever utter a complaint or a reproach against those who had so heartlessly betrayed them. It seems to me impossible that anyone, reading these letters, intended only for my own eyes, can continue to misjudge the lives and the characters of Nicholas II and the Empress Alexandra Feodorovna. What they reveal is their secret selves, unknown except to those who knew them best and knowing them loved them as they deserved to be loved.

The first communication to reach me was a brief message from the Empress, dated October 14, 1917, a short time after the news of my liberation from the fortress reached her in Siberia.

My darling: We are thinking constantly of you and of all the suffering you have had to endure. God help you in the future. How are your weak heart and your poor legs? We hope to go to Communion as usual if we are to be allowed.

Lessons have begun again with Mr. Gibbs also. So glad, at last. We are all well. It is beautifully sunny. I sit behind this wall in the yard and work. Greetings to the doctors, the priest, and the nurses in your hospital. I kiss you and pray God to keep you. .

A week later the Empress wrote me a long letter in which she ventures a few details of life in Tobolsk.

October 21, 1917.

My darling: I was inexpressibly glad to get news of you, and I kiss you fondly for all your loving thoughts of me. There are no real barriers between souls who really understand each other, but still it is natural for hearts to crave expressions of love. I wrote to you on the 14th, and now will try to send this to the same address, but I don't know how long you will remain. I wonder if you got my letter. I had hoped so much that you would see Zina and find comfort in her friendship. The expression in the eyes in the photograph which was brought me [1] has impressed me deeply, and I wept freely as I looked at it. Ah, God! Still He is merciful and will never forget His own. Great will be their reward in Heaven. The more we suffer here the fairer it will be on that other shore where so many dear ones await us. How are our Friend's [2] dear children, how well does the boy learn, and where do they live?

Dear little Owl, I kiss you tenderly. You are in all our hearts. We pray for you and often talk of you. In God's hands lie all things. From this great distance it is a difficult thing to help and comfort a loved one who is suffering. We hope tomorrow to go to Holy Communion, but neither today nor yesterday were we allowed to go to church. We have

[1] The snapshot taken of me by Mr. Gibbs soon after I was released from the fortress.

[2] Rasputine.

had services at home, last night prayers for the dead, tonight confession and evening prayer. You are ever with us, a kindred soul. How many things I long to say and to ask of you. It is strange to be in this house and to sleep in the dark bedroom.[3] I have heard nothing from Lili D. for some time. We are all well. I have been suffering from neuralgia in the head but now Dr. Kostritzky has come to treat me. We have spoken often of you.

They say that life in the Crimea is dreadful now. Still Olga A. is happy with her little Tichon whom she is nursing herself. They have no servants so she and N. A. look after everything. Dobiasgin, we hear, has died of cancer. The needlework you sent me was the only token we have received from any of our friends. Where is poor Catherine? We suffer so for all, and we pray for all of you. That is all we can do. The weather is bad these last few days, and I never venture out because my heart is not behaving very well. I get a great deal of consolation reading the Bible. I often read it to the children, and I am sure that you also read it. Write soon again. We all kiss and bless you. May God sustain and keep you. My heart is full, but words are feeble things.

Yours,   A.

The jacket warms and comforts me. I am surrounded by your dear presents, the blue dressing gown, red slippers, silver tray and spoon, the stick, etc. The ikon I wear. I do not remember the people you are living with now. Did you see the regimental priest from Peterhof? Ask the prayers of O. Hovari for us. God be with you. Love to your parents. Madeleine and Anna are still in Petrograd.

Card from Alexei, November 24, 1917.

[3] This was the house and the room I occupied in my stay in Tobolsk on my second visit to Siberia

I remember you often and am very sad. I remember your little house. We cut wood in the daytime for our baths. The days pass very quickly. Greetings to all.

On the same day the Empress wrote me a short letter in English.

Yesterday I received your letter dated November 6, and I thank you for it from my heart. It was such a joy to hear from you and to think how merciful is God to have given you this compensation. Your life in town must be more than unpleasant, confined in stuffy rooms, steep stairs to climb, no lovely walks possible, horrors all around you. Poor child! You know that in heart and soul I am near you, sharing all your pain and sorrow and praying for you fervently. Every day I read in the book you gave me seven years ago, "Day by Day," and like it very much. There are lovely passages in it.

The weather is very changeable, frost, sunshine, then darkness and thawings. Desperately dull for those who enjoy long walks and are deprived of them. Lessons continue as usual. Mother and daughters work and knit a great deal, making Christmas presents. How time flies! In two weeks more it will be eight months since I saw you last. And you, my little one, so far away in loneliness and sorrow. But you know where to seek consolation and strength, and you know that God will never forsake you. His love is over all.

On the whole we are all well, since I do not count chills and colds. Alexei's knee and arm swell from time to time, but happily without any pain. My heart has not been behaving very well. I read much, and live in the past, which is so full of rich memories. I have full trust in a brighter future. He will never forsake those who love and trust in His infinite mercy, and when we least expect it He will send help, and will save our unhappy country. Patience, faith and truth.

How did you like the two little colored cards? I have not heard from Lili Dehn for three months. It is hard to be cut off from all one's dear friends. I am so glad that your old servant and Nastia are with you, but where are the maids, Zina and Mainia? So Father Makari has left us. But he is really nearer than he was before.

Our thoughts will be very close together next month. You remember our last journey and what followed. After this anniversary it seems to me that God will show mercy. Kiss Praskovia and the children for me. The maid Liza and the girls have not come yet. All of us send tenderest love, blessings and kisses. God bless you, dearest friend. Keep a brave heart.

P. S. I should like to send you a little food, some macaroni for instance.

Up to this time, nearly the end of the year 1917, the Imperial Family in exile were treated with a certain degree of consideration. They had plenty of food and a limited freedom. In the next letter I received from the Empress, dated December 8, she speaks with gratitude of the fact that some of her favorite books were permitted to be retained by her, as a little later she overflows with gratitude to one of the Bolshevist Commissars who sent her a few familiar pictures and trinkets from the old home in Tsarskoe Selo. Little by little, however, privileges were taken from the family, and their status became that of criminal prisoners. I leave this to be shown in the letters which follow. On December 8, 1917, the Empress wrote me, in Russian, a letter which shows how poignantly she and the Emperor felt the desperate situation in Russia.

My darling: In thoughts and prayers we are always together. Still it is hard not to see each other. My heart is so full, there is so much I would like to know, so many thoughts I should like to share with you. But we hope the time will come when we shall see each other, and all the old friends who now are scattered in different parts of the world.

I am sorry you have had a misunderstanding with one of your best friends. That should never happen. This is no time to judge one's friends, every one of us being on such an unnatural strain.

We here live far from everybody and life is quiet, but we read of all the horrors that are going on. But I shall not speak of them. You live in their very center, and that is enough for you to bear. Petty troubles surround us. The maids have been in Tobolsk four days and yet they are not allowed to come to our house, although it was promised that they should. How pitiful this everlasting suspicion and fear. I suppose it will be the same with Isa.[4] Nobody is now allowed to approach us, but I hope they will soon see how stupid and brutal and unfair it is to keep them (the maids) waiting.

It is very cold—24 degrees of frost. We shiver in the rooms, and there is always a strong draught from the windows. Your pretty jacket is so useful. We all have chilblains on our fingers. (You remember how you suffered from them in your cold little house?) I am writing this while resting before dinner. Little Jimmy lies near me while his mistress plays the piano. On the 6th Alexei, Marie, and Gilik (M. Gilliard) acted a little play for us. The others are committing to memory scenes from French plays. Excellent distraction, and good for the memory. The evenings we spend together. He reads aloud to us, and I embroider. I am very busy all day preparing Christmas presents; painting ribbons for book markers, and cards as of old. I also have lessons with the

---

[1] Baroness Buxhoevden, lady in waiting.

children, as the priest is no longer permitted to come. But I like these lessons very much. So many things come back to my mind. I am reading with pleasure the works of Archbishop Wissky. I did not have them formerly. Lately also I have read Tichon Zadonsky. In spite of everything I was able to bring some of my favorite books with me. Do you read the Bible I gave you? Do you know that there is now a much more complete edition? I have given one to the children, and I have managed to get a large one for myself. There are some beautiful passages in the Proverbs of Solomon. The Psalms also give me peace. Dear, we understand each other. I thank you for everything, and in memory I live over again our happy past.

One of our former wounded men, Pr. Eristoff, is in hospital again. I don't know the reason. If possible give hearty greetings to him from us all. Give sincere thanks and greetings to Madame S. and her husband. God bless and comfort him.

Where are Serge (Mme. Viroubova's brother) and his wife? I received a touching letter from Zina. I know the past is all done with, but I thank God for all that we have received, and I live in the memory that cannot be taken from me. Still I worry often for my dearly loved, far distant, foolish little friend. I am glad that you have resumed your maiden name. Give greetings to Emma F., the English Red Cross nurse, and to your dear parents.

On the 6th we had service at home, not being allowed to go to church on account of some kind of a disturbance. I have not been out in the fresh air for four weeks. I can't go out in such bitter weather because of my heart. Nevertheless church draws me almost irresistibly.

I showed your photographs to Valia and Gilik. I did not want to show them to the ladies, your face is too dear and precious to me. Nastinka is too distant. She is very sweet, but she does not seem near to me. All my dear ones are far away. But I am surrounded by their photographs and gifts—jackets, dressing gowns, slippers, silver dish, spoons, and ikons. How I would like to send you something, but I fear it would get lost. I kiss you tenderly, love, and bless you. We all kiss you. He was touched by your letter of congratulation. We pray for you, and we think of you, not always without tears.

Yours.

The next day the Empress wrote again.

This is the feast day of the Virgin of Unexpected Joy. I always read the day's service, and I know that you, dear, do the same. It is the anniversary of our last journey together, to Saratoff. Do you remember how lovely it was? The old holy woman is dead now, but I keep her ikon always near me. . . . Yesterday it was nine months since we were taken into captivity, and more than four months since we came here. Which of the English nurses was it who wrote to me? I am surprised to hear that Nini Voyeikoff and her family did not receive the ikons I sent them before leaving. Give kind regards to your faithful old servant and Nastia. This year I cannot give them anything for their Christmas tree. How sad. My dear, you are splendid. Christ be with you. Give my thanks to Fathers John and Dosifei for their remembrance. I am writing this morning in bed. Jimmy is sleeping nearly under my nose and interfering with my writing. Ortipo lies on my feet and keeps them warm.

Fancy that the kind Kommissar Makaroff sent me my pictures two months ago, St. Simeon Nesteroffs, the little Annunciation from the bedroom, four small prints from my mauve room, five pastels of Kaulbach, four enlarged snapshots from Livadia; Tatania and me, Alexei as sentry, Alexander III, Nicholas I, and also a small carpet from my bedroom.

My wicker lounge chair too is standing in my bedroom now. Among the other cushions is the one filled with rose leaves given me by the Tartar women. It has been with me all the way. At the last moment of the night at Tsarskoe I took it with me, slept on it on the train and on the boat, and the lovely smell refreshed me. Have you had any news of Gaham (Chief of the Karaim)? Write to him and give him my regards. One of our former wounded, Sirobojarski, has visited him. There are 22 degrees of frost today, but bright sunshine. Do you remember the sister of mercy K. M. Bitner? She is giving the children lessons. What luck! The days fly. It is Saturday again, and we shall have evening service at nine. A corner of the drawing room has been arranged with our ikons and lamps. It is homelike—but not church. I got so used to going almost daily for three years to the church of Znamenia before going on to the hospitals at Tsarskoe.

I advise you to write to M. Gilliard. (Now I have refilled my fountain pen.) Would you like some macaroni and coffee? I hope soon to send you some. It is so difficult for me here to take the vegetables out of the soup without eating any of it.[5] It is easy for me to fast and to do without fresh air but I sleep badly. Yet I hardly feel any of the ills of the flesh. My heart is better, as I live such a quiet life, almost without exercise. I have been very thin but it is less noticeable now, although my gowns are like sacks. I am quite gray too.

The spirits of the whole family are good. God is very near us, we feel His support, and are often amazed that we can endure events and separations which once might have killed us. Although we suffer horribly still there is peace in our souls. I suffer most for Russia, and I suffer for you too, but I know that ultimately all will be for the best. Only I don't understand anything any longer. Everyone seems to have gone mad. I think of you daily and love you dearly. You are splendid and I know how wonderfully you have grown. Do you remember

[5] The Empress Alexandra Feodorovna was always a strict vegetarian.

the picture by Nesteroffs, Christ's Bride? Does the convent still attract you in spite of your new friend? God will direct everything. I want to believe that I shall see your buildings (my hospital) in the style of a convent. Where are the sisters of mercy Mary and Tatiana? What has become of Princess Chakoffskaia, and has she married her friend? Old Madame Orloff has written me that her grandson John was killed in the War, and that his fiancée killed herself from grief. Now they are buried beside his father.

My regards to my dear Lancers, to Jakoleff, Father John, and others. Pray for them all. I am sure that God will have mercy on our Russia. Has she not atoned for her awful sins?

My love, burn my letters. It is better. I have kept nothing of the dear past. We all kiss you tenderly and bless you. God is great and will not forsake those encircled by His love Dear child, I shall be thinking of you especially during Christmas. I hope that we will meet again, but where and how is in His hands. We must leave it all to Him who knows all better than we.

During that December I had the happiness of receiving letters from the Emperor, Alexei, and the Grand Duchesses Tatiana, Olga, and Anastasie. The Emperor wrote acknowledging a note of mine written on his name day.

Tobolsk, 10 December, 1917.

Thank you so much for your kind wishes on my name day. Our thoughts and prayers are *always* with you, poor suffering creature. Her Majesty reads to us all your lines. Horrid to think all you had to go through. We are all right here. It is quite quiet. Pity you are not with us. Kisses and blessings without end from your loving friend, N.

Give my best love to your parents.

The children's letters were devoured because they gave so many details of the family life in Tobolsk. On December 9 Tatiana wrote:

My darling: I often think and pray for you, and we are always remembering and speaking of you. It is hard that we cannot see each other, but God will surely help us, and we will meet again in better times. We wear the frocks your kind friends sent us, and your little gifts are always with us, reminding us of you. We live quietly and peacefully. The days pass quickly. In the morning we have lessons, walk from eleven to twelve before the house in a place surrounded for us by a high board fence. We lunch together downstairs, sometimes Mamma and Alexei with us, but generally they lunch upstairs alone in Papa's study. In the afternoon we go out again for half an hour if it is not too cold. Tea upstairs, and then we read or write. Sometimes Papa reads aloud, and so goes by every day. On Saturdays we have evening service in the big hall at nine o'clock. Until that hour the priest has to serve in the church. On Sundays, when we are allowed, we go to a near-by church at eight o'clock in the morning. We go on foot through a garden, the soldiers who came here with us standing all around. They serve mass for us separately, and then have a mass for everybody. On holidays, alas, we have to have small service at home. We had to have home service on the 6th (St. Nicholas' day), and it was sad on such a big holiday not to be in church, but one can't have everything one wants, can one? I hope you at least can go to church. How are your heart and your poor legs? Do you see the doctor of your hospital? You remember how we used to tease you. Greetings to your old servants. Where are your brother and his wife? Have they got a baby? God bless you, my darling beloved. All our letters (permitted letters) go through the Kommissar. I am glad that the parents of Eristoff are kind to you. Him I remember well, but I never saw the parents.

Isa has not come yet. Has she been to see you? I kiss you tenderly and love you.

Your T.

My darling dear Annia, How happy I was to hear from you. Thank you for the letter and the things. I wrote to you yesterday. It is so strange to be staying in the house where you stayed. Remember that we are sending this parcel secretly, so don't mention it. It is the only time probably that we can do it. Yesterday's letter I sent through the Kommissar. I am always thinking of you, my darling. We speak much of you among ourselves and also to Gilik, Valia, Prince Dolgorouky, and Mr. Gibbs. I wear your bracelet and never take it off, the one you gave me on January 12, my name day. You remember that cozy evening by the fireside? How nice it was. Did you ever see Groten and Linevitch?[6] Well, good-bye, my darling Annia. I kiss you tenderly and love you.

Your T.

From the Grand Duke Alexei, December 10, 1917.

My darling, I hope you got my postcard. Thank you very, very much for the little mushroom. Your perfumes remind us so much of you. Every day I pray God we shall live together again. God bless you.

Yours, A.

From the Grand Duchess Olga on the same date.

My darling, what joy it was to see your dear handwriting, and all the little things. Thanks awfully for all. Your perfumes reminded us so of you, your cabin on board, etc. It was very sad. I remember you often, kiss and love you. We

---

[6] Groten and Linevitch were the two aides-de-camp who were so devoted to the family during the trying period before the Revolution. Afterwards they were denied entrance to the palace

four live in the corner blue room, arranged all quite cozily. Opposite to us in the little room is Papa's dressing room and Alexei's, then comes his room with Nagori. The brown room is Papa's and Mamma's bedroom. Then the sitting room, big hall, and beyond Papa's study. When there are big frosts it is very cold, and draughts blow from all the windows. We were today in church. Well, I wish you a peaceful and sunny Christmas. God bless you, darling. I kiss you over and over again.

Ever your own Olga.

From the Grand Duchess Anastasie.

My darling and dear: Thank you tenderly for your little gift. It was so nice to have it, reminding me especially of you. We remember and speak of you often, and in our prayers we are always together. The little dog you gave is always with us and is very nice. We have arranged our rooms comfortably and all four live together. We often sit in the windows looking at the people passing, and this gives us distraction. . . . We have acted little plays for amusement. We walk in the garden behind high planks. . . . God bless you.

An.

From the Empress.

My own precious child: It seems strange writing in English after nine weary months. We are doing a risky thing sending this parcel, but we profit through ———— who is still on the outside. Only promise to burn all we write as it could do you endless harm if they discovered that you were still in contact with us. Therefore don't judge those who are afraid to visit you, just leave time for people to quiet down. You cannot imagine the joy of getting your sweet letters. I have read and reread them over and over to myself and to the others. We all share the anguish, and the misery, and the joy to know that you are free at last. I won't speak of what you have gone through. Forget it, with the old name you have thrown away. Now live again.

One has so much to say that one ends by saying nothing. I am unaccustomed to writing anything of consequence, just short letters or cards, nothing of consequence. Your perfume quite overcame us. It went the round of our tea table, and we all saw you quite clearly before us. I have no "white rose" to send you, and could only scent the shawl with vervaine. Thanks for your own mauve bottle, the lovely blue silk jacket, and the excellent pastilles. The children and Father were so touched with the things you sent, which we remember so well, and packed up at Tsarskoe. We have none of such things with us, so alas, we have nothing to send you. I hope you got the food through ———— and Mme. ————. I have sent you at least five painted cards, always to be recognized by my signature. I have always to be imagining new things!

Yes, God is wonderful and has sent you (as always) in great sorrow, a new friend. I bless him for all that he has done for you, and I cannot refrain from sending him an image, as to all who are kind to you. Excuse this bad writing, but my pen is bad, and my fingers are stiff from cold. We had the blessing of going to church at eight o'clock this morning. They don't always allow us to go. The maids are not yet let in as they have no papers, so the odious commandant doesn't admit them. The soldiers think we already have too many people with us. Well, thanks to all this we can still write to you. Something good always comes out of everything.

Many things are very hard . . . our hearts are ready to burst at times. Happily there is nothing in this place that reminds us of you. This is better than it was at home where every corner was full of you. Ah, child, I am proud of you. Hard lessons, hard school, but you have passed your examinations so well. Thanks, child, for all you have said for us, for standing up for us, and for having borne all for our own and for Russia's sake. God alone can recompense you, for if He has let you see horrors He has permitted you to gaze a little into yonder world. Our souls are nearer now than before. I feel especially near you when I am reading the Bible. The children also are always finding texts suiting you. I am so contented with their souls. I hope God will bless my lessons with Baby. The ground is rich, but is the seed ripe enough? I do try my utmost, for all my life lies in this.

Dear, I carry you always with me. I never am separated from your ring, but at night I wear it on my bracelet as it is so loose on my finger. After we received our Friend's cross we got also this cross to bear. God knows it is painful being cut off from the lives of those dear to us, after being accustomed for years to share every thought. But my child has grown self-dependent with time. In your love we are always together. I wish we were so in fact, but God knows best. One learns to forget personal desires. God is merciful and will never forsake His children who trust Him.

I do hope this letter and parcel will reach you safely, only you had better write and tell ———— that you get everything safely. Nobody here must dream that we evade them, otherwise it would injure the kind commandant and they might remove him.

I keep myself occupied ceaselessly. Lessons begin at nine (in bed). Up at noon for religious lessons with Tatiana, Marie, Anastasie, and Alexei. I have a German lesson three times a week with Tatiana and once with Marie, besides reading with Tatiana. Also I sew, embroider, and paint, with spectacles on because my eyes have become too weak to do without them. I read "good books" a great deal, love the Bible, and from time to time read novels. I am so sad because they are allowed no walks except before the house and behind a high fence. But at least they have fresh air, and we are grateful for anything. He is simply marvelous. Such meekness while all the time suffering intensely for the country. A real marvel. The others are all good and brave and uncomplaining, and Alexeı is an angel. He and I dine *à deux* and generally lunch so, but sometimes downstairs with the others.

They don't allow the priest to come to us for lessons, and even during services officers, commandant and Kommissar, stand near by to prevent any conversation between us. Strangely enough Germogene is Bishop here, but at present he is in Moscow. We have had no news from my old home or from England. All are well, we hear, in the Crimea, but the Empress Dowager has grown old and very sad and tearful. As for me my heart is better as I lead such a quiet life. I feel utter trust and faith that all will be well, that this is the worst, and that soon the sun will be shining brightly. But oh, the victims, and the innocent blood yet to be shed! We fear that Baby's other little friend from Mogiloff who was at M. has been killed, as his name was included among cadets killed at Moscow. Oh, God, save Russıa! That is the cry of one's soul, morning, noon and night. Only not that shameless peace.[7]

I hope you got yesterday's letter through Mme. ———'s son-in-law. How nice that you have him in charge of your affairs. Today my mind is full of Novgorod and the awful 17th.[8] Russia must suffer for that murder too. Dear, I am glad you see me in your dreams. I have seen you only twice, vaguely, but some day we shall be together again. When? I do not ask. He alone knows. How can one ask more? We simply give thanks for every day safely ended. I hope nobody will ever see these letters, as the smallest thing makes them react upon us with severity. That is to say we get no church services outside or in. The suite and the maids may

[7] Brest-Litovsk.
[8] Anniversary of Rasputine's assassination.

leave the house only if guarded by soldiers, so of course they avoid going. Some of the soldiers are kind, others horrid.

Forgive this mess, but I am in a hurry and the table is crowded with painting materials. So glad you liked my old blue book. I have not a line of yours—all the past is a dream. One keeps only tears and grateful memories. One by one all earthly things slip away, houses and possessions ruined, friends vanished. One lives from day to day. But God is in all, and nature never changes. I can see all around me churches (long to go to them), and hills, the lovely world. Wolkoff wheels me in my chair to church across the street from the public garden. Some of the people bow and bless us, but others don't dare. All our letters and parcels are examined, but this one today is contraband. Father and Alexei are sad to think they have nothing to send you, and I can only clasp my weary child in my arms and hold her there as of old. I feel old, oh, so old, but I am still the mother of this country, and I suffer its pains as my own child's pains, and I love it in spite of all its sins and horrors. No one can tear a child from its mother's heart, and neither can you tear away one's country, although Russia's black ingratitude to the Emperor breaks my heart. Not that it is the *whole* country, though. God have mercy and save Russia.

Little friend, Christmas without me—up in the sixth story! My beloved child, long ago I took you to hold in my heart and never to be separated. In my heart is love and forgiveness for everything, though at times I am not as patient as I ought to be. I get angry when people are dishonest, or when they unnecessarily hurt and offend those I love. Father, on the other hand, bears everything. He wrote to you of his own accord. I did not ask him. Please thank everybody who wrote to us in English. But the less *they* know we correspond the better, otherwise they may stop all letters.

Ever your own, A.

The increasing poverty and hardships which surrounded the exiles, to say nothing of the lonely desolation of their lives, could not be kept out of the Empress's letters, although she tried to write cheerfully. I could read, in the growing discursiveness of her contraband letters, the disturbed and abnormal condition of her usual keen and concise mind. On December 15, 1917, she wrote:

Dearest little one: Again I am writing to you, and you must thank ———— and reply carefully. My maids are not yet allowed to come to me, although they have been here eleven days. I don't know how it will come out. Isa (Baroness Buxhoevden, lady in waiting) is ill again. I hear that she will be allowed in when she arrives, as she has a *permis*, but I doubt it. I understand your wounded feelings when she did not go to see you, but does she know your address? She is timid, and her conscience in regard to you is not quite clear. She remembers perhaps my words to her last Autumn that there might come a time when she too would be taken from me and not allowed to return. She lives in the Gorochovaia with a niece. Zizi Narishkine (a former lady in waiting) lives in the Sergievskja, 54.

I hope you will receive the things we sent for Christmas. Anna and Wolkoff helped me to send the parcels, the others I sent through ————, so I make use of the opportunity to write to you. Be sure to write when you receive them. I make a note in my book whenever I write. I have drawn some postcards. Did you receive them? One of these days I shall send you some flour.

It is bright sunshine and everything glitters with hoar frost. There are such moonlight nights, it must be ideal on the hills. But my poor unfortunates can only pace up and down the narrow yard. How I long to take Communion. We took it last on October 22, but now it is so awkward, one has to ask permission before doing the least thing. I am reading Solomon and the writings of St Seraph, every time finding something new. How glad I am that none of your things got lost, the albums I left with mine in the trunk. It is dreary without them, but still better so, for it would hurt to look at them.and remember. Some thoughts one is obliged to drive away, they are too poignant, too fresh in one's memory. All things for us are in the past, and what the future holds I cannot guess, but God knows, and I have given everything into His keeping. Pray for us and for those we love, and especially for Russia when you are at the shrine of the "All-Hearing Virgin." I love her beautiful face. I have asked Chemoduroff to take out a prayer (slip of paper with names of you all) on Sunday.

Where is your poor old Grandmamma? I often think of her in her loneliness, and of your stories after you had been to see her. Who will wish you a happy Christmas on the telephone? Where is Serge and his wife? Where is Alexander Pavlovitch? Did you know that Linewitch had married, and Groten also, straight from the Fortress? Have you seen Mania Rebinder? This Summer they were still at Pavlovskoie, but since we left we have heard nothing of them. Where are Bishops Isidor and Melchisedek? Is it true that Protopopoff has creeping paralysis? Poor old man, I understand that he has not been able to write anything yet, his experiences being too near. Strange are our lives, are they not? One could write volumes.

Zinaida Tolstoaia and her husband have been in Odessa for some time. They write frequently, dear people. Rita Hitrovo is staying with them, but she scarcely writes at all. They are expecting Lili Dehn soon, but I have heard nothing from her for four months. One of our wounded, Sedloff, is also in Odessa. Do you know anything of Malama? [9] Did

---

[9] A wounded officer and friend.

Eristoff give you Tatiana's letter? Baida Apraxin and the whole family except the husband are in Yalta. He is in Moscow at the church conference. Professor Serge Petrovitch is also in Moscow. Petroff was, and Konrad is, in Tsarskoe. There too is Marie Rudiger Belaieff. Constadious, our old general, is dead. I try to give you news of all, though you probably know more than I do.

The children wear the brooches that Mme. Soukhomlinoff sent them. Mine I hung over a frame. Do you ever see old Mme. Orloff? Her grandson John was killed, and her Alexei is far away. It is sad for the poor old woman.

I am knitting stockings for the small one (Alexei). He asked for a pair as all his are in holes. Mine are warm and thick like the ones I gave the wounded, do you remember? I make everything now. Father's trousers are torn and darned, the girls' under-linen in rags. Dreadful, is it not? I have grown quite gray. Anastasie, to her despair, is now very fat, as Marie was, round and fat to the waist, with short legs. I do hope she will grow. Olga and Tatiana are both thin, but their hair grows beautifully so that they can go without scarfs. Fancy that the papers say that Prince Volodia Troubetskoy has joined Kaledin with all his men. Splendid! I am sure that N. D.[10] will take part also now that he is serving in Odessa. I find myself writing in English, I don't know why. Be sure to burn all these letters as at any time your house may be searched again.

[10] A well-known marine officer.

CHAPTER XXII

THROUGH the winter and spring of 1918 I continued to receive letters and parcels, mostly contraband, from my friends in Siberia. I wish I dared to tell how and through whom these precious messages reached me, for it all belongs in the story of Revolutionary Russia. It illustrates the truth, often demonstrated, that tyranny and oppression can never kill the spirit of freedom in human beings. There are always a minority of people who hold their lives cheap by comparison with liberty, and in such people lives deathlessly the inspiration of fidelity to those they love, no matter how relentlessly the loved ones are persecuted. Poor as I was, poor as was the small group of friends who worked with me to communicate with the Imperial Family, we managed to get to them the necessities they lacked. Dangerous and difficult as travel was in those days, every traveler being almost certain to be searched several times along the way, there were three, two officers and a young girl, who at the risk of imprisonment and death by the most unspeakable tortures, calmly and fearlessly acted as emissaries back and forth between Petrograd and remote Tobolsk. They had friends along the way, of course, but how they managed, through months of constant peril, to carry on their work is one of those mysteries which, to my mind, are not wholly earthly.

On January 9, 1918, I received the following Christmas letter from the Empress.

Thank you, darling, for all your letters which were a great joy to me and to us all. On Christmas Eve I received the letter and the perfume, then more scent by little ————. I regret not having seen her. Did you receive the parcels sent through the several friends, flour, coffee, tea, and lapscha (a kind of macaroni)? The letters and the snapshots sent through ————, did you get them? I am worried as I hear that all parcels containing food are opened. I begin today to number my letters, and you must keep account of them. Your cards, the small silver dish, and Lili's tiny silver bell I have not yet been able to receive.

We all congratulate you on your name day. May God bless, comfort, strengthen you, and give you joy. Believe, dear, that God will yet save our beloved country. He will not be unforgiving Think of the Old Testament and the sufferings of the Children of Israel for their sins. And now it is we who have forgotten God, and that is why they[1] cannot bring any happiness. How I prayed on the 6th that God would send the spirit of good judgment and the fear of the Lord. Everyone apparently have lost their heads. The reign of terror is not yet over, and it is the sufferings of the innocent which nearly kills us. What do people live on now that everything is taken from them, their homes, their incomes, their money? We must have sinned terribly for our Father in Heaven to punish so frightfully. But I firmly and unfalteringly believe that in the end He will save us. The strange thing about the Russian character is that it can so suddenly change to evil, cruelty, and unreason, and can as suddenly change back again. This is in fact simply want of character. Russians are in reality big, ignorant children. However it is

[1] Presumably the Soviet Government.

well known that during long wars all bad passions flame up. What is happening is awful, the murders, the persecutions, the imprisonments, but all of it must be suffered if we are to be cleansed, new born.

Forgive me, darling, that I write to you so sadly. I often wear your jackets, the blue and the mauve, as it is fearfully cold in the house. Outside the frosts are not often severe, and sometimes I go out and even sit on the balcony. The children are just recovering from scarletina, except Anastasie, who did not catch it. The elder ones began the new year by being in bed, Marie, of course, having a temperature of 39.5. Their hair is growing well. Lessons have begun again. Yesterday I gave three. Today I am free, and am therefore writing. On the 2nd of January I thought of you and sent a candle to be set before the Holy Seraphim. I have asked that prayers may be said in the cathedral where the relics lie, for all our dear ones. You remember the old pilgrim who came to Tsarskoe Selo. Fancy that he has been here. He wandered in with his big staff, and sent me a prosvera (holy bread).

I have begun your books. The style is quite different from the others. I have got myself some good books, too, but have not much time for reading. I embroider, knit, draw, and give lessons, but my eyes are getting weaker so that I can no longer work without glasses. You will see me quite an old woman! Did you know that the marine officer Nicolai Demenkoff has appendicitis? He is in Odessa. One of our wounded, Oroborjarsky, was operated on there a month ago. He is so sad and homesick, so far away. I correspond with his mother, a gentle, good, and really Christian soul. Lili Dehn went to see her.

I trust you received the painted cards that I put in the parcel of provisions. Not all were successful. If you receive my letters just write, thanks for No. 1, etc. My three maids and Isa are still not allowed to come to us, and they are very

much distressed, just sitting idle. But ——— is of better use
on the outside. Little one, where are your brother Serge
and his wife? I know nothing of them. Your poor sister
Alya, I hope she is not too sad; she has friends, but her husband, has he not become too sad away from her? How are the
sweet children? Miss Ida is with her still, I hope. Did you
know that sister Grekova is to be married soon to Baron Taube?
How glad I am that you have seen A. P. Did he not seem
strange out of uniform, and what did he say about his brother?
Ah, all is past, and will never return. We must begin a new
life and forget self. I must finish, my dear little soul. Christ
be with you. Greetings to all. I kiss your mother. I congratulate you again. I want quickly to finish the small painting, and get it to you. I fear you are again passing through
fearful days. Reports filter through of murders of officers
in Sevastopol. Rodionoff and his brother are there.

Your own,   A.

On the 16th of January the Empress wrote me a
letter in Old Slavonic style to congratulate me on my
name day. In this she addresses me as "Sister Seraphine." I should explain that my hospital in Tsarskoe
Selo bore the name of that saint, because it was on her
day that I suffered the terrible railway accident which
left me lamed for life, but which gave me, in damages,
the funds for founding the hospital.

Dearly beloved Sister Seraphine:
From a full heart I wish you well on your name day! God
send you many blessings, good health, fortitude, meekness,
strength to bear all punishments and sorrows sent by God,
and gladness of soul. May the sun lighten the path you tread
through life, warm all by your love, and let your light shine
forth these sad, gloomy days. Do not despair, suffering sister,

16го Января 1918г.   + ѯі.

"Милая, Дорогая, возлюбленная
Сестрица Серафима!

Отъ нѣжнолюбящаго сердца поз-
дравляю васъ многолюбивая
страдальница моя съ праздником
вашимъ. Да ниспошлетъ вамъ
Господь Богъ всякихъ благъ —
добраго здоровья, крѣпость ду-
ха, кротость, терпѣніе, силы пере-
нести все обиды и гоненіе, ду-
шевную радость. Да освѣтитъ
лучъ солнце ярко и ясно путь вашъ жизненный. Сами погрѣйте
всѣхъ любовию вашей. Да свѣтитъ
свѣтъ вашъ въ отихъ темныхъ,
неясныхъ дняхъ. Не унывай, роди-
мая, скорбящая сестра! Господь
услы-шитъ твои молитвы. Все въ
свое время. Молимся и мы за васъ
Богоизбранную сестру, всюди наемъ
васъ. Уголокъ вашъ убогiй да-
лекъ отъ насъ. — Всѣ любящіе

ONE OF THE EMPRESS'S LAST LETTERS, WRITTEN IN OLD
SLAVONIC TO MME. VIROUBOVA IN 1918.

ЕДРЪ И МЛТИВЪ ГДЬ, БЛГОТЕРПѢЛИВЪ
И МНОГОМЛТИВЪ. НЕ ДО КОНЦА ПРОГНѢ-
БАЕТСА, НИЖЕ ВО ВѢКЪ ВОЛЖДАЕТЪ: НЕ ПО БЕЗ
ЗАКОНIЕМЪ НАШИМЪ СОТВОРИЛЪ ЕСТЬ НАМЪ, НИЖЕ
ПО ГРѢХѸМЪ НАШИМЪ ВОЗДАЛЪ ЕСТЬ НАМЪ. ЯКW ПО
ВЫСОТѢ НЕБЕСНѢЙ WЗЕМЛЙ, ОУТВЕРДИ ГДЬ ... ЕСТЬ ГДЬ

God will hear your prayers, all in good time. Also we pray for thee, sister chosen of the Lord. We have thee in fond remembrance. Your little corner is far away from us. All who love thee in this place send greetings. Do not misjudge the bad writing of thy sister. She is illiterate, an ailing lay sister. I am learning the writing of prayers, but weakness of sight prevents my striving. I read the works of Bishop Gr. Nissky, but he writes too much of the creation of the world. From our sister Zinaida I have received news, so much good will in every word, breathing peace of the soul.

The family known to thee are in good health, the children have suffered from the usual ills of the young, but are now restored to health. The youngest ill, but in good spirits however, and without suffering. The Lord has blessed the weather, beautiful and soft. Thy sister walks out and enjoys the sun, but when there is more frost she hides in her cell, takes a stocking, puts on her spectacles, and knits. Sister Sophia,[2] not long since arrived, has not been granted admittance, those in authority having refused it. She has found hospitality at the priest's with her old woman. The other sisters are all in different places. Dearly loved sister, art thou not weary reading this letter? All the others have gone to dinner. I remain on guard by the sick Anastasia. In the cells next ours is sister Catherina [3] giving a lesson. We are embroidering for church, Sisters Tatiana and Maria with great zeal. Our father Nicholas gathers us around him in the evenings, and reads to us while we pass the time with needlework. With his meekness and good health he does not disdain to saw and chop wood for our needs, cleans the roads, too, with the children. Our mother Alexandra greets thee, sister, and sends her motherly blessings and hopes, sister, that thou livest in the Spirit of Christ. Life is hard but the spirit is strong. Dear

[2] Isa, Baroness Buxhoevden, lady in waiting.
[3] Miss Schneider.

sister Seraphine, may God keep thee. I beg for your prayers.
Christ be with thee.

The Sinful sister FEODORA.

Prayers!

22 of January.

So unexpectedly I received the letter of the 1st and the card
of the 10th. I hasten to reply. Tenderly we thank through
you Karochinsky. Really it is touching that even now we
are not forgotten. God grant that his estates should be spared.
God bless him. I am sending you some food but I do not
know if it will ever reach you. Often we think of you. I
wrote to you on the 16th through the hospital, on the 17th
a card by Mr. Gibbs, and on the 9th two letters by ———.
There! I have dropped my favorite pen and broken it. How
provoking! It is fearfully cold, 29 degrees, 7 in the bathroom,
and blowing in from everywhere. Such a wind, but they are
all out. We hope to see the officer Tamarov if only from a
distance. So glad you received everything. I hope you wear
the gray shawl, and that it smells of vervaine, a well-remembered scent. Kind Zinoschka found it in Odessa, and sent it
to me.

I am so surprised you have made the acquaintance of
Gorky. He was awful formerly. Disgusting and immoral
books and plays he wrote. Can it be the same man? How
he fought against father and Russia when he lived in Italy.
Be careful, my love. I am so glad you can go to church. To
us it is forbidden, so service is at home, and a new priest serves.
How glad I am that all is well with Serge. With Tina it
will be difficult, but God will help her. It is true what they
say about Marie Rebinder's husband? She wrote me, through
Isa, that they are still in Petrograd, and that they threatened
to kill him. It is difficult to understand people now. Sometimes they are with the Bolshevists outwardly, but in their
hearts they are against them.

The cross we hung over the children's beds during their illness but during church service it lies on the table. Bishop Gerogene serves special prayers daily for father and mother— he is quite on their side, which is strange. I must hurry as one waits to take this letter. I am sending you a prayer I wrote on a piece of birchbark we cut. I can't draw much as my eyes are so bad, also my fingers are quite stiff from cold. Such a wind, and it blows so in the rooms. I am sending you a little image of the Holy Virgin. Thanks for the lovely prayer. I wear often the jackets you gave me. I send you all my soul-prayers and love. I believe firmly so I am quite calm. We are all your own and kiss you tenderly.

On the same day Grand Duchess Olga wrote a brief note.

Dearest, we were so glad to hear from you. How cold it is these days, and what a strong wind. We have just come back from a walk. On our window it is written—"Anna darling——" I wonder who wrote it. God bless you, dear. Be well. Your OLGA.

Give my love to all who remember me.

Two other notes from Olga followed in February and just before Easter.

Darling, with all my loving heart I am with you these hard days for you. God help and comfort you, my darling. On Mamma's table stands the mauve bottle you sent her and which reminds us so much of you. There is much sun, but great frosts also and winds, and very cold in the rooms, especially in our corner room, where we live as before. All are well, and we walk much in the yard. There are many churches around here, so we are always hearing bells ringing. God bless you, darling. How sad your brother and sister are not with you. Your own OLGA.

We all congratulate you tenderly with the coming Easter, and wish you to spend it as peacefully as anyone can now. I always think of you when they sing during mass the prayer we used to sing together on the yacht. I kiss you.

OLGA.

The other children also wrote me at this time. Grand Duchess Tatiana wrote two short but characteristic notes, the first one on my name day, January 12. In all these letters it will be seen how confidently the family looked forward to a future of freedom and happiness. This constant optimism in the midst of ever-increasing surveillance and cruelty is my excuse for including notes of slight general interest.

Tatiana wrote first:

"You remember the cozy evenings by the fireside? How nice it was. Did you again see Groten and Linevitch? (the faithful aides-de-camp). Well, good-bye, my darling Annia. God bless you. Good-bye—till when?

Your T.

Also—

My beloved darling. How happy we are to get news from you. I hope you got my letters. I think often of you and pray God to keep you from all harm and help you. I am glad you know the Eristoffs now. We get such good letters from Zina, she writes so well. There are many sadnesses in these days. God be with you. It is very cold. Papa wears his Cossack uniform and we remember how much you liked it. I kiss you tenderly, and love you, and congratulate you on your dear name day.

T.

From the Grand Duchess Marie Nicolaevna.

Good morning, my darling! What a long time since I have written to you, and how glad I was to get your little letter. It is very sad we don't see each other, but God will arrange for us to meet, and what joy it will be then. We live in the house where you have been. Do you remember the rooms? They are quite comfortable when a little arranged. We walk out twice every day. Some of the people here are kind. Every day I remember you, and love you very much. Mr. Gibbs gave us photographs he made of you—it was so nice to have them. Your perfumes remind us so much of you. I wish you every blessing from God, and kiss you tenderly. Don't be sad. Love to all yours.   Your loving MARIE.

My darling beloved, how are you? We are all well, walk much in the yard, and have a little hill down which we can slide. There is much frost these days so Mama sits at home. You will probably get this in February, so I congratulate you on your name day. God help you in future and bless you. We always remember and speak of you. May God guard all your ways. Don't be sad, dear. All will be well, and we shall be together again. I kiss you tenderly.   MARIE.

Alexei wrote that same month of January, 1918:

My darling Annia. We are so glad to have news from you, and to hear that you got all our things. Today there are 29 degrees of frost, a strong wind, and sunshine. We walked, and I went on skees in the yard. Yesterday I acted with Tatiana and Gilik a French piece. We are now preparing another piece. We have a few good soldiers with whom I play games in their rooms. Kolia Deravenko comes to me on holidays. Nagorini, the sailor, sleeps with me. As servants we have Wolkoff, Sednoff, Troup, and Chemoduroff. It is time to go to lunch. I kiss and embrace you. God bless you.   ALEXEI.

The remaining letters from the Empress, dating from the end of January to the last days of April, 1918, are uncomplaining, yet are full of suffering and the prescience of tragic events to come. I do not believe that the Empress ever lost faith in the ultimate happiness of her beloved family, but her keen mind fully comprehended the terrible march of events in the torn Empire, and she knew that trials and still greater trials had to be faced by the Emperor and herself. Her courage in the face of this certain conviction is beyond any praise of mine.

On the 23rd of January she wrote:

My precious child: There is a possibility of writing to you now as ———— leaves here on the 26th. I only hope no one robs him on the way. He takes you two pounds of macaroni, three pounds of rice, and a little ham. It is so well ———— does not live with us. I have knitted stockings, and have knitted you a pair. They are men's size but they will do under valenki and when it is cold in the rooms. Here we have 29 degrees of frost, and 6 in the big room. It is blowing terribly. I was keenly touched by the money you sent, but do not send any more as for the present we have all we need. There have been days when we did not know what to do. I wonder what you are living on. The little money you had I put in the box with your jewels. (My fingers are so stiff I can hardly hold my pen.) I am glad your rooms are so comfortable and so light, but it must be difficult for you to climb the long staircase. How are your poor back and legs?

I know nothing about Lili Dehn, and from my two sisters and my brother I have heard nothing for a year. Only one letter from my sister Elizabeth (Grand Duchess Serge) last summer. Olga Alexandrovna [4] writes long letters to the chil-

[4] Sister of the Emperor.

dren all about her boy whom she adores and nurses herself. The grandmamma I think is getting very old, and is very sad.

Tudles has four in her room. They say that Marie P.[5] lives well in Kisslowdsk, both her sons are with her and she receives all the *beau monde* from Petrograd. Merika[6] lives there also and is expecting a baby. Marianna Ratkova has bought a house there, and receives on Thursdays. Mr. Gibbs asks often about you, also Tudles, and my big Niouta Demidoff. The little doggy lies on my knees and warms them. It is mortally cold, but in Petrograd there is probably worse darkness, hunger, and cold. God help you all to bear it patiently. The worse here the better in yonder world.

It hurts to think how much bloodshed will have to be before better days come. . . . Darling, I send you all my love, and am so sad I can send you little else. I embroider for the church when my eyes allow me, otherwise I knit, but soon I shall have no more wool. We can't get any here—too dear, and very bad. I have had a letter from Shoura Petrovskaia, who is taking care of her brother's children. She sews boots and sells them. In October the children got a letter from their old nurse in England—the first one from there. What rot they publish about Tatiana in the newspapers! Do you see your new friend and saviour often? How is he? Love to your kind parents. I would love to write you certain things of interest, but just now there are many things one can't put in a letter. The little one has put on a sweater, and the girls wear valenki in their rooms. I know how sad you would feel. . . .

The kind servant Sednoff has just brought me a cup of cocoa to warm me up. How do you pray with the rosary, and what prayers do you say on every tenth? I generally say Our Father and to the Holy Virgin, but should one say the same

[5] Grand Duchess Marie Pavlovna.

[6] Princess Galatzine.

prayer to the end? I looked for it in the books but did not get any information. I long so to go to church but they allow us that only on great holidays (feasts). So we hope to go on the 2nd of February, and on the 3rd I shall order prayers at the relics for you. How is poor old Soukhomlinoff? Where is Sacha? I suppose one may completely trust the little officer you sent. I asked him to make the acquaintance of the priest who served us before, a most devoted and energetic man, a real fighting priest—more than spiritual perhaps—yet with a charming face, and a constantly sweet smile, very thin, long gray beard, and clever eyes. His feeling for us is known all over the country now by the good ones, therefore they took him away from us, but perhaps better so, as he can do more now. The Bishop is quite for father and mother, and so is the Patriarch in Moscow, and it seems most of the clergy. Only you must be careful what sort of people come to you. I am so anxious about your seeing Gorky. Be prudent, and don't have any serious conversations with him. People will try to get around you as before. I don't mean real friends, honest-meaning people, but others who for personal reasons will use you as their shield. Then you will have the brutes after you again.

I am racking my brains what to send you, as one can get nothing here at all. Our Christmas presents were all the work of our own hands, and now I must give my eyes a rest. . . . How pleased I was that Princess Eristoff has spoken so kindly of us. Give her and also her son our love. Where does he serve now? The people here are very friendly—lots of Kirghise. When I sit in the window they bow to me, if the soldiers are not looking.

What dreadful news about the robbing of the sacristy in the Winter Palace. There were so many precious relics and many of our own ikons. They say it has been the same in the church of Gatchina. Did you know that the portraits of my parents and of father have been utterly destroyed? Also my Russian Court dresses and all the others as well? But the destruction of the churches is the worst of all. They say it was the soldiers from the hospital in the Winter Palace who did it. . . . We hear that the soldiers in Smolny have seized all available food, and are quite indifferent to the prospect of the people starving. Why was money sent to us rather than having been given to the poor? True, there were for us some very difficult times when we could not pay any bills, and when for four months the servants had to go without any wages. The soldiers here were not paid, so they simply took our money to keep them quiet. All this is petty, but it makes great trouble for the commandant. 'The Hofmarshall Chancelerie is still in existence, but when they abolish it I really don't know what we shall do. Well, God will help, and we still have what we need.

I think often of Livadia and what may be happening there. They say that many former political prisoners are stationed there. Where is our dear yacht, the *Standert?* I am afraid to inquire about it. My God! How I suffered when I heard that you were imprisoned on the *Polar Star*. I cannot think of the yacht. It hurts too much.

It is said that our Kommissar is about to be removed, and we are so rejoiced. His assistant will leave with him. They are both terrible men, Siberian convicts formerly. The Kommissar was in prison for fifteen years. The soldiers have decided to send them away, but thank God they have left us our commandant. The soldiers manage absolutely everything here.

I am lying down, as it is six o'clock. There is a fire burning but it barely warms the room. Soon the little one will be coming in for a lesson. I am teaching the children the Divine Service. May God help me to teach it to them so that it will remain with them through their whole lives, and develop their

souls. It is a big responsibility. . . It is such a blessing to
live all together, and be so near to one another. Still you must
know what I have to endure, having no news from my brother,
nor any idea of what lies in the future. My poor brother also
knows nothing of us. If I thought my own little old home
and the family would have to suffer what we have—it is awful!
Then it might begin also in England. However you remember
that our Friend said that no harm would come to my old home.[7]
I try to suppress all these thoughts that my soul may not be
overwhelmed with despair. I trust all my dear ones to the
Holy Virgin. May she shield them from all evil. I still have
much to thank God for; you are well, and I can write to you;
I am not separated from our own darlings. Thank God we
are still in Russia (this is the chief thing), and we are near
the relics of the Metropolitan John, and we have peace.
Good-bye, my little daughter.

Old friends continued to be very dear to the exiled
Empress, and she kept up her interest in all their affairs. Of my sister-in-law who had her first child
while her husband was fighting on the Rumanian front
the Empress wrote:

How much better it would have been if Tina could have gone
to Odessa to have her baby, not far from Serge, and where kind
Zinotchka could have looked after her and arranged everything.
But now that the Rumanians have taken Kichineff Serge has
probably left, and they are together again. Sharing hardships
will cause their love to increase and strengthen. How is Alyas's
(my sister) health? Was it Mariana's former husband,
Derfelden, who was killed in the south? Her mother and
family live in Boris's house.

I sometimes see Isa in the street (*i.e.* from the window).

[7] Rasputine foresaw this correctly and the Grand Duke of Hesse
retains his old home in peace.

The sister of mercy Tatiana Andrievna is now in Petrograd taking care of her sister. Later she will return to Moscow. She seems rather nervous. Give our greetings to our confessor, father Afanasi, father Alexander, and my poor old Zio. I don't know anything about my second servant Kondratieff. What has become of our chauffeurs and the coachman Konkoff? Is old General Schwedoff still alive?

Holy Virgin, keep my daughter from all danger, bless and console her!

5th of February, 1918.

My own darling little one, How terribly sad I am for you about the death of your dear father, and that I could not be with you to help and console you in your great sorrow. You know that I am with you in my prayers. May Christ and the Holy Virgin comfort you, and wipe the tears from your eyes. May God receive his soul in peace. Tomorrow morning I will ask Anoushka to go and order service for him for forty days near the relics. Alas we can pray only at home. In him we both lost a true friend of many years. Father and the children suffer with you, tenderly kiss you, and know all that your sensitive heart feels.

As your telegram went by post I don't know what day God took him to himself. Is it possible it was the same day you wrote to me? I am so glad you saw him daily, but how did it happen, your poor father? For himself one must thank God—so many hardships to live through—no home, and everything so bad. I remember how it was foretold to us (by Rasputine) that he would die when Serge married. And you two women are all alone now. I wonder if your brother-in-law was there to help you, or your kind uncle. I shall try to write to his address a long letter, and also to your mother. Tell her I kiss her tenderly, and how much we have always loved her and honored your father. He was a rare man. . . . Don't cry. He is happy now, rests and prays for you at the Throne of God.

I am glad that you received my two letters. Now you will get two more. What your little messenger will tell you about your dear ones is for yourself alone. What horrors go on at Yalta and Massandra—My God! Where is the salvation for us all and for the poor officers? All the churches being ruined —nothing held sacred any more—it will finish in some terrible earthquake, or something like it as the chastisement of God. May He have mercy on our beloved country. How I pray for Russia. . . .

They say that the Japanese are in Tomsk and keep good order there. I hope you got our little parcel. As we have no sugar I shall send you a little honey which you can eat during Lent. We live still by the old style, but probably shall have to change. Only I don't know how it will be then with Lent and all the services (festivals and fasts). The people may be very angry if two weeks are thrown out. That is why it was never done before. . . .

The sun shines and even warms us in the day times. I feel that God will not forsake but will save us, though all is so dark and tears are flowing everywhere. . . . My little one, don't suffer too much. All this had to be. Only My God, how sorry I am for the innocent ones killed everywhere. I can't write any more. Ask your mother to forgive the mistakes I shall make in writing to her in Russian, and that I cannot express myself as warmly as I would like to. Good-bye, my darling. I am sending you letters from father and the children.

2nd of March, 1918.

Darling child: Thanks for all from father, mother and the children. How you spoil us all by your dear letters and gifts. I was very anxious going so long without news from you, especially as rumors came that you were gone. Alas, I can't write you as I could wish for fear that this may fall into other hands. We have not yet received all that you have sent (contraband). It comes to us little by little. Dear child, do be careful of the people who come to see you. The way is so slippery, and it is so easy to fall. Sometimes a road is cleared through the snow on which one's true friends are to walk—and then the road becomes still more slippery!

We are all right, and I am now a real mistress of a household, going over accounts with M. Gilliard. New work and very practical. The weather is sunny—they are even sunburned, and even when the frost comes back it is warmer in the sun. I have sat twice on the balcony and sometimes sit in the yard. My heart has been much better, but for a week I have had great pains in it again. I worry so much. My God! How Russia suffers. You know that I love it even more than you do, miserable country, demolished from within, and by the Germans from without. Since the Revolution they have conquered a great deal of it without even a battle. . . . If they created order now in Russia how dreadful would be the country's debasement—to have to be grateful to the enemy. They must never dare to attempt any conversations with father or mother.

We hope to go to Communion next week, if they allow us to go to church. We have not been since the 6th of January. I shall pray to the rosary you have written. Kiss your poor mother. I am glad you took some of your things from the hospital. Best love to poor G. Soukhomlinoff. What terrible times you are all living through. On the whole we are better off than you. . . . Soon spring is coming to rejoice our hearts. The way of the cross first—then joy and gladness. It will soon be a year since we parted, but what is time? Life here is nothing—eternity is everything, and what we are doing is preparing our souls for the Kingdom of Heaven. Thus nothing, after all, is terrible, and if they do take everything from us they cannot take our souls. . . . Have patience, and these days of suffering will end, we shall forget all the anguish and thank God. God help those who see only the bad, and don't try to understand that all this will pass. It cannot be otherwise. I cannot write all that fills my soul, but you, my little martyr, understand it better than I. You are farther on than I. . . . We live here on earth but we are already half gone to the next world. We see with different eyes, and that makes it often difficult to associate with people who call themselves, and really are religious. . . . My greatest sin is my irritability. The endless stupidity of my maid, for instance—she can't help being stupid, she is so often untruthful, or else she begins to sermonize like a preacher and then I burst—you know how hot-tempered I am. It is not difficult to bear great trials, but these little buzzing mosquitoes are so trying. I want to be a better woman, and I try. For long periods I am really patient, and then breaks out again my bad temper. We are to have a new confessor, the second in these seven months. I beg your forgiveness, too, darling. Day after tomorrow is the Sunday before Lent when one asks forgiveness for all one's faults. Forgive the past, and pray for me. Yesterday we had prayers for the dead, and we did not forget your father. A few days ago was the twenty-sixth anniversary of my father's death. I long to warm and to comfort others—but alas, I do not feel drawn to those around me here. I am cold towards them, and this, too, is wrong of me.

The cowardly yielding of the Bolshevist government to the triumphant Germans was a source of constant suffering to the Empress. In subsequent letters written me that spring she speaks almost indifferently of the cold and privations suffered in the house in Tobolsk, but she becomes passionate when she writes of the German invasion.

What a nightmare it is that it is Germans who are saving Russia (from Communism) and are restoring order. What could be more humiliating for us? With one hand the Germans give, and with the other they take away. Already they have seized an enormous territory. God help and save this unhappy country. Probably He wills us to endure all these insults, but that we must take them from the Germans almost kills me. During a war one can understand these things happening, but not during a revolution. Now Batoum has been taken—our country is disintegrating into bits. I cannot think calmly about it. Such hideous pain in heart and soul. Yet I am sure God will not leave it like this. He will send wisdom and save Russia I am sure.

It will always be to me an immense gratification that in the midst of her great pain and sorrow for Russia's piteous plight our small group of friends in Petrograd, and those brave souls who dared to risk their lives as message bearers, were able to get to the forlorn family in desolate Siberia at least the necessities of life of which a cruel and inefficient government deprived them. The Empress who all her life had but to command what she wanted for herself and her children was grateful, pathetically grateful, for the simple garments, the cheap little luxuries, even the materials for needlework we were able to convey to them. She thanks me almost effusively for the jackets and sweaters we sent her and the girls in their cold rooms. The wool was so soft and nice, but the linen, she feared, was almost too fine. This was early in March, but spring was already creeping across the steppes.

The weather is so fine that I have been sitting out on the balcony writing music for the Lenten prayers, as we have no printed notes. We had to sing this morning without any preparation, but it went—well, not too badly. God helped. After service we tried to sing some new prayers with the new deacon, and I hope it will go better tonight.[8]

On Wednesday, Friday and Saturday mornings we were allowed to go to the eight o'clock morning service in church— imagine the joy and comfort! The other days we five women will sing during the home service. It reminds me of Livadia and Oreanda. This week we shall spend the evenings alone with the children, as we want to read together. I know of nothing new. My heart is troubled but my soul remains tranquil as I feel God always near. Yet what are they deciding on in Moscow? God help us.

"Peace and yet the Germans continue to advance farther and farther in," wrote the Empress on March 13 (Russian). "When will it all finish? When God allows. How I love my country, with all its faults. It grows dearer and dearer to me, and I thank God daily that He allowed us to remain here and did not send us farther away. Believe in the people, darling. The nation is strong, and young, and as soft as wax. Just now it is in bad hands, and darkness and anarchy reigns. But the King of Glory will come and will save, strengthen, and give wisdom to the people who are now deceived."

For some reason the Empress seemed to feel that the Lenten season of 1918 was destined to end in an Easter resurrection of the torn and distracted country. At least so her letters indicate. In a mood of fitful kindness and mercy the Bolshevist soldiers in authority in Tobolsk allowed their captives to go rather often to church and to Communion during this season, and the Empress was very happy in consequence. Her letters were full of prayers for the country, in which the whole family joined, and they appeared to look forward to Easter as the day when God would give

[8] Western readers perhaps do not know how indispensable is vocal

some token that the sins of the Russian people, for which they were suffering, were forgiven. Yet never once did she speak of regaining power or the throne. All that was over and forgotten. Neither the Emperor nor the Empress ever indicated in any syllable that they expected to be returned to their former eminence. In fact they never spoke of what might actually happen to the Russian Empire, but they believed that God would hold it together and restore its people to wisdom and strength. For themselves they seemed to look forward to nothing better than an obscure existence with other Russian people. How uncomplainingly they accepted the hard terms of their lives, how grateful they were for the love of distant friends whom they might never see again, is shown in all the last letters I received from the Empress during March, 1918. After receiving one of our parcels of clothing she wrote me:

We are endlessly touched by all your love and thoughtfulness. Thank everybody for us, please, but really it is too bad to spoil us so, for you are among so many difficulties and we have not many privations, I assure you. We have enough to eat, and in many respects are rich compared with you. The children put on yesterday your lovely blouses. The hats also are very useful, as we have none of this sort. The pink jacket is far too pretty for an old woman like me, but the hat is all right for my gray hair. What a lot of things! The books I have already begun to read, and for all the rest such tender thanks. He was so pleased by the military suit, vest, and trousers you sent him,

music in Russian church services where no organ is permitted. All priests are trained musicians, and there is much congregational singing.

and all the lovely things. From whom came the ancient image? I love it.

Our last gifts to you, including the Easter eggs, will get off today. I can't get much here except a little flour. Just now we are completely shut off from the south, but we did get, a short time ago, letters from Odessa. What they have gone through there is quite terrible. Lili is alone in the country with her grandmother and our godchild, surrounded by the enemy. The big Princess Bariatinsky and Mme. Tolstoy were in prison in Yalta, the former merely because she took the part of the Tartars. Babia Apraxine with her mother and children live upstairs in their house, the lower floor being occupied by soldiers. Grand Duchess Xenia with her husband, children, and mother are living in Dulburg. Olga Alexandrovna (the Emperor's sister) lives in Haraks in a small house because if she had remained in Aitodor she would have had to pay for the house. What the Germans are doing! Keeping order in the towns but taking everything. All the wheat is in their hands, and it is said that they take seed-corn, coal, former Russian soldiers—everything. The Germans are now in Bierki and in Charkoff, Poltava Government. Batoum is in the hands of the Turks.

Sunbeam (Alexei) has been ill in bed for the past week. I don't know whether coughing brought on the attack, or whether he picked up something heavy, but he had an awful internal hemorrhage and suffered fearfully. He is better now, but sleeps badly and the pains, though less severe, have not entirely ceased. He is frightfully thin and yellow, reminding me of Spala. Do you remember? But yesterday he began to eat a little, and Dr. Derevanko is satisfied with his progress. The child has to lie on his back without moving, and he gets so tired. I sit all day beside him, holding his aching legs, and I have grown almost as thin as he. It is certain now that we shall celebrate Easter at home because it will be better for him if we have a service together. I try to hope that this attack will pass more quickly than usual. It must, since all Winter he was so well.

I have not been outside the house for a week. I am no longer permitted to sit on the balcony, and I avoid going downstairs. I am sorry that your heart is bad again, but I can understand it. Be sure and let me know well in advance if you move again. Everyone, we hear, has been sent away from Tsarskoe. Poor Tsarskoe, who will take care of the rooms now? What do they mean when they speak of an "état de siège" there? . . .

Darling "Sister Seraphine":

I want to talk to you again, knowing how anxious you will be for Sunbeam. The blood recedes quickly—that is why today he again had very severe pains. Yesterday for the first time he smiled and talked with us, even played cards, and slept two hours during the day. He is frightfully thin, with enormous eyes, just as at Spala. He likes to be read to, eats little—no appetite at all in fact. I am with him the whole day, Tatiana or Mr. Gilliard relieving me at intervals. Mr. Gilliard reads to him tirelessly, or warms his legs with the Fohn apparatus. Today it is snowing again but the snow melts rapidly, and it is very muddy. I have not been out for a week and a half, as I am so tired that I don't dare to risk the stairs. So I sit with Alexei. . . . A great number of new troops have come from everywhere. A new Kommissar has arrived from Moscow, a man named Jakovleff, and today we shall have to make his acquaintance. It gets very hot in this town in Summer, is frightfully dusty, and at times very humid. We are begging to be transferred for the hot months to some convent. I know that you too are longing for fresh air, and I trust that by God's mercy it may become possible for us all.

They are always hinting to us that we shall have to travel either very far away, or to the center (of Siberia), but we hope that this will not happen, as it would be dreadful at this season. How nice it would be if your brother could settle himself in Odessa. We are quite cut off from the south, never hear from anybody. The little officer will tell you—he saw me apart from the others.[9] I am so afraid that false rumors will reach your ears—people lie so frantically. Probably the little one's illness was reported as something different, as an excuse for our not being moved.[10] Well, all is God's will. The deeper you look the more you understand that this is so. All sorrows are sent us to free us from our sins or as a test of our faith, an example to others. It requires good food to make plants grow strong and beautiful, and the gardener walking through his garden wants to be pleased with his flowers. If they do not grow properly he takes his pruning knife and cuts, waiting for the sunshine to coax them into growth again. I should like to be a painter, and make a picture of this beautiful garden and all that grows in it. I remember English gardens, and at Livadia you saw an illustrated book I had of them, so you will understand.

Just now eleven men have passed on horseback, good faces, mere boys—this I have not seen the like of for a long time. They are the guard of the new Kommissar. Sometimes we see men with the most awful faces. I would not include them in my garden picture. The only place for them would be outside where the merciful sunshine could reach them and make them clean from all the dirt and evil with which they are covered.

God bless you, darling child. Our prayers and blessings surround you. I was so pleased with the little mauve Easter egg, and all the rest. But I wish I could send you back the money I know you need for yourself. May the Holy Virgin guard you from all danger. Kiss your dear mother for me. Greet-

[9] By this the Empress meant that the secret messenger would give me particulars she dared not write in her letter.

[10] To a convent as they desired.

ings to your old servant, the doctors, and Fathers John and Dosifei. I have seen the new Kommissar, and he really hasn't a bad face. Today is Sacha's (Count Voronzeff, aide-de-camp) birthday.

March 21.

Darling child, we thank you for all your gifts, the little eggs, the cards, and the chocolate for the little one. Thank your mother for the books. Father was delighted with the cigarettes, which he found so good, and also with the sweets. Snow has fallen again, although the sunshine is bright. The little one's leg is gradually getting better, he suffers less, and had a really good sleep last night. Today we are expecting to be searched— very agreeable! I don't know how it will be later about sending letters. I only hope it will be possible, and I pray for help. The atmosphere around us is fairly electrified. We feel that a storm is approaching, but we know that God is merciful, and will care for us. Things are growing very anguishing. Today we shall have a small service at home, for which we are thankful, but it is hard, nevertheless, not to be allowed to go to church. You understand how that is, my little martyr.

I shall not send this, as ordinarily, through ———, as she too is going to be searched. It was so nice of you to send her a dress. I add my thanks to hers. Today is the twenty-fourth anniversary of our engagement. How sad it is to remember that we had to burn all our letters, yours too, and others as dear.[11] But what was to be done? One must not attach one's soul to earthly things, but words written by beloved hands penetrate the very heart, become a part of life itself.

I wish I had something sweet to send you, but I haven't anything. Why did you not keep that chocolate for yourself? You need it more than the children do. We are allowed one

---

[11] All purely personal letters were burned in the palace at Tsarskoe Selo as soon as the news of the Emperor's abdication reached us, the Empress being determined that her most sacred possessions should

and a half pounds of sugar every month, but more is always given us by kind-hearted people here. I never touch sugar during Lent, but that does not seem to be a deprivation now. I was so sorry to hear that my poor lancer Ossorgine had been killed, and so many others besides. What a lot of misery and useless sacrifice! But they are all happier now in the other world. Though we know that the storm is coming nearer and nearer, our souls are at peace. Whatever happens will be through God's will. Thank God, at least, the little one is better.

May I send the money back to you? I am sure you will need it if you have to move again. God guard you. I bless and kiss you, and carry you always in my heart. Keep well and brave. Greetings to all from your ever loving, A.

This letter, written near the end of March, 1918, was the last I ever received written by her Majesty's own hand. A little later in the spring of that year she and the Emperor were hurriedly removed to Ekaterinaburg—the last place from which the world has received tidings of them. The children and most of the suite were left behind in Tobolsk, the poor little Alexei still ill and suffering, and cruelly deprived of the solace of his mother's love and devotion. In May I received a brief letter from Grand Duchess Olga who with difficulty managed to get me news of her parents and the family.

Darling, I take the first opportunity to write you the latest news we have had from ours in Ekaterinaburg. They wrote
not be made public by the Provisional Government. She never recovered from the grief of destroying her youthful love letters, which were more to her than the most costly jewels she possessed, the richest of any sovereign in Europe. To me this is a singular revelation of the real character of the Empress.

on the 23rd of April that the journey over the rough roads was terrible, but that in spite of great weariness they are well. They live in three rooms and eat the same food as the soldiers. The little one is better but is still in bed. As soon as he is well enough to be moved we shall join them. We have had letters from Zina but none from Lili. Have Alya and your brother written? The weather has become milder, the ice is out of the river Irtish, but nothing is green yet. Darling, you must know how dreadful it all is. We kiss and embrace you. God bless you.

OLGA.

After this short letter from Olga came a card from Ekaterinaburg written by one of the Empress's maids at her dictation. It contained a few loving words, and the news that they were recovering from the fatigue of their terrible journey. They were living in two rooms—probably, although this is not stated, under great privations. She hoped, but could not tell yet, that our correspondence could be continued. It never was. I had a card a little later from Mr. Gibbs saying that he and M. Gilliard had brought the children from Tobolsk to Ekaterinaburg and that the family was again united. The card was written from the train where he and M. Gilliard were living, not having been allowed to join the family in their stockaded house. Mr. Gibbs had an intuition that both of these devoted tutors were soon to be sent out of the country and such proved to be the case. This was my last news of my Empress and of my Sovereigns, best of all earthly friends.

In July short paragraphs appeared in the Bolshevist newspapers saying that by order of the Soviet at

Ekaterinaburg the Emperor had been shot but that the Empress and the children had been removed to a place of safety. The announcement horrified me, yet left me without any exact conviction of its truth. Soviet newspapers published what they were ordered to publish without any regard whatever to facts. Thus when a little later it was announced that the whole family had been murdered—executed, as they phrased it—imagine "executing" five perfectly innocent children!—I could not make myself believe it. Yet little by little the public began to believe it, and it is certain that Nicholas II and his family have disappeared behind one of the world's greatest and most tragic mysteries. With them disappeared all of the suite and the servants who were permitted to accompany them to the house in Ekaterinaburg. My reason tells me that it is probable that they were all foully murdered, that they are dead and beyond the sorrows of this life forever. But reason is not always amenable. There are many of us in Russia and in exile who, knowing the vastness of the enormous empire, the remoteness of its communications with the outside world, know well the possibilities of imprisonment in monasteries, in mines, in deep forests from which no news can penetrate. We hope. That is all I can say. It is said, although I have no firsthand information on the subject, that the Empress Dowager has never believed that either of her sons was killed. The Soviet newspapers published accounts of the "execution" of Grand Duke Michail, and strong evidence has been presented that he was murdered in Siberia with others of the family, including the Grand Duchess Serge. These same newspapers, however, officially stated that Grand Duke Michail had been assisted to escape by English officers.

The most fantastic contradictions concerning all these alleged murders have from time to time cropped up. When I was in prison in the autumn of 1919 a fellow prisoner of the Chekha, the wife of an aide-de-camp of Grand Duke Michail, told me positively that she had received a letter from the Emperor's brother, safe and well in England.

Perhaps the strangest incident of the kind happened to me when I was hiding from the Chekha after my last imprisonment and my narrow escape from a Kronstadt firing squad. A woman unknown to me approached me and calling me by my name, which of course I did not acknowledge, showed me a photograph of a woman in nun's robes standing between two men, priests or monks. "This," she said mysteriously and in a whisper, "is one you know well. She sent it to you by my hands and asks you to write her a message that you are well, and also to give your address that she may write you a letter."

I looked long at the photograph—a poor print— and I could not deny to myself that there was something of a likeness in the face, and especially in the long, delicate hands. But the Empress had always been slender, and after her ill health became almost emaciated. This woman was stout. I might, had I had the slightest assurance of safety, have taken the risk of writing my name and address for this stranger. But no one in Russia takes such risks. The net of the Chekha is too far flung.

I have one word more to say about these letters of the Empress Alexandra Feodorovna. I have translated them as faithfully and as literally as possible, leaving out absolutely nothing except a few messages of affection and some religious expressions which seem to me too intimate to make public, and which might appear exaggerated to western readers. I have included letters which may be thought trivial in subject, but I have done it purposely because I yearned to present the Empress as she was, simple, self-sacrificing, a devoted wife, mother, and friend, an intense patriot, deeply and consistently religious. She had her human faults and failings, as she freely admits. Some of these traits can be described, as the French express it, as "the faults of her quality." Thus her great love for her husband, which never ceased to be romantic and youthful, caused her at times cruel heart pangs. Because this has nothing to do with her life or her story I should not allude to the one cloud that ever came between us—jealousy. I should leave that painful, fleeting episode alone, knowing that she would wish it forgotten, except that in certain letters which have been published she herself has spoken of it so bitterly that were I to omit mention of it entirely I might be accused of suppressing facts.

I have, I think, spoken frankly of the preference of the Emperor for my society at times, in long walks, in tennis, in conversation. In the early part of 1914 the Empress was ill, very low-spirited, and full of morbid reflections. She was much alone, as the Emperor was occupied many hours every day, and the children were busy with their lessons. In the Emperor's leisure moments he developed a more than or-. dinary desire for my companionship, perhaps only because I was an entirely healthy, normal woman, heart and soul devoted to the family, and one from whom it was never necessary to keep anything secret. We were much together in those days, and before either of us realized it the Empress became mortally jealous and suspicious of every movement of her husband and of myself. In letters written during this period, especially from the Crimea during the spring of 1914, the Empress said some very unkind and cruel things of me, or at least I should consider them cruel if they had not been rooted in illness, and in physical and mental misery. Of course the Court knew of the estrangement between us, and I regret to say that there were many who delighted in it and did what they could to make it permanent. My only real friends were Count Fredericks, Minister of the Court, and his two daughters, who stood by me loyally and kept me in courage.

That this illusion of jealousy was entirely dissipated, that the Empress finally realized that my love and devotion for her precluded any possibility of the things she feared, her letters to me from Siberia amply demonstrate. Our friendship became more deeply cemented than before, and nothing but death can ever sever the bond between us.

Other letters written by the Empress to her husband between 1914 and 1916 have within this past year found publication by a Russian firm in Berlin. Some of them have been reproduced in the London *Times,* and I have no doubt that they will also be published in America. These letters reveal the character of the Empress exactly as I knew her. It is balm to my bruised heart to read in the London *Times* that whatever has been said of her betrayal, or attempted betrayal of Russia during the war, must be abandoned as a legend without the least foundation. So must also be discarded accusations against her of any but spiritual relations with Rasputine. That she believed in him as a man sent of God is true, but that his influence on her, and through her on the Emperor's policies, had any political importance I must steadfastly deny. Both the Empress and Rasputine liked Protopopoff and trusted him. But that had nothing to do with his ministerial tenure. The Empress, and I think also Rasputine, disliked and distrusted Grand Duke Nicholas. But that had nothing to do with his demission. In these affairs the Emperor made his own decisions, as I have stated. The strongest proof of what I have written will be found in the letters of the Empress, those she wrote to the Emperor, to her relations in Germany and England, and those included in this volume. Nothing contradictory, nothing inconsistent has ever been discovered, despite the efforts of the Empress's bitter enemies, the Provisional Government and the Bolshevists. Before all the world, before the historians of the future, Alexandra Feodorovna, Empress of Russia, stands absolved.

CHAPTER XXIII

TOWARDS the close of the summer of 1918 life in Russia became almost indescribably chaotic and miserable. Most of the shops were closed, and only the few who could pay fantastic prices were able to buy food. There was a little bread, a very little butter, some meat, and a few farm products. Tea and coffee had completely disappeared, dried leaves taking their places, but even these substitutes were frightfully dear and very difficult to find. The trouble was that the Bolshevist authorities forbade the peasants to bring any food into Petrograd, and soldiers were kept on guard at the railway stations to confiscate any stocks that tried to run the blockade. Frequently the market stalls were raided, and what food was there was seized, and the merchants arrested. Food smuggling went on on a fairly large scale, and if one had money he could at least avoid starvation. Most people of our class lived by selling, one by one, jewels, furs, pictures, art objects, an enterprising class of Jewish dealers having sprung up as by magic to take advantage of the opportunity. There was also a new kind of merchant class, people of the intelligentsia, who knew the value of lace, furs, old china and embroideries, who dealt with us with more courtesy and rather less avarice than the Jews.

My mother and I fell into dire poverty. A home

we had, and even a few valuable jewels, but we clung
to everything we had as shipwrecked sailors to their
life belts.   We could not look far ahead, and we viewed
complete bankruptcy with fear and dread.   I recall one
bitter day in that summer sitting down on a park bench
weary and desolate as any pauper, for I had not in
my pocket money enough to go home in a tram.   I
do not remember how I got home, but I remember
that in that dark hour a former banker whom we had
long known called at our lodgings and told us that he
had a little money which he was about to smuggle to
the Imperial Family in Siberia.   He wanted us to accept twenty thousand rubles of this for our immediate
needs, and gladly we did accept it.   Very soon afterwards the banker suddenly and mysteriously disappeared, and his fate remains to this day a profound
mystery.   I do not even know if he succeeded in getting the money to Siberia.   However, with the hope
he inspired in me I began to think of possible resources
which I might turn to account.   My hospital in Tsarskoe Selo had been closed by the Bolsheviki, but its
expensive equipment of furniture, instruments, horses
and carriages still remained, and I employed a lawyer
to go over the books and to estimate what money I
could realize from a sale of the whole property.   To
my dismay I learned that the place with everything
in it had been seized by my director and head nurse
who, under the Bolshevist policy of confiscation,
claimed all, ostensibly as state property but really as
their own, for they had become ardent Bolshevists.   I
made a personal appeal to these old employees of mine
to let me have at least one cow for my mother who, be-

ing very frail, needed milk. They simply laughed at me. My lawyer took steps to protect my rights, and the result of this rash action was that the former director denounced me to the Chekha as a counter-Revolutionist, and in the middle of an October night our home was invaded by armed men who arrested me and my nursing sister, and looted our rooms of everything that caught their fancy. Among other things they took was a letter from the Emperor to my father explaining the conditions which led him to assume supreme command of the army. This letter, treasured by me, seemed to them somehow very incriminating.

Driven ahead of the soldiers, I went downstairs and climbed into a motor truck which conveyed us to the headquarters of the Chekha in Gorohvaia Street. After my name had been taken by a slovenly official I followed the guard to one of two large rooms which formed the women's ward of the prison. There must have been close to two hundred women crowded in these rooms. They slept sometimes three to a narrow bed, they lay on the tables and even on the bare floor. The air of the place was, of course, utterly foul, for many of the women were of the class that never washes. Some were of gentle birth and breeding, accused of no particular offense, but held, according to Bolshevist custom, as hostages and possible witnesses for others who were under examination or who were wanted and could not be found. In the early morning all the prisoners got up from their narrow beds or the hard floor and made their way under soldier escort to a toilet where they washed their faces and hands. As

I sat miserably on the edge of my bed a woman came up to me introducing herself as Mlle. Shoulgine, the oldest inhabitant of the place, and therefore a kind of a monitor. It was her business, she said, to see that each prisoner received food and to handle any letters or petitions the women might desire to send out. I told her that I desired to send a petition to the head of the Chekha, or to whatever committee was in charge of the prison, asking the nature of the charges against me, and begging for an early trial. This petition was duly dispatched, and very soon after a very large man, a Jew, came to see me and promised that my affair would be promptly investigated. The soldiers on guard spoke to me kindly and offered, if I had money, to carry letters back and forth from my home. I gave them money and was comforted to hear from my mother that Dr. Manouchine was once more working for my release. Although not a Bolshevist, the doctor's skill was greatly respected by the Communists, who had appointed him head physician of the old Detention House. There was a student doctor attached to our prison, and merely because he was a friend of Dr. Manouchine and knew that I was also, he was courteous and attentive to me. So potent is the influence of a truly great character.

The five days I spent in that filthy, crowded cell will never leave my memory. Every moment was a nightmare. Twice a day they served us with bowls of so-called soup, hot water with a little grease and a few wilted vegetables. This with small pieces of sour black bread was all the food vouchsafed us. Some of the prisoners got additional food from outside, and usually these fortunate ones divided what they had with the others. There was one beautiful woman of the half-world who daily received from some source ample food, and like most of the women of her class she was generous. I was told that she had been arrested because she had hidden and helped her lover, a White officer, to escape, and that she felt proud to be suffering for his sake. Perhaps it was from friends of his that she received the food, yet women of her kind, God knows, very seldom meet with gratitude even from those who owe it most.

Although I was accused of no crime and had no idea what accusations could be brought against me, I lived as all the others lived, in a state of constant anxiety and fear. All day and all night we heard the sound of motors and of motor horns, we saw prisoners brought in, and from our windows we could see great quantities of loot which the Bolshevist soldiers had collected, silver, pictures, rich wearing apparel, everything that appealed to them as valuable. In the courtyard we could see the men fighting like wolves over their spoils. It was like living in a pirates' den rather than a prison, and yet we were often enough reminded that we were prisoners. One day all the women in my room were roughly ordered into a larger room literally heaped with archives of the Imperial Government. With soldiers standing over us we set to work like charwomen to sort the papers and tie them up in neat bundles. Very often in the night when we were sleeping exhausted in our cell rooms the electric lights would suddenly be turned on, guards would call out names, and half a dozen frightened women would get up, gather their rags about them, and go out. Some returned, some disappeared. No one knew whose turn would come next or what her fate would be.

The name of my nursing sister was called before mine, and within a short time she returned smiling to say that she was to be sent home at once and that I should soon follow. Two hours later soldiers appeared at the grating and one called out my surname: "Tanieva, to Viborg Prison" I had spirit enough to demand the papers consigning me to this dread women's prison, but the soldiers merely pushed me back with the butts of their guns and bade me lose no time in obeying orders. I still had a little money with which I paid for a cab instead of walking the long distance to the prison, and I begged the soldiers to stop on the way and let me see my mother. For this privilege I offered all the money remaining in my purse, which the soldiers took, also bargaining for the ring I wore on my hand. This I declined to give so they philosophically said: "Oh, well, why not?" And stopped the cab at the door of my mother's lodgings. Of course my poor mother was overjoyed to see me, even for a moment, and so was old Berchik, now almost at the end of his life. Both assured me that everything was being done in my behalf and that at the Viborg prison I would be in less danger of death than at the Chekha headquarters. I might even hope to be admitted to the prison hospital.

A little heartened in spite of myself I went on to Viborg, which lies in a far quarter of the town on what is known as the Viborg side of the Neva. A rather pretty Bolshevist girl was in charge of the receiving office, and when I pleaded ill health and asked to be sent to the hospital she promised to see what could be done. Viborg prison was one of many which during the first frenzied days of the Revolution were thrown open, the prisoners released, and the wardresses murdered. I do not know how other women were induced to take their places, but I do know that the women in whose charge I was placed were so kind and considerate that had any attempt been made against them the prisoners themselves would have fought in their defense. The wardress who locked me in my cell stopped to say a comforting word, and because she saw that I was shivering with cold as well as nervousness, she brought me bread and a little hot soup.

After some hours I had another visitor, Princess Kakouatoff, accused of being the ringleader of an anti-Bolshevist plot, who had been six months in Viborg and was regarded as a "trusty." Among other privileges she had the right to telephone friends of new prisoners, and at my request she telephoned messages to friends who could be of use to my mother if not to me. The princess brought me a little portion of fish which I ate hungrily, and I think she was also instrumental in finally getting me into the prison hospital. This was after I had fainted on the floor of my cell, and everyone in authority, including the prison doctor, knew that I was in no condition to endure the noisy confusion of the huge cell house. The hospital was a little cleaner than the rest of the prison, but it was a pretty dreadful place just the same. For nurses we had good-conduct prisoners, women of low type who stole food and everything else they could lay hands on. They stripped me of my clothes, substituting the prison chemise and blue dressing gown, and took away all my hairpins. I was given a bed in a room with six other women, one of them a particularly awful syphilis case, and two others, very dirty, who spent most of their time going over each other's heads for vermin. I stayed in this ghastly place a very short time, a woman doctor and a prisoner of my own class, Baroness Rosen, succeeding in getting me transferred to a better ward. Nevertheless the whole prison hospital was horrible. The trusties in charge of the wards were in the habit of eating the meat out of the prisoners' bowls, and fighting for food among prisoners throughout the institution was a daily occurrence. I can describe Viborg prison and most of its inmates in one word—beastly. Many of the women were syphilitic, most were verminous, some were half mad. One who slept near me had murdered her husband and burned his body. Nearly all sang the most obscene songs and held unrepeatable conversations Mostly they were so depraved that the doctor in his rounds showed that he was afraid of them. Yet there were among them a few women who, like myself, had led sheltered and religious lives, and who were only now learning that such abandoned specimens of womanhood existed on the earth. There was no attempt at reforming the women. Once there had been a church attached to the prison, but this the Bolsheviki had closed, substituting a cinema to which on special occasions some of the prisoners were admitted. Not many political prisoners had this privilege because they were treated much more rigorously than common criminals. It was the common criminals also, the thieves, murderers, prostitutes, who were released in advance of "counter-Revolutionists," those accused, however vaguely, of political activities.

All the prisons of Petrograd by this time were so crowded with so-called political prisoners that even the women's prison was obliged to receive an overflow of sick men prisoners. This wholesale imprisonment of anti-Bolshevists naturally led to the shooting of thousands of citizens, shooting being simpler than feeding and housing, and in addition an economy of effort on the part of those charged with the mockery of trials. Later the Chekha dispensed with this mockery, but in those days prisoners were given the pretense of a hearing. I can testify to their futility, because I went through more than half a dozen trials and in no case was I accused of any crime, tried for any definite offense, or given anything like a fair hearing. On September 10, 1918, word was brought to the Viborg prison that on the next morning I was to be taken away not to return. This seemed to be a death sentence, and all that night I lay awake thinking of my poor mother and wondering what would become of her alone in the midst of the Bolshevist inferno. Silently and long I prayed for her and for the peaceful release of my own tried soul.

Very early in the morning I was summoned, my own clothes were given me, and I was led to the receiving office of the prison. Here two soldiers waited, and I was taken out between them and marched to the headquarters of the Chekha. In a small, dirty room I underwent an examination by two Jewish Communists, one of whom, Vladimirov—nearly all Jewish Communists assume Russian names—being prominent in the councils of the Communist central committee. For fully an hour these men did everything they could to terrorize me. They accused me of being a spy, of plotting against the Chekha, of being a dangerous counter-Revolutionist. They told me that I was to be shot at once and that they intended to shoot all the intellectuals and the "Bourju," leaving the proletariat in full possession of Russia. They continued this bluster until from sheer weariness they stopped, then one of the men leaned his elbows on the table and with a smile that was meant to be ingratiating said confidentially: "I tell you what. You relate the *true* story of Rasputine and perhaps we won't have you shot, at least not today." I assured the man that I knew no more about Rasputine than they did, perhaps not as much, since I had no access to police records and they had. Then they wanted to know all about the Czar and the life of the Court. As well as I could I satisfied their curiosity, which was that of ignorant children, and at the end of an exhausting interrogation they actually sent me, not to a wall and a firing squad, but back to the filthy cell in the Viborg prison. I dropped on my dirty bed, swallowed a little food brought me by a sympathetic fellow prisoner, and resigned myself for what next might happen to me. What happened was astonishing. A soldier came to the door and called out: "Tanieva, with your things to go home."

Within a short time I stood trembling and weak on the pavement in front of the prison. I could not have walked to my lodgings, in fact I felt incapable of walking at all, but a strange woman observing me and my piteous condition approached, put her arm around me, and helped me into a drosky. I had a little money, perhaps fifty rubles, and I gave it all to the ischvostik to drive me home. Here I found an amazing state of affairs, the general immorality and demoralization into which Bolshevism was driving the people having penetrated our own place. Everyone was turning thief, and my nursing sister, who had been with me since 1905, whom my mother had treated like a daughter, had become inoculated with the virus of evil. The woman had not only appropriated almost all the clothes I possessed, but had stolen all the trinkets and bits of jewelry she could lay hands on. She had even taken the carpets from the floors and stored them in her room. Not daring to attempt to regain any of this property I asked the nurse to please take what she wanted and leave the apartment. "Not at all," she replied. "This place suits me very well and as long as I choose I shall remain." She had embraced Bolshevism, not I am sure from principle, but as the safest policy, and in time she became rich in jewels, finery, and miscellaneous loot. It was months before we finally induced her to leave, and after her departure I have reason to believe that she did everything she could to keep me in trouble with the Bolshevists.

By this time the Communist régime was fully organized. The whole town was divided into districts, each one under command of a group of soldiers who had full license to search—and rob—houses, and to make arrests. Every night the search went on. At seven o'clock all electric lights were turned off, and when, two or three hours later, they suddenly flashed up again, every soul in the district was seized with fear, knowing that this was the signal for the invasion. Often women were included in the searching parties, terrible women dressed in silks and strung with jewelry, stolen of course from the hated "Bourju." Seven times our home was raided, once on the authority of an anonymous letter charging that we were in possession of firearms. Once more I was dragged off to an interminable examination, this time before the staff of the Red Army in a house in Gogol Street. The close connection between the Chekha and the Red Army was apparent because in the two hours during which I sat in the ante-chamber waiting examination a Lettish official of the Chekha passed freely in and out of the committee room, occasionally throwing me a reassuring word. My case would be settled favorably, he said, and it was, for the committee after bullying me for a length of time, dropped the subject of concealed firearms, assumed the snobbish and half cringing air with which I was becoming familiar to the point of nausea, and began asking questions about the Imperial household. They produced a large album of photographs and made me go through it and identify each picture. Finally the head inquisitor told me magnanimously that I could go home, cleared by the highest authority, but that soldiers would go with me and make sure that there were no revolvers or pistols in the house. The search was made anew, and then the men left, obviously disappointed that practically nothing worth stealing had come to light.

Two things of importance were happening in those days. The White Army was approaching Petrograd, and in all the streets soldiers were drilling in anticipation of a battle. Airplanes whirred overhead, and once in so often a shell screamed over the housetops. We prayed for the coming of the White Army, and at the same time dreaded the massacres we knew would precede its entry into the town. The second thing that marked this date was the Communist system of public feeding, free food being furnished by cards distributed according to the status of the individual. The Bolshevist authorities and the soldiers of course had the most food and the best. Next came the proletariat, so-called, and last of all the "Bourju" was provided for. These of the lowest strata in society got hardly anything at all and would have starved, most of them, had it not been for the food smuggling which constantly went on, the peasants from out of town boldly bringing in bulky parcels, and taking back in return for their food, not Bolshevist money, which they disdained, but everything they could accumulate in the way of furniture or dress materials. They even accepted window curtains and table linen, anything, in fact, that could be fashioned into clothing. These same peasants before the Revolution had been expert spinners and weavers, but now they scorned such plebeian occupations because it was easier to barter grains, milk, vegetables, and other produce for the last possessions of the townspeople.

We went on living, somehow, parting with clothing and furniture, burning boxes and even chairs for fuel, walking miles for stray bits of wood, praying for the success of the White forces, praying for protection against what must happen before that success could be achieved. My mother all these days was very ill with dysentery, which was rife in Petrograd, and I had that additional suffering, for I knew that it would take little to bring her frail life to an end.

CHAPTER XXIV

O N September 22 (October 6, New Style) I went in the evening to a lecture in a church. At that time every non-Bolshevist spent as many hours every day as possible in the churches, praying or listening to words of hope and comfort from the priests. The church was, in fact, the only home of peace and rest in the whole of the distracted country. That particular night in church I met some old friends who invited me to go home with them rather than walk the long and dreary, even the dangerous way back to my lodgings. I stayed with my friends that night, and the next morning early I went to mass in the little church where Father John of Kronstadt lies buried. I reached home about midday, and found the place in the possession of soldiers, two of whom had waited the entire night to arrest me, this time as a hostage, the White Army being reported within a few miles of Petrograd. My sick mother prepared me a little food, made a parcel of my scanty linen, and once more we bade each other the despairing farewell of two who knew that they might never meet again on earth. I was quickly conveyed to the headquarters of the Chekha where I was greeted with the exultant welcome: "Aha! Here we have the bird who has dared to stay out a whole night."

Thrust into the old filthy, ill-smelling cell room I found a spot near a dirty window from which I could

get a far glimpse of the golden dome of St. Isaac's
Cathedral. During my whole term in this place I
kept my eyes and my whole mind on that golden dome,
trying to forget the hell that whirled around me. The
woman in charge of the room was a Finnish girl who
had committed the crime of trying to run away to
Finland. She was a stenographer and clerk, and the
Chekha used her by night as an office assistant.
Whether by nature or by association she had become
as hard and as ruthless as her captors, and her imprisonment had many mitigations. It was her pleasant
duty to make out the lists of those who, twice a week,
were taken to Kronstadt to be shot, and her reports
on the subject which she confided regularly to her
chosen comrade, a Georgian dancer named Menabde,
were enough to sicken even those of us who had become
accustomed to wholesale slaughter of unoffending
human beings. We heard little else except death and
threats of death in this place. There was an official
named Boze in the prison, and often we heard him
screeching through the telephone to his wife that he
would be late to dinner that night because he had a
load of "game" to get off to Kronstadt. Under such
conditions pity and sympathy become strangely dulled.
On occasions when I was sent to the kitchens for hot
water I used to get glimpses of the "game," huddled
wretchedly in their seats or restlessly pacing their cells
—waiting. Often when I returned with the water I
found the seats and the cells empty, and although my
heart sank and my senses swam, I never felt the screaming horror a normal person would have felt. This
dulling of the emotions, I suppose, is nature's way of

keeping the mind from giving way entirely. Of course nature took away all human dignity and self-respect, this, too, in mercy. Any prisoner who went to the kitchens was greeted with jeers and foul abuse from the cooks who threw us handfuls of potato parings and withered cabbage leaves, quite as one would throw bones to dogs. Like dogs we eagerly snatched at these leavings, because the prisoners' regular rations were nothing half as palatable, being mostly wormy dried fish and a disgusting substitute for bread.

One day I was called up for examination, and this time a real surprise awaited me. My judge was an Esthonian named Otto, not altogether a brutal man, as it turned out. As I approached his desk he regarded me grimly and without a word handed me a letter, unsigned, and reading about as follows: "To the Lady in Waiting, Anna Viroubova. You are the only one who can save us from this terrible Bolshevik administration, as you are at the head of a great organization fully equipped with guns and ammunition." Sternly the Esthonian judge commanded me to tell him the truth about the organization of which I was the head. Of course I told him that the whole thing was an invention, and he astonished me by saying that although the letter had been posted to my address he had very much doubted its verity. Then he asked, almost gently: "Are you very hungry?" Taken off my guard as much by the kindness as by the prospect of food, I fell against the desk murmuring only half aloud: "Hungry? Yes, oh, yes." Whereupon he opened a drawer of his desk and handed me a large piece of fresh, sweet bread. "Go now," he said, "and

I will discuss your case with my colleague Vikman. In the evening we will see you again."

At eleven that night I was again summoned, this time before the two men. The Esthonian, still kind and courteous, gave me a glass of steaming tea, which did much to lend me courage. Both he and Vikman then put me through a searching examination especially about my relations, real and assumed, with the Imperial Family and with persons of the Court. At three in the morning they released me, more dead than alive with fatigue, Otto telling me heartily that he thought I would be set free within a few days. Vikman, however, declared that my case would have to be referred to Moscow and that I need not expect an early release. I went back to my evil cage expecting nothing. I knew that the threat of the White Army advance filled with terror the whole Bolshevist population, and that in case of actual battle no life outside the slim Communist ranks would be worth the smallest scrap of their worthless paper money.

Very shortly after my return to the cell room I began to hear my name whispered from one wretched woman to another, and I accepted this without much emotion as a prelude to a boat journey to Kronstadt. Early on a certain morning a soldier approached the door and bawled out: "Tanieva, you to Moscow." I happened to be exceedingly ill that day, but mechanically I picked up my little handkerchief containing my few possessions, including a Bible, and followed the escort of two soldiers down the steep steps, as I believed, to my death. Perhaps they had orders to take me to Kronstadt, I cannot be sure of that, but I do know that the route we followed did not lead to the Moscow station. We had walked but a short distance when one of the soldiers said to the other: "What's the good of two of us bothering with one lame woman? I'll take care of her and you can go along. It will soon be over anyway." Nothing loath the other soldier, glad to get out of anything resembling work, took himself off while I, in charge of one armed man, mounted the crowded tram and rode on toward an unknown destination. At a certain point we had to change trams, and here occurred an incident so extraordinary that I almost hesitate to strain the credulity of a non-Russian reader by relating it. The second tram had been delayed for some reason, and a considerable crowd of passengers was waiting for it on the street corner. My soldier stood at my side waiting with the rest, but soon he became impatient. Ordering me not to move an inch in his absence, he ran down the street a short distance to see if the tram were in sight. As soon as he turned his back, people in the crowd began to speak to me. A girl in whom I recognized a former acquaintance asked me where I was going, and when I told her she took a bracelet I gave her and promised to carry it, with news of my fate, to my poor mother. An officer of the old army came up to me saying: "Are you not Anna Alexandrovna?" And when I said yes, he too asked me where I was being taken. "Kronstadt, I think," I answered, but he said: "Who knows?" and pressed into my hands a roll of bills saying that they might be of use to me.

Other people surrounded me, mostly strangers, but

two of them women whom I had often seen at mass in the small church of Father John. They said: "Why should you be shot? The soldier has not come back. Run while the chance is yours. Father John will surely help you." Encouraged by their sympathy, yet hardly knowing what I was doing, I limped off on my crutch much faster than I could have believed possible, the whole street-corner crowd spreading out to shield my flight. I limped and stumbled down Michel Street as far as the Nevski Prospekt weeping and praying all the time: "God save me! God save me!" until I reached the old shopping arcade known as the Gostiny Dvor Here I caught sight of my soldier running in frantic pursuit of his escaped prisoner. It seemed all over with me then but I crouched in a corner of the deserted building and miraculously the soldier ran on without seeing me. As soon as I thought it at all safe I crept out of the old arcade and turned into the Zagorodny Prospekt, where I found a solitary cab. "Take me quickly," I cried to the ischvostik. "My mother is dying." The man replied indifferently that he had a fare waiting, but I thrust into his hands the entire roll of bills given me by the friendly officer, at the same time climbing into the drosky.

Said the ischvostik, "Where shall I drive you?" I gasped out the address of a friend in the suburbs of the city, and the man lashed his half-starved animal into a walk. After what seemed to me many hours we reached the place, I rang the doorbell and fell across the threshold in a dead faint.

My friend and her husband courageously took me

in, fed, warmed me, and put me to bed. They even dared to send word to my mother that I was for the moment safe from pursuit, but they warned her not to come near the house as soldiers would certainly be watching her every movement. As a matter of fact my mother was visited by Red soldiers, arrested in her bed, and closely guarded for three weeks. Our maid also was arrested, as was everyone who came to the house. The old Berchick who had spent almost his entire lifetime in the service of our family was taken ill during this period and died. For five days his body lay uncoffined in the house, the Bolshevist authorities refusing him a burial permit. It was for my mother an interval of utter despair, since in addition to the death of Berchick she lived in constant fear of my re-arrest. In the opinion of the Bolshevist soldiers, however, I had escaped to the White Army, and photographs of me were posted conspicuously in all the railway stations.

The kind friends who had taken me in dared not for their lives keep me long, and wishing them nothing of harm I set out on a dark night without a kopeck in my pockets and with no certain idea where I could find a bed. I had in mind a religious hostel, a place where a few students, men and women, lived under the chaperonage of an old nun. There I went, begging them for Christ's sake to take me in, and there I was hidden for five perilous days. A girl student volunteered to go to see my mother, and go she did, but when hours passed, a day passed, and she did not return, a panic of fear seized all of us, and rather than expose these kind people to risk of imprisonment and death I voluntarily left the place.   What else could I do?

How shall I describe the horrors of the next few months?   Like a hunted animal I crept from one shelter to another, always leaving when it seemed at all possible that my protectors might be punished for their charity.   Four nights I spent in the cell of an old nun whom I knew, but pitying her fears I put on the black head kerchief of a peasant woman and started in a cab, on borrowed money, for the house of a friend near the Alexandra Lavra on the outskirts of the town.   All unknown to me a decree had that day been issued that no one could ride in a cab without written permission from the authorities.   Consequently before we had traveled half the journey the cab was stopped by two women police, fierce creatures armed with rifles, who called out to the ischvostik: "Halt! We arrest you and your passenger."   Hastily I crammed all the money I had into the ischvostik's hand and begged the women to let me go as I had just been discharged from hospital and knew nothing of the new rule.   Oddly enough they let us drive on, but very soon the ischvostik, sick with terror, stopped his horse and told me that he would take me no further.   I got out and staggered on through the muddy snow, for it was now late in the autumn of 1919.   A former officer whom I had once known well met and recognizing me asked if he might not accompany me to my destination.   "No, no," I cried.   "It would be madness for you to be seen with me.   I cannot explain, only go, go, as fast as you can."   I staggered on, dripping with rain until I reached my friend's house.   To my now customary greeting: "I am running away. Will you hide me?" she replied: "Come in. I have two others." Thus did brave Russians in those days risk their lives to save those of others. Under her protection I lived ten days, and in her house I met a woman, a servant in one of the Communist kitchens, who having access to food and supplies, afterwards more than once saved me from starvation.

From one such kindly haven to another I fled in the dead of night. Once I was received in the home of an English woman who out of her scanty stores gave me warm stockings, gloves, and a sweater. Another day or two I spent in the rooms of a dressmaker whose husband was an unwilling soldier in the Red Army. Once I ventured back to the student hostel, where they welcomed me and fed me well, one of their number having just returned from the country with a stock of smuggled food. Here I had news from my dear mother from the girl who had gone to her on my behalf, and had, after ten days' detention by the Chekha, got back to the hostel. Some members of the Chekha, she informed me, looked forward to shooting me instantly when I was caught, but others said that it was certain that I was with the White Army and would never be caught.

From the hostel I sought a paid lodging with the family of a former member of the orchestra of the Imperial Theater. These people, however, were very mercenary and would receive me only on advance payment of a large sum of money. Almost everything my mother and I had owned had been sold long before, but I retained a pendant of aquamarines and diamonds, a wedding present from the Empress, safely hidden in the house of a friend. This I had sold for fifty thousand rubles, giving half the money to the musician's wife in return for a few days' shelter in a wretchedly dirty, unheated room. Here I had to cut my hair short to get rid of vermin, and feeling unable to endure the hole I left it. Yet finding my next lodgings even worse, I returned, and here in the midst of discomfort and bitter cold, I had the joy of meeting my mother and also my aunt Lashkeroff, who brought me the welcome news that they thought they had at last found me a permanently safe retreat. It was miles from where I was staying, and I had to walk every step of the way, but when I arrived I found my hostess a lovely woman belonging to the Salvation Army. Gladly would I have stayed with her indefinitely but that was impossible as I had no passport and the police began to haunt the neighborhood. She did not abandon me for all that, but got me a new shelter in the home of a good priest and his wife. From here I was handed on from one to another of the priest's parishioners to whom he confided the story of my harried career. Once an Esthonian woman told me that her sister had found a Finnish woman who, for a good price, was willing to take fugitives over the frontier, and she strongly advised me to attempt the flight. Some instinct forbade, and it turned out a good instinct, for the Finnish woman, after taking the money, had abandoned the Esthonian's poor sister in the midst of a wood, from which she had to return, empty of purse and in deadly peril of arrest.

Cutting the story of my fugitive existence short, I

finally found something like a permanent abode in the tiny and happily obscure woodland cottage of a working engineer, who kindly offered to take me in to his bachelor quarters a mile or two outside of Petrograd. Here I became once more the happy possessor of a passport, true not in my own name but perfectly legal otherwise. In Russia when a girl marries she gives up her passport to the priest, receiving a new one in the name of her husband. My kind old priest gave one of these maiden passports to the engineer, at the same time reporting to the Commissar of his neighborhood that such a passport had been lost. This was to prevent any possible trouble or inquiry. The Commissar obligingly gave the priest a duplicate, signed and sealed by Bolshevist authority. Now again I was a human being, for no one in Russia can be said to have any identity unless he is in possession of a passport. Mine described me as a teacher, and as such I was henceforth entitled to the Communist rations. For the time being I was less a teacher than an unskilled household servant, for naturally I wanted to do everything possible to repay the good engineer for affording me a safe shelter. I knew nothing whatever of cooking or housework, yet I attempted to do both. The engineer himself was absent all day, but when he returned at night he carried in wood enough to last twenty-four hours, and also water which had to be brought from a great distance. Food, of course, was very scarce. My mother and the friendly priest brought all they could, but even so I would often have suffered had it not been for my old acquaintance, the woman who worked in the Communist kitchen. And here I have to tell another incident which may seem impossible to some readers. One day I was sitting in the little house in the wood, feeling as secure as an escaped prisoner can feel, when I heard a sudden loud knocking at the door. There was no possible place where I could hide, but I sat absolutely still in my chair, hardly breathing for fear of disclosing the fact that the house was not empty. Again came the knocking at the door, this time louder and more peremptory than before. Realizing that it was useless to resist, I arose and with a prayer on my lips, I went to the door and opened it. No one was there. Nothing was in sight save the wintry trees and the frozen path that led to the highway. But yes! There almost at the end of the path stood the shivering figure of a little girl, the daughter of the woman in the Communist kitchen.

"Oh!" she cried, seeing me in the doorway. "I have been looking everywhere for your house and I could not find it."

"But you knocked," I said.

"No, I didn't," declared the child. "I haven't been near the house. I just this minute turned into the pathway to get out of the wind. I'm so glad I've found you. Mother has sent you something."

Who knocked at my door twice? The wind? It never did before or afterwards. If you believe in Providence, as I do, you may agree with me that God did not intend me at that time to starve in the depths of a desolate forest. If you prefer another explanation seek it.

In January, 1920, my kind friend the engineer told me reluctantly that he was about to marry and that the tiny room I occupied would have to be given up. I had not the remotest idea where I was to go. Above all things I desired to embrace a religious life, but in those perilous days no convent in Petrograd dared receive me. The convents were constantly being raided, and the younger nuns were frequently taken out and forced to work on the streets. No religious house could shelter a fugitive even though she possessed a false passport. Again I became a vagrant, spending a night here, a day there, sleeping in any refuge that opened to me. Towards the end of March I again found a home in the house of a priest and his wife who were as parents to me, and to whom I owe a lifetime of gratitude. Here I found not only safety but work, that blessed anodyne against all trouble. My passport, as I have said, described me as a teacher, and a teacher I now became, thanks to my new friends, who found me plenty of pupils among the working-class children of the neighborhood. I taught them the simple elements, and to children of the more intellectual classes languages and music. My pay was in food, but food in the Bolshevist paradise is worth much more than money, so I was completely satisfied.

By this time my appearance was so changed that I lost all fear of the police or the Chekha. One day when I was slowly walking the long distance across the river to my favorite church, the resting place of Father John, a motor car stopped in my path and I recognized as its occupant the Chekha inquisitor Boze, the man who had several times been my brutal jailer. "Grazhdanka (Citizeness)," he addressed me, "please tell me where to find——" he named a street and number whither he was bound, doubtless on some errand of terror. Giving him the direction, I moved on as fast as my crippled legs could carry me, but I need not have been afraid for he did not know me at all.

So went the year 1920, my mother and I and the good priest's family often discussing the possibilities of escape from the increasing starvation, death, and terror which everywhere surrounded us. People did escape, we knew, but how were we to do it—two women, one old and the other lame? It seemed altogether impossible. Besides, we had almost nothing with which to buy our way out of the country. My only shoes were homemade affairs of carpet, and I was so careful of them that often when walking I took them off and carried them in my hands to preserve them. Another thing, beset with dangers as we were in Russia we were no longer hungry, because I had an increasing number of pupils, and each one meant a tiny portion of food and firewood for my mother, my friends, and myself. But here is a strange and a universally human thing. Food and warmth do not bring content to prisoners, they create courage, and when one day in late October we received a letter from my sister, safe in a near-by country which I may not name, the flame of adventure blazed up in the soul of my brave little mother and in my own heart. My sister suggested the possibility of our getting out by one of the ways that persist in flourishing in spite of Bolshevism and the Chekha, and she offered us, if we succeeded in escaping, the shelter of her own home. I cannot reveal any detail of those secret ways of escape, because they still exist, and must not in any way be placed in jeopardy. Enough it is to say that Petrograd is separated from Finland by only a few versts of land, carefully guarded, and by a narrow arm of the Baltic Sea which cannot be quite as successfully guarded. In winter this water freezes, not as unsalted water freezes, smooth and thick and safe for passage, but in rough and treacherous hummocks of mixed ice and snow, with unexpected gaps of half-frozen water opening here and there between the ice masses. Still, the icy Baltic does at times admit of sledge passage, and there are men who make a business of taking over—for a price far beyond what most Russians can afford—refugees who have friends waiting for them in Finland or in countries to the west and south. Sometimes Red soldiers have to be bribed, and often they sell out the people whose money they accept. Sometimes also the men who contract to take refugees over the ice betray their passengers to the Bolshevik guards. Any way you look at it, escape from Bolshevik Russia is about as perilous as going unarmed into a tiger's cage. Yet people dare it, and we did.

It was about the first of December in our calendar, in the year 1920, when we received a second smuggled letter from my sister: "Be ready whenever we send for you." For that promised summons we waited in desperate suspense until two days after Christmas. Then to my mother's lodging came a fisherman and his little boy with the whispered news that we were to go with them on the day following. My mother found means of sending the news to our friend the priest, and he brought it to me. "Tomorrow at four o'clock you go abroad."

The next day at the appointed hour my mother and I, two shivering creatures facing death, but ready, met at a small railway station leading along the Baltic shores. The fisherman's son was also at the station, but obeying instructions, we did not notice him but simply followed wherever he led. Our train journey was short, and at five o'clock, pitch dark in the Russian winter, we alighted at a poor village, following the boy who carried on his back a bag of potatoes. Alas! In the darkness and confusion we lost him, and stood in the icy cold like lost souls, not knowing where to turn. Suddenly out of the shadows a peasant woman approached us. "Are you looking for a boy with a bag of potatoes?" she said in a low voice, and to our frightened assent she murmured: "Follow me." We followed, although, for all we knew, it was to a Chekha prison. Anybody in Russia may be Chekha, the friend who invites you to dinner, the man who buys your last jewel, the woman who offers to guide you over an unknown road. You can trust no one, consequently, when you must, you trust anyone. We followed the peasant woman into a dim hut, and there we found two fishermen who assured us that they were ready that night to take us across the frozen Baltic to a village on the Finnish side. Their horses and sledges, they told us, were safely hidden, but they would be ready to take us and three other fugitives, a lady, a child, and a maid, as soon as we could safely venture to leave the village. As luck would have it there was a festival and a dance going on that night, and we had to sit in that stifling hut in complete silence until two o'clock. Also we had to pay for our shelter and escape one hundred thousand rubles, which my mother had secured by selling her last treasure, a pearl necklace.

When the last peasant had gone to bed and silence wrapped the village, we stole out through the mud and the snow, and got into the rough sledge. Hardly had we struck the rough ice of the Baltic when the sledge overturned, waking the child who, silent before, now began to cry and to beg to go home. The little thing spoke only French and I can still hear him repeating over and over again in a high baby voice which he did not know imperiled the lives of all of us: "Maman, Maman, à la maison, à la maison." For six hours we drove thus, slowly and cautiously over the rotten ice, one of the men driving, and the other running ahead with a long pole testing the ice for a safe pathway. Often we stopped to listen for possible sentinels, and once in the neighborhood of Kronstadt we had such a fright that I wonder the men dared go farther. Plainly to our ears came the grinding of machinery, and we knew that where there was machinery there were men. We stopped long and listened, until our driver suddenly remembered that the noise was that of an ice breaker several miles out of our highway. By this time I was so stiff and drowsy with cold, so nearly frozen, in fact, that I hardly cared what happened to us. Seeing my wretched state, one of the men took off an extra pair of woolen socks he wore and slipped them on my feet. The unknown lady who accompanied us also spared me a warm wrap, and by rubbing and holding me close to their bodies they kept me alive. At eight o'clock of a pale winter morning they lifted me out of the sledge and with the others I stood trembling on the snowy shores of Finland.

"Now you are out of Sovdepia" (Soviet land), said the fishermen cheerfully, "but we are not safe yet, for the Finnish police may catch us and send us back." Hurriedly we climbed the hill to the cottage of one of the smugglers. Here we met his wife, who, gray with fear, came out to meet her husband after his night of peril on the ice. The woman gave us hot coffee, bread, and cheese, but she would not keep us long in her house. We knew that we must report as soon as possible at the quarantine station, and we knew, besides, that the sorely tried Finnish authorities would not be any too glad to see us coming. Do not blame the Finns for this. Every Russian refugee is a burden on their slender resources, and too often a pretended refugee is merely a Bolshevik agent sent to stir up trouble among disaffected workmen. However, on this occasion the Finns received our wretched group with infinite kindness, and made us comfortable during the required period we spent in the quarantine station. Then we went to our separate destinations, all of us to poverty, obscurity, homesickness, to that sunless clime which waits the exile wherever he may go. In the country where my mother and I finally arrived we found my sister, happier than ourselves, because she left Russia before the great horror began, thus saving part of her fortune. My sister gave us food, clothing, a lodging. Except for her bounty we had lost everything we ever owned, home, friends, possessions, country, for Russians now have no country, no flag, no place in the wide world. The best any of us can hope for is an obscure corner in some foreign land where we can earn enough to buy our daily bread, and a quiet place in which to pray every day of our lives: "God save Russia."

I am told, although I can hardly believe it, that in other lands, even in free America, there are beings so deluded that they wish to bring about revolution and Bolshevism. I do not wish for any of them the long nightmare of suffering that I, one of millions, have suffered under revolution and Bolshevism. I pray only that there may be revealed to them the fate of the betrayed who have died and are dying under the criminal administration of the Provisional Government and, later, of Lenine and his fanatical followers. If they can be made to know only in part what my poor, ravished country is today, they will forget their delusions and pray with the exiles: "God save Russia."

APPENDIX A

THE TRUTH CONCERNING THE RUSSIAN IMPERIAL FAMILY

Statement of Vladimir Michailovitch Roudneff, appointed by Minister
of Justice Kerensky Special High Commissioner for Revision and
Investigation of the actions of Ministers and other High Personages of the Imperial Government.

"I was acting as Procureur of the Court of Assizes of
Ekaterinoslav when I received orders from Minister of Justice
Kerensky to become a member of the High Commission of
Inquiry charged with an examination of the acts and abuses of
ministers and other high personages of the former Government.
While working with this Commission in Petrograd I was espe-
cially assigned to examination of sources of secret influences at
Court which were known as Dark Forces. My work with the
Commission lasted until August, 1917, when I was forced to
leave because the President, Mourvavieff, insisted upon my
making reports of a plainly prejudicial character.

"As an Attorney General (*juge d'instruction*) I had access to
all documents, and the right to be present at the examination
of all witnesses, with the view of establishing impartially the
part played by persons accused by society and the public press of
exerting influence on foreign and domestic politics. I was
assigned to read all the papers and letters found in the Winter
Palace, the palace at Tsarskoe Selo, and at Peterhof, especially
the personal correspondence of the Emperor and Empress, certain of the Grand Dukes, and also the correspondence seized
in the course of examination of the house of Archbishop
Varnava, also of Countess S. S. Ignatieff, Dr. Badmaeff,
Voyeikoff, and Anna Viroubova, and also to the relations

383

existing between the Imperial family and the German Imperial family. Being aware of the importance of my inquiry in throwing light on historical events preceding and following the Revolution, I made copies of all documents and letters, *dossiers,* and statements of witnesses. In leaving Petrograd I took with me all these copies, concealing them in my home in Ekaterinoslav, but it is probable that these documents were destroyed when the Bolsheviki raided my house. If by happy chance I find that they still exist I shall certainly publish them in full, without any comments of my own.

"In the meantime I consider it my duty to write a short account of the principal persons who were accused of being Dark Forces. I must, however, warn the reader that as I write from memory some details may escape my mind. When I went to Petrograd to begin my work with the High Commission I admit that I was influenced by all the pamphlets and newspaper articles on the subject of the Rasputine influence, and other rumors and gossip, and I began my work under the domination of preconceived prejudices. But careful and impartial investigation soon forced me to the opinion that these rumors and newspaper accounts were based on slender foundations.

"The most interesting person charged with exercising a malign influence on political affairs was Gregory Rasputine, therefore this person was the central figure of my investigations. The account of the surveillance under which he lived, up to the very day of his death, is of great importance. This surveillance was exercised by the ordinary as well as the secret police, special agents noting all his goings and comings, some of these agents being disguised as policemen or as servants. Everything concerning the movements of Rasputine was carefully recorded every day. If he left his house, even for an hour or two, the moment of his departure and his return was noted, and also every person he met on the road.

"The secret agents kept strict account of all people he met

and of all who visited him. In cases where the names of these persons were not known their full descriptions were taken. After having read all papers and examined many witnesses I reached the conclusion that Rasputine was a person more complex and less comprehensible than had been previously represented. In studying his personality I naturally paid attention to the chronological order of circumstances which finally opened to the man the doors of the Tsar's palace, and I discovered that the first preliminary was his acquaintance with the well known, pious, and learned churchmen Bishops Theofan and Hermogen. I noted also that it was afterwards due to the influence of Rasputine that these two great pillars of the Orthodox Church fell into disfavor. He was the cause of the relegation of Hermogen to the Monastery of Saratoff, and of the disgrace (demotion) of Theofan, after these two archbishops, discovering Rasputine's low instincts, openly turned against him. All the evidence pointed to the conclusion that in the inner life of Rasputine, a simple peasant of the Government of Tobolsk, there occurred suddenly a complete change transforming him and turning him toward Christ. Only in this way can I explain to myself his intimacy with these two remarkable bishops. This hypothesis is moreover confirmed by Rasputine's story of his journey to the Holy Land. This book is marked by extreme naïveté, simplicity, and sincerity. On the recommendation of the exalted churchmen mentioned Rasputine was received by the Grand Duchesses Anastasie Nicholaevna and Melitza Nicholaevna, and it was through them that he made the acquaintance of Mme. Viroubova, *née* Tanieff, then maid of honor. He made a deep impression on this very religiously inclined woman, and gained at last an entry to the Imperial Palace. It was then that awoke in him his worst instincts, hitherto repressed, and it was then that he began adroitly to exploit the religious fervor possessed by very high personages. It must be admitted that he played his part with astonishing cleverness.   Correspondence bearing on the subject and the testimony of various witnesses prove that Rasputine refused all subsidies, gratuities, and even honors which were freely offered him by their Majesties, indicating thus his integrity, his disinterestedness, and his profound devotion to the Throne, insisting that he was an intercessor for the Imperial family before God's throne.   He alleged that everyone envied him his position, that he was surrounded by intriguers and slanderers, and that therefore evil reports concerning him were unworthy of belief.   The only favor he accepted was the rental of his lodgings, paid by the personal Chancellor of his Majesty.   He also accepted presents made by the hands of the Imperial family, such as shirts, waist-bands, etc.

"Rasputine had free entry to the apartments of the Emperor, saying prayers, addressing the Emperor and Empress with the familiar 'thou,' and greeting them in the Siberian peasant manner (with a kiss).   It is known that he warned the Emperor, 'My death shall be thine also,' and that at Court he was regarded as a man gifted with the power of forecasting events.   His predictions were couched in mysterious phrases like those of the Pythons of antiquity.

"Rasputine's income was derived from numerous persons who desired positions and money, and used Rasputine as their intermediary with the Emperor.   Rasputine asked favors for his clients, promising, if these were granted, all kinds of blessings to the Imperial family and to Russia.

"To this must be added that Rasputine possessed within himself a strange power by which he was able to exercise hypnotic suggestion.   I have been able to establish the fact that he cured by hypnotism the disease of St. Vitus Dance which afflicted the son of one of his friends, Simanovitch.   The young man was a student in the College of Commerce, and his malady completely disappeared after two séances in which Rasputine plunged the patient into hypnotic slumbers.

"Another case establishing the hypnotic power of Rasputine may be noted. During the winter of 1914-15 he was called to the house of the superintendent of railways in Tsarskoe Selo where lay, entirely unconscious, Anna Alexandrovna Viroubova, who had been seriously injured in a railroad accident. She was suffering from broken legs and a fracture of the skull. Their Majesties were in the room when Rasputine arrived, and he, simply raising his arms, said to the unconscious woman: 'Anushka, open your eyes,' which she instantly did, looking intelligently around her. This naturally made a deep impression on everyone present, including their Majesties, and it served to increase the prestige of Rasputine. Although Rasputine could barely read and write, he was far from being an inferior person. He had a keen and observant intellect, and a rare faculty of reading the character of any person with whom he came in contact. The rudeness and exaggerated simplicity of his bearing, which lent him the appearance of a common peasant, served to remind observers of his humble origin and his lack of culture.

"As so much was bruited in the public press about the immorality of Rasputine, the closest attention was given to this phase of his question. From the reports of the secret police it was proved that his love affairs consisted solely in night orgies with music-hall singers and an occasional petitioner. It is on record that when he was drunk he sometimes hinted of intimacies in higher circles, especially in those circles through which he had risen to power, but of his relations with women of high society nothing was established, either by police records or by information acquired by the commission. In the papers of the Bishop Varnava was found a telegram from Rasputine as follows: 'My dear, I cannot come, my silly women are shedding tears and won't let me go.' As for the accusation that in Siberia Rasputine was accustomed to bathe in company with women, and that he was affiliated with the 'Khlysty' sect, the Extraordinary Commission referred these charges to Gramoglassoff, professor in the Ecclesiastical Academy (of Moscow), who after examination of all the evidence, testified that among peasants of many parts of Siberia the common bath was a usual custom, and that he found no evidence in the writings or preachings of Rasputine of any affiliation with the 'Khlysty' doctrines.

"Rasputine was a man of large heart. He kept open house, and his lodgings were always crowded with a curiously mixed company living at his expense. To acquire the aureole of a benefactor, to follow the precepts of the Gospels according to which the generous hand is always filled, Rasputine took the money offered by his petitioners, but he gave generously to the poor and to people of the lower classes who begged his assistance. Thus he built up a reputation of being at once a generous and a disinterested man. Besides these alms Rasputine spent large sums in restaurants, cafés, music halls, and in the streets, so that when he died he left practically nothing. The investigation disclosed an immense amount of evidence concerning the petitions carried by Rasputine to Court, but all these, as has been said, referred merely to applications for positions, favors, railway concessions, and the like. Notwithstanding his great influence at Court not a single indication of Rasputine's political activity was disclosed.

"Many proofs of his influence were found in the papers of General Voyeikoff, Commandant of the Palace, as for example the following: 'My dear, Arrange this affair. Gregory.' These letters were annotated by Voyeikoff, with the names and addresses of the petitioners, the nature of their demands, the results of their applications, and the date of the replies. Many letters of the same kind were found among the papers of President of the Council of Ministers, Sturmer, and of other high personages. All the letters concerned themselves exclusively with favors and protection for the people in whom Rasputine interested himself. He had special names for various persons with whom he was in frequent contact. Sturmer was called

'The Old Man,' Archbishop Varnava 'Butterfly,' the Emperor 'Papa,' and the Empress 'Mama.' The nickname of Varnava, 'Butterfly,' was found in a letter to Mme. Viroubova.

"The inquiry into the influence of Rasputine on the Imperial family was intensive, but it was definitely established that that influence had its source in the profound religious sentiments of their Majesties, joined to their conviction that Rasputine was a saint, and was the sole intermediary between God and the Emperor, as well as of all Russia. The Imperial family believed that they saw proofs of his sanctity in his psychic power over certain persons of the Court, such as bringing back to life and consciousness the desperately injured Mme. Viroubova, whose case has been described; also in his undoubtedly benign influence on the health of the heir, and on a whole series of fulfilled forecasting of events.

"It is evident that sly and unscrupulous people did everything in their power to profit by Rasputine's influence on the Imperial family, thus waking up in the man his worst instincts. This is particularly true of the former Minister of the Interior, A. N. Khvostoff and of Belezky, Director of the Police Department. To consolidate their position at Court they came to an understanding with Rasputine whereby they agreed to pay him, out of the private funds of the Police Department, the sum of three thousand rubles monthly, besides other sums, that he might require, provided he helped them to place candidates agreeable to them. Rasputine accepted these conditions, and for three months filled his engagements, but finding that the arrangement was not advantageous to himself, returned to his independent manner of work. Khvostoff, fearing that Rasputine would betray him, began openly to oppose him. He knew that he stood well with the Imperial family, and he counted also on the coöperation of the Duma, of which he was a member, and in which Rasputine was cordially hated. This put Belezky in a difficult position, because he doubted Khvostoff's power at Court, and he had no doubt at all concerning Rasputine's power. Belezky decided therefore to betray his chief, and range himself on the side of Rasputine. His object was, to use the words of Rasputine himself, to throw down the Khvostoff ministry. The struggle between these two officials culminated in the famous plot against the life of Rasputine, which created such a sensation in the press during the year 1916. The plot was laid by Belezky in the following manner. An engineer named Heine, owner of several private gambling houses in Petrograd, was hired to go to Christiania to meet the unfrocked monk Illiador Troufanoff, a former friend of Rasputine. The result of this journey was a series of telegrams addressed to Heine and signed by Illiador covertly alluding to a conspiracy against the life of Rasputine. In one of these telegrams it was stated that the forty men engaged in the conspiracy were dissatisfied to wait longer, and it was necessary to send them immediately thirty thousand rubles. These telegrams, coming in war time from a neutral country, were delivered to the police, only after having been read being passed on to the person addressed. Finally, after receiving all the telegrams, Heine presented himself to Rasputine in the guise of a repentant sinner, giving him full details of the plot, in which he owned himself concerned, but which he vowed Khvostoff to be the leading spirit. The result was that Rasputine took the story to the Imperial family, and the dismissal of Khvostoff quickly followed. It is an interesting fact that Heine's telegrams from Christiania mentioned a number of names of persons living in Tsaritzine, former friends of Illiador, who were supposed to be in Christiania busy with the details of the plot. The evidence given at the inquiry proved beyond doubt that the persons concerned had never left their homes.

"Personally the official Khvostoff was highly esteemed by both the Emperor and the Empress, they believing him to be sincerely religious, and devoted to the interests of the Imperial family

and to Russia, but the evidence shows that he was really devoted only to his personal interests. He once invited the head
of the Gendarmerie, General Komissaroff, to go with him in
civilian dress, and to introduce Rasputine to the Metropolitan
Pitirim. They were received by a novice who went to the
Metropolitan's study to announce them. When the Metropolitan appeared Rasputine introduced General Komissaroff, and
disagreeable as it was to see a gendarme officer in his house, his
Eminence invited the men to follow him into his study. There
they discovered Khvostoff sitting on a sofa. Seeing Rasputine
Khvostoff laughed rather nervously, but continued his conversation with the Metropolitan, then, rising to take his departure,
asked General Komissaroff to drive home with him. Komissaroff found himself in an awkward position, and when Khvostoff
suddenly asked him if he understood the affair he answered in
the negative. 'Well,' said Khvostoff, 'it is now clear in what
relation Pitirim stands with Rasputine. When you were announced he was just telling me that he had nothing in common
with Rasputine, and that the person who was waiting to see him
was an eminent Georgian. "Permit me," he said, "to leave you
for a few minutes." Now we see who the "eminent Georgian"
really was.' This was testified to by Komissaroff himself.

"Of all the ministers Khvostoff was the closest to Rasputine.
Rumors of the intimate relations between Sturmer and Rasputine were found to be without foundation. There was between
them, it is true, a friendship. Sturmer understood Rasputine's
great influence, and did what he could to advance the interests
of his clients. He sent fruit, wine, and delicacies to Rasputine,
but there is no evidence that he allowed him to influence political affairs. The relations between Rasputine and Protopopoff, who, for some reason, Rasputine called 'Kalinine' were
no more intimate, although Protopopoff liked Rasputine, and it
is certain that Rasputine defended Protopopoff when the position of the latter was menaced. This was done usually in the

absence of the Sovereigns, Rasputine addressing himself to the Empress, at the same time uttering predictions.

"Protopopoff distinguished himself by an extraordinary lack of will power, representing at different times quite opposing organizations. He was even at one time elected vice-president of the Duma. Protopopoff has publicly been accused of initiating and carrying out an attempt to put down the popular uprising of the first days of the Revolution. He is accused of having placed machine guns on the roofs of houses to shoot down the armed insurgents. However, the *juge d'instruction* Jousvik-Kompaneitz, after having interrogated many witnesses, and examining all the machine guns found in the streets of Petrograd in the first days of the Revolution, has testified that all the machine guns belonged to different regiments, and none, not even those found on the roofs of houses, to the police. Generally speaking, there were no machine guns on roofs, except those placed there at the beginning of the war as a defense against airplane attacks. It must be said that during the critical days of February, 1917, Protopopoff showed a complete incapacity, and from the legal point of view, his absolutely criminal weakness. Among his papers were found intimate and even affectionate letters from Rasputine, but not one letter contained anything more than recommendations in favor of his protégés. Nor in the papers of any other high personages were found letters of different tenor signed by Rasputine. Both press and public seem to have been persuaded that Rasputine was very intimate with two political adventurers, Dr. Badmaeff and Prince Andronnikoff, and that through him these men were able to exercise wide political influence. Evidence has established, however, that these rumors were without any foundation. The two adventurers were, in fact, nothing more than the hangers-on of Rasputine, glad to gather up the crumbs from his table, and falsely representing to their clients that they had influence over Rasputine, and through him influence at Court."

(Here follows at some length the result of the High Commission's inquiry into the activities of Dr. Badmaeff and Prince Andronnikoff, but as they have nothing whatever to do with this history they are omitted. A. V.)

"Badmaeff was the physician of Minister Protopopoff, but the Imperial family had no confidence in his methods—any more than had Rasputine—and in an examination of the servants of the Imperial household, it was demonstrated clearly that the Thibetan doctor had never been called in his professional capacity to the apartments of the Emperor's children.

"General Voyeikoff, Commandant of the Palace, I examined many times in the Fortress of Petropavlosk where he was imprisoned. He did not play a very powerful rôle at Court, but according to letters from his wife, daughter of Court Minister Fredericks, covering the years 1914-15, and found in his house, he was esteemed by the Imperial family as a man devoted to the throne, an impression which I, after several interviews with him, did not share. From letters of Voyeikoff to his wife it is plain that he was hostile to Rasputine. In certain of the letters he calls Rasputine the evil genius of the Imperial family and of Russia, and he believed that his intimacy at Court discredited the throne and gave strength to humors and opinions and slanderous stories by which the anti-Government party profited. Nevertheless he took full advantage of the influence of Rasputine. He had not the courage to reject his petitions, which is proved by the annotations in his handwriting on the letters of Rasputine."

(High Commissioner Roudneff adds that, in his opinion, Voyeikoff thought badly of Rasputine, and that his wife hated the man, but that neither of them communicated their views to the Imperial family. A. V.)

"Having heard a great deal of the exceptional influence at Court of Mme. Viroubova, and of her relations with Rasputine, and having read and believed what was said about her in society and the press, I must admit that when I went to examine her in the Fortress of Petropavlosk I was frankly prejudiced against her. This hostility remained with me up to the moment of her entrance into the office of the Fortress under the escort of two soldiers. As she entered the room I was struck with the expression of her eyes, an expression of more than earthly gentleness and meekness. This first impression was confirmed in all my subsequent interviews with her. From the first conversation which I had with her I became convinced that, given her individuality and her character, she could never have had any influence on politics either foreign or domestic. I believe this in the first place because of the essentially feminine point of view shown by her on all political matters of which we talked, and in the second place because of her loquacity and her complete incapacity to keep secret even facts which might reflect on herself. I became convinced that to ask Mme. Viroubova to keep anything a secret was equivalent to proclaiming it from the housetops, because anything that she thought important she felt impelled to communicate, not only to friends but to possible foes. Noting these two characteristics of Mme. Viroubova, I asked myself two questions—why she stood in close relations with Rasputine, and what was the secret of her intimacy with the Imperial family.

"I found the answer to the first question in conversations with the parents of Mme. Viroubova, M. Tanieff, chief of the private Chancellory of his Majesty, and his wife, *née* Countess Tolstoy. From them I learned of an episode in the life of their daughter which, in my opinion, explained why Rasputine obtained later such an influence over the will of the young woman. At the age of thirteen Mme. Viroubova fell gravely ill of typhus, the illness being complicated with peritonitis, and her condition, according to the physicians, was desperate. Her parents called to her bedside the famous priest, Father John of Kronstadt. Following his prayers the illness took a favorable turn, and the young girl was soon pronounced out of danger. This made a deep impression on her mind, and thereafter strongly inclined her to a religious life.

"Mme. Viroubova first met Rasputine in the house of the Grand Duchess Melitza Nicholaevna (wife of Grand Duke Peter), and that meeting was not a happy event. The Grand Duchess had prepared Mme. Viroubova for the meeting by conversations on the subject of religion, and had given her certain French books on occult subjects. Later the Grand Duchess invited Mme. Viroubova to her house, promising to introduce her to a great intercessor before God in favor of Russia, a man who possessed gifts of prophecy, and the faculty of curing the sick. This interview by Mme. Viroubova, then Mlle. Tanieff, made a great impression on the young woman who was then on the eve of marriage with Lieutenant Viroubova. Rasputine spoke only on religious subjects, and when the young girl asked him if he approved her marriage he answered allegorically saying that the pathway of life was strewn not only with roses but with thorns, and that man progressed towards perfection only through sufferings and trials.

"The marriage of Mme. Viroubova was from the first unhappy. According to the testimony of Mme. Tanieff, the man was completely impotent, addicted to perverted practices and saddistic habits, causing her daughter the most frightful moral sufferings and physical disgust. Nevertheless, believing in the Biblical injunction 'Whom God hath joined let no man put asunder,' Mme. Viroubova for a time kept her sufferings a secret even from her parents, and only after she had been nearly killed by her husband did she reveal to them the tragedy of her marriage. The result was, of course, a divorce. The testimony of Mme. Tanieff concerning the moral character of her son-in-law was confirmed by a medical examination of Mme. Viroubova, ordered by the Commission of Inquiry, and by which was established the virginity of the young woman. This examina-

tion was held in May, 1917. In consequence of her shocking
marital experience the religious inclinations of Mme. Viroubova
were increased and were developed into something approaching
religious mania. She became the purest and most sincere ad-
mirer of Rasputine, who, up to the last day of his life, she
considered a holy man, and one completely disinterested from
every worldly point of view.

"In regard to the question of the intimacy of Mme. Viroubova with the Imperial family, I concluded that it had its roots
in the wholly different mentalities of the Empress and Mme.
Viroubova, that attraction of opposites which so often seems
necessary to complete a balance. The two women were entirely
different, and yet they had many things in common. Both, for
example, were devotedly fond of music, and as the Empress
possessed an agreeable contralto voice and Mme. Viroubova a
good soprano, they occupied many leisure hours singing duets.

"Such were the conditions which produced in the minds of
persons ignorant of the nature of the intimacy between the
Empress and Mme. Viroubova, belief in the exceptional influence of Mme. Viroubova on Court affairs. As has been said,
Mme. Viroubova possessed no such influence, nor could she have
possessed it. The Empress dominated the intelligence and the
will of Mme. Viroubova, but the attachment between the two
women was very strong. The religious instincts deeply rooted
in their two natures explains the tragedy of their veneration of
Rasputine. The relations between the Empress and Mme.
Viroubova could be likened to those of a mother and daughter,
nothing more.

"My opinions regarding the moral qualities of Mme. Viroubova, resulting from interviews with her in the Fortress of
Petropavlosk and in the Winter Palace were entirely confirmed
by the forgiving and Christian spirit displayed by her towards
those who had caused her, in the course of her imprisonment,
the most horrible suffering. Of the insults and tortures to

which she was subjected in the Fortress I did not learn, in the first instance, from Mme. Viroubova herself, but from her mother. Only on direct examination did Mme. Viroubova confirm her mother's testimony, and even then she spoke calmly and with astonishing meekness, saying that her persecutors should not be blamed too severely because they did not realize what they were doing. These tortures of the prison guards, such as spitting in her face, dealing her blows on the head and body, accusing her of being the mistress of the Emperor and of Rasputine, tearing off her clothes and threatening to murder a sick woman who could walk only with the aid of crutches, caused the Commission of Inquiry to transfer the prisoner to a house formerly occupied by the Director of the Gendarmerie (House of Detention). The testimony of Mme. Viroubova presented a complete contrast to that of Prince Andronnikoff. Her statements were all candid and sincere, and their truth was subsequently established beyond doubt by documentary evidence. The only fault I found with Mme. Viroubova was her tendency to wordiness, and her amazing habit of skipping from one subject to another, without regard to the fact that she might be hurting her own cause. Mme. Viroubova appears to have interceded at Court for various persons, but her petitions were received with a certain distrust because of her known goodness and her simplicity of mind.

"The character of the Empress Alexandra was shown clearly in her correspondence with the Emperor and with Mme. Viroubova. This correspondence, in French and English, is filled with sentiments of affection for her husband and children. The Empress occupied herself personally with the education of her children, and she often indicates in her letters that it is desirable not to spoil them or to give them habits of luxury. The correspondence reveals also the deep piety of the Empress. In her letters to her husband she often describes her emotions during religious services, and speaks of the peace and tranquillity of her soul after prayer. Hardly ever, in the course of this long correspondence, are any allusions made to politics. The letters concern intimate and family affairs only. In passages in which Rasputine is mentioned she speaks of him as 'that holy man,' and shows that she considers him one sent of God, a prophet, and a man who prays sincerely for the Imperial family. Through the whole correspondence, which covers a period of ten years, I found not one single letter written in German. According to the testimony of Court adherents I have proof that before the War German was never spoken at Court. Because of public rumors of the sympathy of the Empress for Germany and of the existence in the Palace at Tsarskoe Selo of private wires to Berlin, I made a careful examination of the apartments of the Imperial family, and I found no indications at all of communications between the Imperial household of Russia and the Imperial household of Germany. I also examined the rumors concerning the beneficence of the Empress towards the German wounded and prisoners of War, and I found that the Empress showed compassion for the sufferings of Germans and Russians alike, without distinction, desiring to fulfill the injunction of Christ who said that whoever visited the sick and suffering also visited Himself.

"For these reasons, and above all on account of the frail health of the Empress, who suffered from a disease of the heart, the Imperial family led a very retired life, which favored the development, especially in the Empress, of extreme piety. Inspired by her devotion the Empress introduced into certain churches attached to the Court a régime of monastic services, and followed with delight, in spite of her ill health, up to the very end, masses which lasted for hours on end. This same excessive religious zeal was the foundation for her admiration for Gregory Rasputine, who, possessing an extraordinary power of suggestion, exercised an undeniably salutary effect on the invalid Tsarevitch. Because of her extreme piety the Empress was in no proper state of mind to understand the real source of the amazing influence of Rasputine on the health of the Heir, and she believed the explanation to be due, not at all to hypnotism, but to the celestial gifts which Rasputine owed to the sanctity of his life.

"A year and a half before the Revolution of 1917, the former monk, Illiador Troufanoff, sent his wife from Christiania to Petrograd with the proposal that the Imperial family purchase the manuscript of his book, which later appeared under the title of 'The Holy Devil,' in which the relations of the Imperial family with Rasputine were scandalously represented. The Police Department interested itself in the matter, and at its own imminent risk entered into negotiations with the wife of Illiador concerning the purchase of the manuscript for which Illiador demanded, I am assured, sixty thousand rubles. The affair was finally submitted to the Empress Alexandra who repudiated with indignation the vile proposition of Illiador, saying that 'white could never be made black, and that an innocent person could never be assoiled.'

"In terminating this inquiry I believe it necessary to repeat that Bishops Theofan and Hermogen contributed importantly to the introduction of Rasputine at Court. It was because of their recommendations that the Empress, in the beginning, received Rasputine cordially and confidently. Her sentiments towards him were fortified only by the reasons indicated in the course of this document."

APPENDIX B

Copy of certificate of acquittal of Anna Viroubova issued by the High Commission of Inquiry, August, 1917.

Ministry of Justice

The High Commission of Inquiry into the acts and abuses of Ministers and other High Personages of the Former Government.

25th of August, 1917.

No. 3285

Petrograd

Winter Palace

Tel. 1-38-20 and 186.

(Seal)

Testimonial

This testimonial delivered to Anna Alexandrovna Viroubova at the end of the investigation of the High Commission of Inquiry, certifies that she was found not guilty and that she will not again be called to judgment. This statement is given under the signature and seal of the President of the High Commission.

(*Signed*) N. MOURVAVIEFF.

CPSIA information can be obtained
at www.ICGtesting.com
Printed in the USA
LVHW080310110221
678929LV00035B/135